The Horned God of Wytches

Also by Zan Fraser

*A Briefe Historie of Wytches:
As Told Through Examples of Burning Times Drama*

The Burning Times: The Fifteenth Century

The Goddess of Wytches

A Briefe Historie of Magi

The Horned God of Wytches

Zan Fraser

Three Moons Media

Copyright © 2007 Bruce Alex Skidmore

All rights reserved. No part of this book may be reproduced or transmitted in any form or by any means, electronic or mechanical, including photocopying, recording or by any information storage and retrieval system, except for brief quotations within a review, without permission in writing from the author.

Published by Three Moons Media
1610 Valley Brook Lane
Longview, Texas 75605-2676

www.threemoonsmedia.com

Printed in the United States of America

ISBN 1-933514-08-6
ISBN-13 978-1-933514-08-6

This book is dedicated to Mario, Casey, Asher, Vincent, and Nick, who have crossed over.

The Horned God of Wytches

The Horned God of Wytches

The records of the Middle Ages show that the ancient god was known in many parts of the country, but to the Christian recorder he was the enemy of the New Religion...
—Margaret Murray, *The God of the Witches*

Mano cornuta: "Hand held like Horns"; the Italian name for the magical gesture made by holding the middle two fingers beneath the thumb in the palm of the hand, extending the first and last fingers forward—so that the hand resembles the head of a horned beast. It is very familiar to pop culture today as the "Rock and Roll Forever!" gesture flashed by hipster rockers. It also known as the "Hook 'em Horns" of the University of Texas at Austin

The Italians have a custom of gifting one another with tiny horn-shaped amulets, which are worn on a chain about the neck as a talisman to ward away misfortune. My Italian-American friend Mike wears one that was given to him by his mother. He remembers being in Catholic School in the Italian-American enclave wherein he grew up. There was a very strict nun, who asked the class if any of them had or knew anyone who had such a horn-shaped amulet. Most of the boys shot up their hands, exploding into a babble about whose uncle wore one that was two inches big and solid gold; whose older brother wore two; whose cousin had one brought over by his grandmother from the Old Country. The nun became very angry and lectured the boys fiercely about the sin of idolatry.

The Scottish version of *mano cornuta:* "Highland fingers." I was at PSG (Pagan Spirit Gathering) one year and there was a woman there who conducted a workshop on the Highlands dancing of Scotland. Seems that because of the ancient alliance of Scotland and France against England, Highlands dancing is very similar to ballet, involving as it does holding the arms up in the air whilst executing great leaps and intricate footwork. However, in Highlands dancing, one holds the hand in what is called "Highlands fingers"—the second of the four fingers on the hand is pressed against the extended thumb, pointing away from the palm. This pulls the first and third fingers into the points of the "Highlands fingers" (it also leaves the pinky kind of pointed upwards). As with *Mano cornuta*, the point of "Highlands fingers" is to imitate the horns of a horned animal.

Trois Freres

The Horned God of the European witches was perhaps born 20,000 years ago, when the so-called *Trois Freres Sorcerer* was painted onto a cavern wall in Ariege, France. A curious and compelling image, the Sorcerer resembles nothing so much as a half-man, half-beast hybrid—or perhaps a man in the process of changing into a beast—or perhaps a beast in the process of becoming a man.

He stares back at the viewer, unabashed by the space of thousands of years. He is possessed of great, round eyes—eyes that unquestionably recall the unruffled look of an owl. He holds his hands folded daintily in front of him and crouches in a stance that we would without hesitation call a "bunny-hop." He has a little tail going on behind. The most noticeable features of all are the two great antlers that rise above his head.

It has been suggested that the Animal-Man may be wearing a costume of animal-skins—his odd, blank stare suggests a mask. His demeanor is so uncanny he has been dubbed "the Sorcerer." It is supposed that he may be a tribal shaman of some prehistoric people—dancing perhaps to bring rich hunts to his social group. Perhaps he represents an identification with the animals hunted by the people of the caves. Perhaps the hopping Sorcerer is acting out some Stone Age Mystery Religion of life and death, imagined through the life cycles of animals.

Prehistoric humans in France and Spain crawled deep inside caves, to paint extraordinary murals of breath-taking visual art—vistas of teeming animal-life. Impressions on the floor indicate that

they moved around on their hands and knees—perhaps acting out some ritual? It seems as if the caves must have served as churches or temples to them—Joseph Campbell connects the urge to paint animal-murals on the walls of caverns with the desire to decorate the walls of a cathedral.

In like manner, another Stone Age painting from the Fourneau du Diable, Dordogne, shows an odd bull-man apparently dancing like the Trois Freres Sorcerer. In his hoofed hand he holds either a bow or some sort of instrument. As with his brother wizard, the Bull-Man of Dordogne is surrounded by animals, the favored subject of the masterful Paleolithic artists. As Margaret Murray indicates, the fact that the men can be viewed only from the most inaccessible spots in the caves suggests "a great degree of sanctity...attached to this representation."[1] (Murray also refers to smaller figures of horned and masked men, rendered on bone and horn, dating from the Paleolithic.)

In other words, one must undergo a determined *quest-journey* in order to view the Animal-Men. If one must venture deep into

---

[1] Margaret Murray, *The God of the Witches* (London: Faber and Faber, Ltd., 1952 ed.), p. 23

the recesses of cavern—armed with only a flickering torch or a lamp made of animal-grease—what a terrifying trip that would be. How one must master one's fear as one creeps deeper and deeper within a rocky hole inside the earth. Finally—after one has inched one's way to the very most removed section of stone tunnel—one can glimpse in the skipping light—the Beast-Man Wizard of Life.

Horns and antlers

Horns and antlers have been long associated with power, divinity, and with mystically enlightened states. Celtic, Viking, Teutonic, and Samurai warriors all wore horns on their helmets, as did African and Native American shamans on their headdresses. One cannot think of Germanic opera without imagining everyone with horns on their heads. I once met someone who worked for the Smithsonian, who described to me how she interpreted the spell-workings of a nineteenth-century Native American shaman, based upon materials inserted into the horns of his headdress. Moses is famously depicted as horned by Michaelangelo, supposedly due to a mistranslation of Biblical text, but perhaps instead representative of an earlier symbology (the Hebrew *keren* can mean both "horn" and "power").[2]

Men horned with the keratinous protuberances of *goats, cattle,* and *sheep* are found during the Bronze Age in the Near and Middle East; William Anderson observes that the same imagery can be found in prehistoric societies from Stonehenge and Avebury to India, and that one recurrent archetypal figure, the diminutive son-lover to the wide-hipped Mother-Goddess, often wears a bull-mask with horns.[3] Bulls were apparently creatures of fascination to the people of Catal Huyuk in Turkey, one of the intrepid first cities of humans. Dated to the precocious period of 6700 BCE (this is some 3000 years before Egypt and Sumer and is comparable only to Jericho in Palestine, which, at 7000 BCE, was already fortified by a stout wall and overseen by a watchtower), Catal Huyuk consisted of mud-brick houses arranged in streets (one, curiously, entered the houses through the roof). The houses had painted murals on

---

2 Jeffrey Burton Russell, *Witchcraft in the Middle Ages* (Ithaca, New York: Cornell University Press, 1972), p. 316

3 William Anderson, *Green Man: The Archetype of our Oneness with the Earth* (New York: HarperCollins, 1990), p. 34

the walls; some were reserved as temple-spaces; and the horns of bulls were utilized predominantly as a decorative motif.

Sumer and Egypt
The mighty gods of Sumer, the first human society to organize itself into a civilization c. 3000 BCE, wore horns as a sign of importance, as did later deities in Babylonia and Assyria.[4] According to Margaret Murray, who was ceded to be a credible Egyptologist:
Originally the gods wore only two horns; such is the case of a copper head found in a gold-tomb at Ur that possibly predates the first Egyptian dynasty. When gods deemed superior to those worshipped by primitives were introduced over the centuries of Babylonian civilization, their greater importance was emphasized by the increased number of horns which they bore. While the old-fashioned gods wore but two horns (and there were plenty of these), the grander gods such as Asshur and Ishtar (as well as their priests on earth) bore seven horns. *This is probably the reason why the Lamb in the* Book of Revelation *has seven horns.*[5]

Beginning with the Bronze and Iron Ages horned gods appear in Egypt (Murray's conceded arena of expertise). A slate palette, dated just prior to the beginning of Egyptian history, shows a man with the head and tail of a jackal (the ears of jackals are often depicted as horn-like in Egyptian art). Like the Ariege dancer, his body, hands, and feet are human. He plays a flute and is in the midst of animals. *Chief of the Egyptian gods was* Amon, *the god of the life-force.* Originally the local god of Thebes, he is usually imagined in human form with the curved horns of the Theban ram; Herodotus recalls that at the annual festival at Thebes, Amon's figure is wrapped in a ram's skin. Down to the "latest period of pharaonic history," the horned Amon was associated with the divine father of the king.[6]

The greatest of the Egyptian horned gods is Osiris, *an earth-god and a god of renewal.* The crown of Osiris is also the monarch's crown; the Pharaoh is thus symbolized as God and as the giver of fertility. In addition, many Egyptian headdresses represent two curved

---

4   Diane Wolkstein and Samuel Noah Kramer, *Inanna, Queen of Heaven and Earth: Her Stories and Hymns From Sumer* (Harper and Row, 1983), p. 185n
5   Murray, *The God of the Witches*, p. 24–26
6   *The God of the Witches*, p. 26

horns with the disc of the sun between them (or, as in the matter of *Isis's* crown, with the moon-disc between). On great occasions the Pharaoh wore a bull's tail attached to his girdle. The Tail-festival, the *sed-heb*, wherein the Pharaoh was invested with the tail, was an occasion of grave importance; the Pharaoh's performing a sacred dance, wearing the bull's tail, was often shown as taking place before *Min*, the god of human regeneration. The horned goddess *Isis* is another important Egyptian deity, whose worship continued in Egypt until Christian times and was spread far throughout the Roman Empire. In *The God of the Witches*, Murray includes details of an Egyptian priest wearing a horn-like jackal's mask and a woman worshipping a seated ram.

India and the Aegean

During the Bronze Age horned gods proliferate in both India and the Aegean. At Mohenjo-Daro, the first Indian city to rise, there are many examples of humans either masked or horned, some possibly wearing a bull's hide. The most famous is a steatite seal c. 2700 BCE, which apparently depicts an ithyphallic male sitting cross-legged in a posture of yogic meditation. He is possibly masked; has a majestic set of buffalo horns rising from his head; and is surrounded by game-animals.

The man is thought to be an early version of *Shiva*, one of the most important of Hindu deities, called the "Lord of Yoga" and frequently shown in the ascetic contemplation of his yoga-pose. Lord Shiva is also frequently shown meditating atop a deer or tiger's skin. (At first, I thought this was to represent the animalistic side of humans, which we transcend through the enlightenment of the higher functions. However it seems as if Hindu holy books advise meditating upon an animal-skin because apparently crawling reptiles will not cross the skin of a dead creature. There seem to be many snakes in India, which I guess would otherwise be an impediment to tranquility, if one had to be anxiously mindful of them during one's meditation session.) Because the seal-figure is surrounded by animals, which he appears to control through the harmony of his enlightenment, he is sometimes known as *Pasupati*, the "Lord of Animals."

Widespread distribution throughout the first Indus-Sarasvati cities of *rishi-images* (yogic sages or seers) like the Shiva-seal indicates that yoga was already developed in India 4700 years ago.

This would mean that yoga is in fact extremely old—as old as the Pyramids of Gisa or Stonehenge, as old as Egypt or Sumer—and that it must have been invented by Neolithic Indian shamans—what today we would call *swamis* or *gurus*. The Mohenjo-Daro Shiva connects yogic meditation with the archetypal motif the "Lord of Animals"—and with a man powerful enough to wear the horns of a beast.

Of the Aegean, the *Minotaur*, the Minoan bull, was worshipped in Crete, which seems to have had a cult of bull-worship, to judge from depictions of the famous bull-dancers painted on palace walls. The theory is that the legend of the Minotaur relays a custom of ceremonial combat between the Minotaur (represented as a man with a bull's head or mask) and Theseus (shown with the flowing locks of the Cretan athlete). The Cretan queen-moon priestess, who weds the bull-man in the sacred marriage, was supposed (like the original Hera) to be identified with cows.

Pagan Pan
The most famous representation of the classical horned god is Pan, *the forest god of Greece*. His worship originated in Arcadia, a region regarded as primitive and remote even by the ancient Greeks. We therefore have no knowledge of Pan before the late Iron Age (the fifth century BCE). His worship seems to be indigenous to Greece and of great antiquity; Arcadian customs must descend from the Stone Age. Scenes of his worship show him playing his namesake pipes, followed by an enthusiastic procession of dancing nymphs and satyrs. Artistic depictions often show him in hot pursuit (and fully erect), after either a lissome young maiden or a comely youth. *It is significant that, in examining the Christian Devil, we find most of Pan's attributes:* hoofs, horns, and sexuality.

Of equal interest is Bull Dionysos, *who, like the Minotaur, was slain. This makes Osiris, Dionysos, and the Minotaur representative of the sacri-*

ficed god, or of the dying god-king. Dionysos was said to have come to Greece from the north, indicating that his worship was imported from foreign soil. Murray points out that this implies that the worship of horned beings was prevalent in the countries outside Greece, probably before the Iron Age.[7] Euripedes describes Dionysos as horned; in Crete he was called *Dionysos-Zagreus* ("wild goat with enormous horns"), in Thrace he was represented as a bull, and in Arcadia it was said that Hermes transformed him into a ram.

Mithra *was a notable Persian sun/light-god, and god of purity.* He was associated with the ritual slaying of a bull, from whose blood vegetation grew (Green Man motif). His cult was advanced throughout the Roman Empire; ruins of a temple to Mithra are to be seen in London. *So immensely popular was Mithra, with such a wide following, the cult of Mithra could conceivably have been chosen as the Imperial religion, instead of Christianity. It might have been that we would just now be coming off a two thousand-year history of* Mithraism *or* Mithra-anity. We'd all be Mithrans. "Our Father, who art Mithra—"

Feyrey King

A form taken by the god of the European witches was that of the *Feyrey King*—a male being analogous to the Feyrey Queen and descended from the old gods of Celto-Teutonic legend.[8] A Celtic example of the Fay King (and an example of the Celtic belief in reincarnation) would be *Midhir,* the faerey husband to the mortal woman Etain, who reawakens her memories of her former life as his wife and consort. Another would be *Fin Bheara* (Finvarra; also Findabair/Finnavar), an especially Celtic sort of divinity. Despite two wives (Nuala and Oonagh), Finnavar was sometimes the thief of beautiful mortal women. (Finnavar may well have inspired the Faery King in the Middle English verse romance *Sir Orfeo,* which concerns the seduction of a beautiful mortal woman into the Land of Ferey; otherwise *Sir Orfeo* is a retelling of the Orpheus/Eurydice myth.) In the story of *Ethna, the Loveliest Woman in Ireland,* the woman Ethna (like the lovely lady Herodias in *Sir Orfeo*) falls into a swoon, from which she cannot be awakened. *When she revives, she*

---

7   *The God of the Witches*, p. 29
8   I have this thing whereby I try to be very variable in spelling the name of the very variable fees.

says that she has been in a beautiful country, to which she longs to return. As is the situation with Herodias in *Sir Orfeo*, nothing can prevent Finnavar from stealing away Ethna to be his Faerey Bride. Many Celtic divinities are imagined as being rulers of an extra-dimensional realm. *Gwynn ap Nudd* is a Welsh mythic figure who became a medieval Feyre King. In the Welsh *Mabinogion* story of *Pwyll, Lord of Dyved*, Arawn is king of *Annwvyn*, the Otherworld or the Not-world, while Pwyll serves as sort of "honorary Underworld Lord," ruling in Arawn's stead for a year (during which, he politely refrains from knowledge of Arawn's wife). In the story of *Manawydan, son of Llyr*, Llwyd is the king of the Not-world, implicitly responsible for the dimension-hopping which Rhiannon and Manawydan undergo.

As with the night-flying pagan goddess of the Middle Ages, the god of pagans ruled the *realm of the dead*. The stories of *Herne* and *Hakelbrand* tell of hunters who returned from the dead; *Harlequinus/Herlichin, Herla*, and *Hekla* all led processions of the dead. (The British king *Hecla/Hekla* was said to drive the *hell-wain*, the wagon of the dead.) The feryie-king *Midhir* lives within a fairy-mound, or *sidh*, the home of the dead. Like the Plutonian faery-king in the ballad *Sir Orfeo*, the Irish fayrie-king *Fin Bheara* was regarded as king of the dead; a story features Finnavar as a rider on a black horse, who presides over a banquet of the departed.[9]

Oberon

An exceptionally well-known manifestation of the Faery King is *Oberon*, also known as *Auberon* or *Alberon*, from a Teutonic species of name for "elf," *alp* or *alb*.[10] Some further derive Oberon from the German dwarf-king *Alberich*.[11] (The Germanic poem of *Orendel* cites a dwarf *Alban*.) Since Teutonic legend associates dwarfs (for being subterranean) with the Otherworld and with death, this makes Oberon something of a mortuary deity.

The story of *le roi de la feerie* is first known in the fifteenth-century French romance *Huon of Bordeaux*. Part of the Charlemagne

---

9 Katharine Briggs, *An Encyclopedia of Fairies* (New York: Pantheon Books, 1976), p. 175

10 Jacob Grimm, *Teutonic Mythology*, vol. II (Gloucester, Massachusetts: Peter Smith, 1966 ed.), p. 453

11 Briggs, *Encyclopedia of Fairies*, p. 314

sagas, the story of the Crusader Huon was translated into English in 1548. (Although *Huon* is the first literary use of Oberon as the faerey-king, an old poem which describes how three fays prophesy at the birth of Auberon proves that the name was in common parlance before the sixteenth-century translation.)[12]

Huon and his companion are traveling through the forest of Oberon, a wood "full of the fairy and strange things," *located eccentrically somewhere in Arabia, when they meet apparently a five year-old child, driving a chariot. This child is Oberon, the feryie-king.* Although of "angelic visage," Oberon is but three-feet high, as the result of a spell cast by a faerie. All the faereys had been invited to attend Oberon's birth but one; that one cursed him so that he would never grow beyond five years of age: "I have thus continued infantile in appearance, though full of years and experience."[13] (This is like the vampire-child in the Anne Rice novel.) Repenting of her curse, the fay also made Oberon the *"fairest ever that lived."* (This is like the very well-known faerey-story motif "Mirror, mirror, on the wall.") Oberon is probably presented as magically stunted because of the memory of his derivation from the German Alberich; it would seem logical to show Oberon as a mutant-child, if he was originally a dwarf.[14] Other guests endowed Oberon with the shamanic powers of clairvoyance; the ability instantaneously to travel; to tame birds or beasts; and to make castles grow at command. He can plague with ferocious storms (witchcraft-story motif) and has a magic bow that can bring down any animal (hunting-mythology motif). Oberon has pledged to make use of all his abilities by *"promoting justice and rewarding virtue."*

Oberon has an impressive genealogy. He was sired by Julius Caesar, with the feyrey-woman Glorianda, lady of the Secret Isle—which makes Oberon part of the European "supernatural parent" tradition, like Mother Shipton and Cu-chulaidh and Merlin. Oberon makes a point to speak to all who enter his wood—anyone who responds is lost forever, transformed into a hobgoblin (fayre-tale motif), although apparently he takes a shine to Huon.

Oberon favors Huon with two gifts. One is a horn that, when blown, will instantly summon Oberon to his side; it has the ad-

---

12   Grimm, *Teutonic Mythology*, vol. IV, p. 1401
13   Thomas Bulfinch, *Bulfinch's Mythology: The Age of Chivalry and Legends of Charlemagne or Romance in the Middle Ages* (Meridian Books, 1995), p. 563
14   Briggs, *Encyclopedia of Fairies*, p. 228

ditional benefit of causing any priests in the vicinity to break into a helpless jig (motif: enjoyment of the discomfiture of the clergy). Oberon also makes present of a rich goblet, which furnishes wine and fare when (interpolation alert) the sign of the cross is made over it. Huon eventually joins the supernatural Feyrey Host, with whom (so the story says) he will remain until the Day of Judgment.

Midsummer
Oberon is most famously presented as the fayrey-lord in Shakespeare's *A Midsummer Night's Dream* (c. 1595), one of the most classic comedies ever devised. Fifty percent of the show concerns the antics of the characters of England's famous faery-mythology, ingeniously incorporated by Shakespeare into one play; pagan motifs run all over the place. Like the Irish Ghost Queen *Morrighu*, Oberon is the *"king of shadows"* (III.ii.347); Oberon becomes invisible in the course of the show (II.i.186), an old theme in Celtic legends known as *feth fiadha*. (The Tuatha de Danaan understood its secret, as did certain Druids. The *Lorica* of St. Patrick and the legend of Diarmid and Grainne both describe people who escape their enemies at the last moment by turning invisible.)[15]

Oberon is a magician, who releases Titania from her charm: *"Be as thou wast wont to be; see as thou wast wont to see."* (IV.i.70–1) He is a priest of nature otherwise: *"I know a bank where the wild thyme blows, where oxlips and the nodding violet grows; quite o'er-canopied with luscious woodbine, with sweet musk-roses, and with eglantine: there sleeps Titania sometime of the night."* (II.i.249–53) Purkiss calls Shakespeare's Oberon "in essence a classical deity of the seasons," a *vertumnus*. (Vertumnus was a Roman god of the changing year, who wins Pomona the goddess of ripening fruit—the Romans clearly had gods for everything.)[16]

Oberon demonstrates that he, like the young lovers, and (we suspect) like Old Will himself, enjoys the moonlit revels in the woods on a summer's night: *"we are spirits of another sort: I with the morning's love have oft made sport."* (III.ii.388–9) Finally (IV.i.85–98),

---

15 Jean Markale, *Merlin: Priest of Nature* (Rochester, Vermont: Inner Traditions, 1995), p. 152
16 Diane Purkiss, *At the Bottom of the Garden: A Dark History of Fairies, Hobgoblins, and Other Troublesome Things* (New York: NYU Press, 2001), p. 176

the night has flown and night-spirits must away. Oberon: *"Come, my queen, take hands with me... Now thou and I... will to-morrow midnight solemnly dance in Duke Theseus' house triumphantly and bless it to all fair prosperity."*
Puck: *"Fairy king, attend and mark: I do hear the morning lark."*
Oberon: *"Then, my queen, in silence sad, trip we after night's shade: we the globe can compass soon, swifter than the wandering moon."*
At the play's conclusion (V.i), we find the same mythic situation as is preserved in the testimonies of the Friulian benandanti, concerning roving bands of the dead (here, feyries), led by the Good Mothers or the Night Women (here, the King and Queen of Faeryes), entering the home at night, in a nocturnal visit that brings blessings to the home and (fertility-motif) physical perfection to the children born of the newly consummated marriage.
Oberon: *"Through the house give glimmering light, by the dead and drowsy fire: every elf and fairy sprite hop as lightly as bird from brier; and this ditty, after me, sing and dance it trippingly."*
Titania: *"First, rehearse your song by rote, to each word a warbling note: hand in hand, with fairy grace, will we sing and bless this place."*
Oberon: *"Now, until the break of day, through this house each fairy stray. To the best bride-bed will we, which by us shall blessèd be; and the issue there create ever shall be fortunate. So shall all the couples three ever true in loving be; and the blots of Nature's hand shall not in their issue stand; never mole, hare lip, nor scar, nor mark prodigious, such as are despised in nativity, shall upon their children be. With this field-dew consecrate, every fairy take his gait; and each several chamber bless, through this palace, with sweet peace, ever shall in safety rest, and the owner of it blest. Trip away; make no stay; meet me all by break of day."*

Oberon was to become a popular choice for invocations in rituals of scholarly or ceremonial magic, especially after *Huon of Bordeaux* made *Auberon* a familiar name. A man was pilloried in London in 1444, *"the whyche wrought by a wycckyd spyryte, the whych was called Oberycom."*[17] In other words, the man wrought magic by means of a spryte—a "wycckyd" one—named *Oberycom*. A 1528 letter to Thomas Cromwell (quoted in the *Norfolk Archaeology* of 1847)

---

17   George Lyman Kittredge, *Witchcraft in Old and New England* (New York: Russell and Russell, 1956 ed.), p. 59

explains how the parson of Lesingham (a truant monk and magician) raised three spirits, *Andrew Malchus, Incubus,* and *Oberion*.[18] This is significant, because it was not until later that Lord Berners's translation of *Huon of Bordeaux* make Auberon familiar to the literate; also predating the English *Huon* is the 1510 account of a man raising *Oberion* near Halifax.[19]

A sixteenth-century book of magic preserved in the Bodleian Library contains the *"Call of Oberion into a Crystal Stone,"* a bit of conjuration utilizing Catholic prayers in Latin. One Amylion recorded in 1521 that George Dowsing *"dede aryse in a glasse a litull thing of the length of an ynche or ther about, but whether it was a spiret or a shadowe he cannot tell."* In other words, he called up into a crystal a little thing perhaps an inch in length, but remained uncertain as to whether it was a spirit or a shadow.[20]

Magic-use was plainly such a popular subject in England after Elizabeth came to the throne that Briggs warns, "It is difficult to over-estimate the number of magical manuscripts which must have been scattered about the country in the sixteenth and seventeenth centuries."[21] The huge amount of printed instruction must have encouraged a number of people, such as the intrepid quartet who conducted a magical experiment in 1510 at Knaresborough. Four citizens—two clerics, an ex-schoolmaster (and professional cunning-man) and a client of his, a leading citizen—embarked upon a scheme to find treasure.

Late at night the four met at an agreed-upon spot. There, they laid three circles of virgin parchment, thirty feet in circumference, to protect themselves from spirits (motif: magical circle-casting). *One of the group, who had been a scryer or crystal-gazer in his youth, had a book of magic from which they were going to read and one of the clerics was prepared to perform an invocation. Unfortunately, there was fog that night, they lost their way—the whole thing came to naught. But their exploit generated so much talk in the town that one of the men was questioned.*[22] The point is—they

---

18 Katharine Briggs, *The Anatomy of Puck: An Examination of Fairy Beliefs among Shakespeare's Contemporaries and Successors* (New York: Arno Press, 1977 ed.), p. 114
19 *Anatomy of Puck*, p. 114
20 *Anatomy of Puck*, p. 114–5
21 *Anatomy of Puck,* p. 113
22 Kittredge, *Witchcraft in Old and New England*, p. 207

had prepared lead tablets, on which they had inscribed the names of demons—two of which were *Oberion* and *Storax* (which may be an early version of the Shakespearean wytch *Sycorax's* name).

Elsewhere, Oberon continued his fame as king of the fays— Drayton makes Oberon his fayrie-king, even though he uses Mab as the feyry-queen.[23] The drama of Greene's *The Scottish Hystorie of James the Fourth, Slaine at Flodden* (c. 1590) is intermittently interrupted by Oberon the King of the Feyreys, accompanied by a band of disguised *"Antiques"* or *"Antics,"* who dance *"rownds"* (rounds) and *"prittie daunces."* The legend of Oberon bears no relation to anything at all in the eponymous masque written by Jonson for the young Prince Henry (oldest boy to James I), except to show the Faery Prince (Henry) in the very pagan circumstance of reveling in moonlit woods, dancing in a circle ("rownds") with satyrs and sylvans (forest-beings) and Silenus (the forest-god).

Crowds in procession

In 1622 a denunciation was registered in Cividale against Minena Lambaia. On *"Thursdays of the Ember Days she goes out in procession, candle in hand... and... they go up into the mountains, and there is food there, and they* [the dead] *walk around her house, moaning, so that she must go out to them..."*[24] Thursdays, and the Ember days, are periods associated with the supernatural night-ladies. Also related to the night-ladies is the belief in wandering bands of spirits. Minena Lambaia, although she does not mention the night-women, refers to similar phenomena—the roaming of the dead during the *seasonal periods of the Ember times*. Minena is able to see and hear the dead during these times.

In 1626 Fra Domenico d'Auxerre received a complaint against a woman, which mentioned *"crowds... in procession,"*[25] another reference to the dead traveling in great throngs. A woman of Prutars, named Morosa, was denounced in 1645 for having ecstatic impressions of the dead. On the *"night of San Giusto she saw processions that began near her home and went as far as Anconeta, and all the marchers were clutching candles in their hands, and on one*

---

23   Briggs, *Encyclopedia of Fairies*, p. 314
24   Carlo Ginzburg, *The Night Battles: Witchcraft and Agrarian Cults in the Sixteenth and Seventeenth Centuries* (New York: Penguin Books, 1985), p. 68
25   *The Night Battles*, p. 68

occasion she had even seen her father and mother in a procession, and they begged for alms..."[26] Maria Panzona, tried for witchcraft in 1619, recalled vivid spiritual experiences. She made journeys *"in body and spirit,"* to *"heaven [where] I saw God and the Madonna with many small angels, and everything was filled with roses; and in hell I saw devils and smaller devils being boiled and I also saw one of my godmothers."*[27] A shepherd reported of ghosts frolicking in night-time coventicles in 1621: *"both men and women cavorted, and sometimes ate, and... they were also accustomed to go with lighted candles to the small church* [of San Canziano] *inside and out."*[28]

The thing that all of these accounts have in common is the idea of the *wandering dead*, a detail noted in the chronicles of the *night-ladies*. Just as the *Canon Episcopi* describes women who fly with the goddess of pagans on certain nights—and as women describe assemblies in honor of the night-goddess, which take place on certain nights—other people claim periodically to see processions of the dead on certain nights. (Some Christian influence may be seen, in the references to heaven, hell, and candle-lit processions to churches.)

A Tyrolese woman named Wyprat Musin was tried in 1525. She testified that, during the Ember season two years previously, a multitude appeared to her, led by *Fraw Selga*, sister to *Fraw Venus*. Fraw Selga told Wyprat that she (Wyprat) had to follow them on Thursdays and Saturdays or face death, since Wyprat had been predestined from birth to do so.[29] (A mistress whose commands must be obeyed is one of the characteristics of the night-bands; Selga and Venus are names associated with the Germanic good women, such as Holdr/Holle and Bertha/Perchta.) A weaver named Giuliano Verdena was tried in Mantua in 1489. Gazing into a vase of water, he would see the *"mistress of the game,"* who revealed to him *"the properties of herbs and the nature of animals."* With her were a *"great multitude of people some of whom were on foot, others mounted..."*[30]

From the Swabian region of southwest Germany comes a sixteenth-century tale borrowed from an earlier chronicle. A 1544

---

26 *The Night Battles*, p. 68
27 *The Night Battles*, p. 67
28 *The Night Battles*, p. 67
29 *The Night Battles*, p. 51
30 *The Night Battles*, p. 49

Annales described *clerici vagantes*, who, in something of the manner of the night-ladies, wandered about the countryside. They told the peasantry that they had traveled to the Venusberg (a mythic mountain in Germanic folklore), where they had seen marvelous things. They boasted of *charms* which protected humans and beasts from witchcraft; *knowledge* of both the past and the future; the power to discover *lost objects* and treasure; and the power to keep *hail* away. They also claimed charms which would affect the prices of grain and wine, an application of a *fertility motif*. In a seeming departure from the benevolent philosophy of the night-women, however, the clerici vagantes would periodically extort money from the intimidated locals, threatening to unleash storms and what-not upon them.[31]

Furious Horde

A special talent of these spiritual bandits was the ability to call forth the *"Furious Horde."* This they described as comprised of the souls of *unbaptized children* (a common source of superstition in the Middle Ages), the spirits of men who *died in battles*, and the souls of other *ecstatics* such as themselves. These souls, so they said, gathered during the Ember seasons, on Thursdays and Saturdays. Through the journey to the mythic mountain the Venusberg (identified with the Roman Venus, another classical name, like Diana's, inserted into this scheme), the clerici vagantes gained the power to cure spells and to summon the ranks of the dead. Groups of clerici vagantes appeared in Lucerne in 1576, in 1599, and in 1600. A group called the *Johannesbruderschaft* ("the Brotherhood of John") was tried in 1694 in Leopoli, Italy. They too searched for treasures and saw the souls on the magical Venusberg.[32]

Spread across Europe is the legend of the itinerant *good-goddess*, who flies about nights with multitudes. Women are said to fly with her; also joining the goddess in her night-flights are *spirits of the dead*. The dead attend the assemblies of Oriente; people who have ecstatic experience of the goddess receive information concerning the dead. These spiritual traditions are found across centuries and across a wide area of Europe. Clustered around a

---

31 *The Night Battles*, p. 55
32 *The Night Battles*, p. 56

"nucleus of fairly consistent and compact beliefs," these traditions are identified, in addition to other places, over Alsace, Heidelberg, Bavaria, the Tyrol, and Switzerland.[33] What links these traditions together is the identification of *souls of the dead*. Bands of the dead join the multi-named goddess in her night-travels; this goddess is a goddess of the dead. Just as women report ecstatic experience of the good-goddess, various people describe visions of the roaming dead.

The two beliefs, in a wandering *night-goddess* and in processions of the *restless departed,* are related, but are not interdependent. What links them are specific *seasonal dates,* such as the Ember times of the *solstices* and *equinoxes*. Across Europe, certain specific dates are regarded as ones on which certain phenomena were likely to occur. These included nomadic bands of spirits and the travels of the night-goddess. These folk beliefs, and the periods of certain specific dates, combine in another European belief, known as the *Wild Chase* or the *Furious Ride*.

In the case of Burchardt and his *Decretum* (1008–12 CE), Diana and her nocturnal bands were identified with *"the witch Holda"* and her Wild Hunt; likewise with Nicholas of Cusa and Herolt, in their respective sermons. The sermons of Geiler von Kaisersberg, collected in Strasbourg in the early sixteenth century, reference witches and women who go at night to see *"Fraw Fenus"* (Venus, the classical love-goddess associated with Frau Holda in Teutonic legend, due to scholastic interpolation). Von Kaisersberg also describes women who, during the Ember Days, fall into swoons, during which they are insensible to pricking or scalding.[34] When they revived, they told stories of being in heaven; they related information gathered there. Von Kaisersberg goes on to speak of another superstition, also associated with the Ember Days—the migration of the "Furious Horde."[35]

Popular belief (according to von Kaisersberg) regards the time of the *winter solstice* (Yule-tide) as the holiest time of all, regarding these "sorts of things." This is also the time when

---

33   *The Night Battles*, p. 54
34   *The Night Battles*, p. 44
35   *The Night Battles*, p. 44

Holda and Berchta made their processions and when the folk-goddess Hera (or a goddess identified thereby) flew about the world. During these Ember times, the dead roamed the earth. "So then, the nights of the Ember Days in which the journeying of the women condemned by Nider and Geiler took place...were also, according to a tradition widespread in central Europe, the nights in which the 'Furious Horde' appeared."[36] The *Furious Horde*, or *Wild Hunt*, is another manifestation of the *night-traveling traditions*.

Wild Ride
> *Another class of spectres will prove more fruitful for our investigation: they, like the ignes fatui, include* unchristened babes, *but instead of straggling singly on the earth as fires, they sweep through forest and air in* whole companies *with a horrible din. This is the widely spread legend of the* furious host, the furious hunt, *which is of high antiquity, and interweaves itself, now with gods and now with heroes. Look where you will, it betrays its connexion with heathenism.*
> —Jacob Grimm[37]

Throughout Europe—France, Spain, Italy, Germany, England, and Scandinavia—from the eleventh century onwards, various texts (in Latin and the vulgate) begin to speak of the "Savage Ride."[38] Sometimes called the Wild Hunt *(Wilde Jagd, Chasse sauvage, Chasse Arthur)*, sometimes called the Furious Army *(Wutischend Heer, Mesnie furieuse, Mesnie Hellequin, exercitus antiquus)*, it is a deafening, overwhelming mob. It is marked by a sudden roar and howl of winds. You hear the horses pounding their hoofs—the blasting of horns—the hunters calling *"hollo hoho"* to each other. It may be seen in the thrashing tree-tops or in night-shadows against fleeting clouds.

It was wise to clear quickly out of the way if one saw or heard the Chase approach. Otherwise, one risked being trampled or

---
36   *The Night Battles*, p. 47
37   Grimm, *Teutonic Mythology*, vol. III, p. 918
38   Carlo Ginzburg, *Ecstasies: Deciphering the Witches' Sabbath* (New York: Pantheon Books, 1991), p. 101

dragged under the horses' stampeding hoofs. Sometimes the Hunt chases the *moss-folk* and the *wood-wives* (the gentle forest-beings), who run terrified before it—perhaps a metaphor for the way leaves are driven by the wind before a storm. Legend indicates that no good comes to anyone rash enough to echo the hunters' calls or to blow a bugle which might be found at the scene. Bundles of oats were left to appease the horses, so that the Wild Riders would not trample the crops.[39]

The Ride can have definite, sinister, portentous overtones. Even until the early part of the twentieth century, on stormy winter's nights, when the wind roared about the eaves, English country people were said to comment by their firesides that "the Hunt's about"; the Wild Hunt was apparently recorded as sighted on Halloween as late as the 1940s.[40] This is significant, Halloween being a mortuary holyday and the Hunt being identified with the dead. In Wales and in the western British Isles, the legendary *Hecla* was said to lead the procession that included the *Hellwain*, the wagon of the dead—a significant detail, as both Celtic and Nordic traditions associate death with wagons, burying people in carts, for instance.

From Ditchling Beacon, the highest point of the South Downs in Sussex, it is said that one can hear the galloping horses, the baying hounds, the hunters' shouts, as the deathly visitation sweeps by, although, of course, nothing can be seen.[41] An American cowboy song became popular in 1949, playing upon kind of the same theme; it was called *"Riders in the Sky,"* and was about a ghostly cowboy doomed to round up cows across *"the endless skies."*

The Hunt remained a vital ingredient in folk custom for centuries. It seems that the *"Christians had not so quickly nor so completely renounced* [the people's] *faith in the gods of their fathers, that these imposing figures could all at once drop out of their memory,"* comments Mr. Grimm.[42] The common theme uniting all these different, distant,

---

39 Grimm, *Teutonic Mythology*, vol. III, p. 944
40 Rosemary Ellen Guiley, *The Encyclopedia of Witches and Witchcraft* (New York: Facts on File, 1989), p. 366
41 Doreen Valiente, *Witchcraft for Tomorrow* (Custer, Washington: Phoenix Publishing, 1978), p. 51
42 Grimm, *Teutonic Mythology*, vol. III, p. 918

and ancient stories, is that of the dead.[43] The dead attend the assemblies of the ecstatic women and fly through the skies in the multitudes of the night-women. A goddess commanded Wyprat Musin to join her multitude, which included the dead. The dead are among the participants of the Wild Hunt, the "throng of the dead" led by "mythical or mythicized" figures.[44]

These "throngs" of dead, like Celtic goddesses, will take on different characters in different places. In certain sections of Europe, ecstatic assemblies and swarming multitudes are associated with a female deity. In Milanese trials and others, we find a "female aspiration to a separate world composed only of women and governed by a maternal, wise goddess."[45] However—in the case of the Wild Hunt, the apparitions "appeared almost exclusively" to men, "hunters, pilgrims, wayfarers."[46] Both manifestations are connected with specific times of the year, including the period between Christmas and Epiphany, the *Twelves* of the year. In certain places, these conceptualizations overlap—Herolt's sermons (collected in 1418 and reprinted throughout the latter fifteenth century) discuss *"Diana with her army"*; Herolt connects the medieval bands of women with the rowdy throngs of the dead.[47] According to Ginzburg, Herolt seems to be acting upon a perception of different "aspects of a single mythical image."[48] "There is no doubt that the nocturnal cavalcades of Diana's female followers are a version of the Wild Hunt."[49] As Russell notes, the reference to riding on beasts, the reference to being a part of a band, are, in fact, "full reference to the wild ride of folk tradition."[50]

But, whereas the night-goddess may be understood as a primarily Celtic manifestation, the Wild Ride leads into Teutonic Europe. Unlike the nocturnal bands (which are associated with a multi-named goddess) the Hunt is associated mostly (although not exclusively) with men. As with the night-bands, the Wild Hunt is

---

43 Ginzburg, *Ecstasies*, p. 101
44 *Ecstasies*, p. 102
45 *Ecstasies*, p. 102
46 *Ecstasies*, p. 102
47 *Ecstasies*, p. 102
48 *Ecstasies*, p. 102
49 Ginzburg, *The Night Battles*, p. 40
50 Russell, *Witchcraft in the Middle Ages*, p. 79

organized around a center of divine beings. "The traditions concerning the 'furious army' have been interpreted as a coherent mythical and ritual configuration, in which, through implicit or explicit reference to the figure of Wotan, a remote and persistent warrior vocation of German men is expressed."[51]

All-father Odinn

> [W]hen Odinn sat there on his high seat he saw over the whole world and what everyone was doing, and he understood everything he saw... He may well be called All-father for this reason—he is the father of all the gods and men and of everything that he and his power created. The earth was his daughter and his wife; by her he had his first son, Asa-Thor ["Thor-the-charioteer"]. Might and strength were Thor's characteristics, by these he dominates every living creature.[52]
> —The Prose Edda

Odinn may be accepted as "a Primitive West European god known to all the tribes of the group."[53] He was the ancient Teutonic father-god, king of the Nordic heavens and parent to the subsequent generations of gods. To the early west Europeans, he was *Wodenaz*. In Old High German, he was *Wuotan;* in Old Saxon, *Wodan;* in Old Norse *Voden* (Odinn); and *Woden* in Old English. The whole of Odinn's character may be understood in the original conception of *Wodenaz*. The name may describe a storm or wind-god, with power over the dead. It may also describe a magician who, through self-sacrifice, brought wisdom to the people.[54]

Odinn was credited with the invention of the *runes*, a magical, divinatory alphabet, carved on sticks and rocks, of great significance to the Scandinavians and Germans. In order to achieve this feat, Odinn lost an eye, and serves as an example of self-sacrifice and of the price that must be paid for wisdom and knowledge. His

---

51 Ginzburg, *Ecstasies*, p. 102
52 Jean I. Young, *The Prose Edda of Snorri Sturluson: Tales from Norse Mythology* (Berkeley: University of California Press, 1954), p. 37
53 Brian Branston, *Lost Gods of England* (London: Thames and Hudson, 1957), p. 93
54 *Lost Gods of England*, p. 94

various names relate to words (Old Norse: *odr,* German: *wutend,* Old English: *wood*) which mean "mad," "possessed," or "seized by ecstatic inspiration."[55] The description by eleventh-century chronicler Adam of Bremen is famous: *Wodan, id est furor;* "Wodan, that is to say, Fury." The worship of the shaman-magician god, the one-eyed, the bringer of the runes, is apparent in many Germanic traditions, including the firmly rooted custom of the "Need-fire," a special, sacred flame.[56] Many curses and spells make reference to Wode, such as this ninth-century German charm: *"Phol* [Baldr] *and Woden rode to the wood where Baldr's foal wrenched her foot... then Woden charmed as he well knew how... bone to bone, blood to blood, limb to limb, as if they were glued."* A Christian interpolation may be seen in a later version: *"Our Lord rade/His foal's foot slade... heal in the name of the Father, Son, and Holy Ghost."*[57]

The importance of Odinn's worship is seen in his commemoration in numerous place-names. To judge from the English countryside, the Anglo-Saxons paid homage to Odinn in various places throughout Kent, Essex, Hampshire, Wiltshire, Somerset, Staffordshire, Bedfordshire, and Derbyshire.[58] At the Vale of Pewsey, a notable earthwork is the *Wansdyke* ("Wodnes dike"). Otherwise, *Wednesbury* ("Woden's fortress") and *Wednesfield* ("Woden's Plain") are to be found above the Thames. *Woodnesborough* (near Sandwich) and *Wornshill* (near Sittingbourne) must have been at one time vital centers of worship. The fourth day of the week is another example of Wotan's influence.

A popular nickname for Odinn was *Grimr,* or *Grimnir* ("Masked one"). This refers to a person wearing a hood which masks the face and is applied to Odinn in connection with his habit of wandering the earth in disguise. Southern England boasts many earthworks called *Grimsdyke;* the name appears in Jutish Kent, Saxon Essex and Wessex, and Anglian Mercia.[59] Other names for Odinn include "Deep-hooded one" and "Very wise one."[60] *"I am called*

---

55 Ralph Metzner, *The Well of Remembrance: Rediscovering the Earth Wisdom Myths of Northern Europe* (Boston: Shambhala, 1994), p. 112
56 Grimm, *Teutonic Mythology,* IV, p. 1283-4
57 Branston, *Lost Gods of England,* p. 49-50
58 *Lost Gods of England,* p. 41
59 *Lost Gods of England* p. 42
60 Young, *The Prose Edda,* p. 49

Mask, I am called Wanderer, Warrior and Helm-Wearer...War-merry...Weak-eyed, Flame-eyed...Mask and Masked one, Maddener and Much-wise...Broadhat, Broadbeard, War-father...Father of All, Father of the Slain...by one name I have never been known since I went among the people...Grimnir they called me...Odinn I am called now, Terrible One I was called before..."[61] ("Grimnir's Sayings," from the Verse Edda, 46–54)

As *"Father of All, Father of the Slain,"* Odinn reveals himself as the receiver into the afterlife. According to the Eddas, he welcomed half of those fallen in battle (sharing the other half with the goddess of magic Freyya) and directed the valkyries in ferrying the valiant dead to the hero's paradise of Valhalla.

Associated with Wodan's connection with the dead, and his identification with divine madness, is his identification with the Hunt. The "longer duration of heathenism, especially of Wodenworship, among the Saxons, is perceptible in the legend of the Wild Host..."[62] Parallel phrases and folktales in Scandinavia give "full assurance" of a connection between this Saxon *Wode* and the old northern god.[63] In areas of Nordic influence, the hunt is strongly linked to Wuotan: *wutende heer*, the "wild army."[64] Also, *Odens jagt*, otherwise known as "Woden's Hunt," known in Anglo-Saxon as *wodendream*.[65] Wuotan, the god of war and victory, appears army-like with valkyries and *einheriar* in a train. They are oft accompanied by a howling wind, or a *"crying and whooping."*[66]

It is significant that sometimes (as in Bavaria) the Devil takes the place of Wuotan in the Wild Chase, as does a giant in Switzerland.[67] Devil-like, when Wod happens across unwary travelers after dark, he sometimes vows to "make them his own," and, Wodan-like, the Devil sometimes disguises himself and travels amongst humanity incognito.[68] The Devil's army is called a *"swarm"* in Ger-

---

61 Carolyne Larrington, trans. *The Poetic Edda* (Oxford: Oxford University Press, 1996), p. 58–9
62 Grimm, *Teutonic Mythology*, vol. IV, p. 1283–4
63 *Teutonic Mythology*, vol. III, p. 919
64 *Teutonic Mythology*, vol. III, p. 918
65 Branston, *Lost Gods of England*, p. 94
66 Grimm, *Teutonic Mythology*, vol. III, p. 919
67 *Teutonic Mythology*, vol. III, p. 920
68 *Teutonic Mythology*, vol. III, p. 924

manic folk-stories, as is Diana's band in the *Canon Episcopi*.[69] And the Devil periodically pulls people through the air, as the goddess of pagans and the Wild Hunters were said to do.[70] (Perhaps others have heard the ominous expression, *"to ride with the Devil."*) The Devil and Odinn are further linked in expressions and customs of phrase associating them with unruly weather. All of this strongly suggests (to me at any rate) that the Devil was an import into European mythology, very incorrectly misinterpreted by European pagans, who (having no native conception of a figure of *Evil* such as the Devil, which implies that they lived in a world in which people could sometimes *do* bad things, but in which *Evil* as a giant, pervasive thing did not exist) appear originally to have accommodated the Devil to their own conception of pagan gods, having no other real context for him.

Initiation

One starts to understand the Wild Chase as a metaphor for spiritual experience. One is alone in the woods. It is still. Suddenly—a ripple and a murmur, a breeze, a stir in the trees. Suddenly—the storm of Odinn falls upon one, and when it is over, one is —different, somehow. Everything is as it was, but it is all—different. *Shamans frequently say that the shamanic introduction can strike one with as devastating effect as the Fury of Odinn's storm—as suddenly and as unpredictably.*

Other Hunt leaders

In Lower Saxony and Westphalia the Hunt is led by *Hackelbernd*, *Hackelberg*, or *Hackelblock*, a huntsman who, at the time of his death, asked leave to continue to ride for eternity. Hackelberg is associated with a specific forest, the Hackel, near Halberstadt and Groningen.[71] Those fateful few who happen across Hackelnberg (like those who stumble across faerie revels) must fall on their faces and not dare look as the Host passes by. The clothes Hackelberend wears are notably similar to Odinn's traditional garb—the wide-brimmed hood which hangs over the blind eye, the great cloak. *Hakolberand* is, in fact, an Old Saxon epithet for *Wodan*, gradually

---

69 *Teutonic Mythology*, vol. IV, p. 1606–7
70 *Teutonic Mythology*, vol. III, p. 1028
71 *Teutonic Mythology*, vol. III, p. 921–2

taking on independent life as the hunter.[72] *Hakol* seems familiar as well to the Old Norse *Hekla*, associated with mountains, woods, highlands, and the name of another Hunt-leader.[73]

The Ride, first the occupation of the gods and goddesses of heathen times, began to be associated with heroes as the centuries wore on. The French and Germans imagined *Charlemagne* leading the Chase, as the English did *Arthur*. Gervaise of Tilbury comments thus, and *The Complaynt of Scotland* reveals that, "*Arthour knycht he raid on nycht with gyldin spur and candillycht.*"[74] Eckhardt the faithful goes before frau Holle's train to warn people of her coming (also in legends, he faithfully sits guard outside the mount of Venus). In Frankfurt therefore, as late as 1688 (according to a Lutheran minister's dissertation) youths escorted a large cart filled with leaves (vegetation motif) from house to house to the accompaniment of song, in memory of *Eckhard's army*.[75] *Dietrich Bern* is another native hero associated with the Wild Band, as is Danish *Waldemar*.[76] Other mythological characters mentioned in connection with the Furious Horde are associated with the Ember Days upon which the Horde was expected to appear. Southern Austria, Carinthia, and the Slovenes identify *Quatembermann* ("the man of the four Ember Days"), otherwise called *Kwaternik*, as the Hunt Leader; Baden, Swabia, Switzerland, and the Slovenes deify *Frau Faste* ("the lady of the Ember Days") or similar characters such as *Posterli* or *Quatemberca*.[77] In Switzerland, *Frau Saelde*, also called *Frau Zalti* or *Frau Selten*, guides the procession of children who died before baptism, which travels on Wednesday night of the Ember Days of winter.[78]

The Swabian specter *Berchtold* or *Berhtolt* ("the bright") leads that hunt, clothed in white; he is a male version of the white-robed *Berhta*, Apollo to her Artemis, as t'were. Otherwise, the goddess *Holda* holds her own against the bad-boys of Teutonic mythology, whipping up her own Wild Hunt on occasion. As the *Decretum* and

---

72 *Teutonic Mythology*, vol. III, p. 923
73 *Teutonic Mythology*, vol. III, p. 923
74 *Teutonic Mythology*, vol. III, p. 942
75 Ginzburg, *Ecstasies*, p. 182
76 Grimm, *Teutonic Mythology*, vol. III, p. 943
77 Ginzburg, *The Night Battles*, p. 189–90
78 *The Night Battles*, p. 190

Nicholas of Cusa attest, the *"witch Holda"* is as associated as any with the Furious Chase. Her mistress-ship of the Hunt is noted by the fact that her hair is frequently messed from night-flying, *meatt der Holle farn.* A man with shaggy hair is likewise called *holle-kopf.* Teutonic stories describe how the *"unholden" "fared to the woods"* to join the Wild Ride; the phrase "faring to the woods" recalls phrases used in connection with forest outlaws.[79] In the woods, the unholden drove even hunters before them, blowing horns like *Tutosel,* who, as an owl, flew ahead of the Furious Host. Jacob Grimm: *"Such* unholden *are much more night-dames,* bonae dominae, *than devil's partners."*[80] *Perahta,* the bright, the luminous, similar to *Selene, Lucina, Luna, Artemis, Diana,* and the later *Bensozia* and *Abundia,* makes her appearance (Hecate-like, accompanied by hounds) in the areas where Holda leaves off—Alsace, Switzerland, Bavaria, and Austria.

⌇

Ginzburg finds the *Hunt mythology* to be a phenomenon related to the *Night-Ladies cult* of Europe, which subject is covered with exhaustive thoroughness in *Ecstasies,* along with the whole shebang's probable origin in *Eurasian shamanism.* Areas in Europe where the Hunt mythology is found—a supernatural *movement* of exultant *participants*—are also the parts of Europe where: women flock in *nighttime assemblies* in honor of a beneficent *goddess;* processions of men and boys disguised as *animals* take place; the spirits of the *dead* were thought to roam during the *Ember times* of the year, periods also associated with all of the above. As well, all of these phenomena are connected to occurrences of *ecstasy*—the churchman Nider says women claim to *see souls* during the Ember times; women say that they see and visit with *pagan goddesses;* persons in Italy and Central Europe say that their *souls slip free* of their bodies.

Contemporary thought believes that the purpose for a lot of Europe's strange, prehistoric earthen constructions—the spiral of Glastonbury Tor; stone rings such as Stonehenge and Avebury; linear ditches that can run for several miles—is to serve as avenues for ritual *procession* somehow. (This is also imagined to be the solution to similar land-works in other parts of the world, such as

---

79 Grimm, *Teutonic Mythology,* vol. III, p. 1061
80 *Teutonic Mythology,* vol. III, p. 1061

the famous Nazca Lines of Peru.) Whereas the procession traditions of the Wandering Mistress are heavily identified with women, the traditions of the rough, unruly Wild Hunt are stereotypically masculine—and mixed up to more then a small degree with an activity of primal importance—the *hunt of animals* for food.

Fertility-god

> *The Horned god represents powerful, positive male qualities that derive from deeper sources than the stereotypes and the violence and emotional crippling of men in our society. If man had been created in the Horned God's image, he would be free to be wild without being cruel, angry without being violent, sexual without being coercive, spiritual without being unsexed, and able to truly love.*
> —Starhawk, The Spiral Dance[81]

Spread throughout the ancient world are networks of archetypal religious imagery. The cult of the Mother-Goddess is the most famous of these, the Mother and Her youth-consort. But—appearing in tandem—is the *Fertility-God*, the life-force god, a god of vegetation and nature. He is identified with animals, whatever animal seems vital and impressive to the native populace: stags, bulls, goats. He is specifically identified with the horns of animals, regarded as symbolic of virility and strength.

Bronze Age rock carvings in Scandinavia and in the Italian Alps suggest a fascination with horned men. The Teutons will eventually become proverbially identified with horns; the Celts, in like fashion, made powerful associations with horns. In Celtic art, horns are often found on gods in human form; to express power and divinity, the Celts often combined the human and the animal form. As Miranda Green notes, "The tradition of horned and zoomorphic imagery was very strong in the Celtic world." "There appears to have been no rigid division, in Celtic perceptions of divinity, between the human and animal form. Thus, gods could be depicted with hooves, antlers or the horns of a bull, goat, or ram."[82]

---

[81] Starhawk, *The Spiral Dance: A Rebirth of the Ancient Religion of the Great Goddess* (HarperSan Francisco, 1989 ed.), p. 109

[82] Miranda J. Green, *Dictionary of Celtic Myth and Legend* (Thames and Hudson, 1992), p. 120

A rock carving from the seventh century BCE at Camonica Valley depicts a half-man, half-stag figure, whose antlers are emphasized. An early (600–500 BCE) German pillar-stone shows horned sculpture, as does La Tene metalwork. A Celtic horned helmet is recovered from the Thames at Waterloo Bridge and horned helmets are carved over the first century CE arch at Orange; Iron Age coins depict horned beings, particularly a Hungarian coin which depicts a *horned horseman*. In the Romano-Celtic world, we find horns widely distributed. Horns were added to Roman gods such as Mercury and Mars; a horned Mercury in bronze is recovered from the shrine at Uley (Glos). Gallic horned gods are found at Blain near Nantes, and at the Burgundian shrine of Beire-le-Chatel. Horned gods predominate among northern England, especially in the areas held by the Brigantes tribes. Frequently, as at Maryport in Cumbria, warriors are shown (in good Celtic fashion) nude, with dicks, spears, shields, and horns. And—in Icklingham, Suffolk, and at Richborough, Kent—women deities are shown as horned.[83] This connects with old fayry stories of *horned women*, who are identified as *witches*, and who have various adventures (such as told by Briggs, in Appendix II to *Anatomy of Puck*).

Horned men, with a combination of human and animal characteristics, are painted on the walls of caves in southern France thousands years ago. Horned beings are next found in Europe during the Celtic period. As Murray notes, "It is highly improbable that the cult of the Horned God should have died out in southwestern Europe in Neolithic times and have remained unknown through the Bronze and Iron Ages, only to be revived before the arrival of the Romans. It is more logical to suppose that the worship continued through the unrecorded centuries..."[84] *If, then, this religious identification of horned men continued throughout Europe from the Stone Age to the coming of the Romans, it is equally unlikely that this same ingrained religious tradition will die out suddenly four hundred years later, when Rome goes Christian.* As Murray says, "Such a cult must have had a strong hold on the worshippers, and among the illiterate, and in the less accessible parts of the country it would

---

83   *Dictionary of Celtic Myth and Legend*, p. 120
84   Murray, *The God of the Witches*, p. 29

linger for many centuries after a new religion had been accepted elsewhere."

Cernunnos

The Christians, seeking to replace the "barbaric" faith of the heathen Europeans with the "enlightened" faith of Christ, frequently erected shrines and chapels at popular sites of pagan worship. The idea was that pagans, already accustomed to visiting these spots, slowly would come to associate them with God the Father, instead of with Thor or with Nemetona or with Brighida or whomever. *It is the curious case, then, that places of Christian worship are often also the same sites of still-older pagan worship.* It was not altogether surprising, then, that when repairs were being performed in Notre Dame Cathedral during the eighteenth century, workers unearthed a four-sided stone altar, dedicated to a pagan god. This altar was dedicated by sailors to *"Cernunnos"* during the reign of Tiberius, and was carved with a man's face, bearing two proud *stag's antlers* on his head.

From each horn hangs a torq (a Celtic neck-ring, which may have a variety of important connotations). The man has also the ears of a stag. *Although this is the only artifact uncovered which gives* Cernunnos *as the man's name, the symbology is repeated in enough other places to make it seem that he was a generally recognized deity.*

During the fourth century BCE, he was carved on a rock at Paspardo in Camonica Valley in northern Italy, with a torq on each arm, accompanied by a ram-horned snake and an ithyphallic being.[85] The *Gundestrup Cauldron*, a lovely silver bowl recovered from a peat-bog in Denmark, into which it was apparently thrown as an offering, contains a famous representation of an antlered Cernunnos-figure. The vessel could date from 400–300 BCE. *The figure appears to be sitting cross-legged. He holds a torq in one hand. He is accompanied by a stag, a ram-horned snake, and by other animals. Note: it has been pointed out that the figure is beardless, an unusual trait for a Celtic man. This may indicate that the figure is either a woman or represents some sort of shamanic transgendered state.* There are many surprising similarities between the Mohenjodaro Shiva and the Celtic being fashioned onto the Gundestrop Cauldron. Both are horned and both are sitting cross-legged, in apparently

---

85 Green, *Dictionary of Celtic Myth and Legend*, p. 59

the same yoga-posture. Both are surrounded by animals and—like innumerable Celtic figures—Shiva is possibly three-faced. How a 2400-year-old Celtic/Danish metal-worked bowl so closely resembles a 4700-year-old proto-Indian ornament has led to much speculation.

T.C. Lethbridge, in *Witches*, noted various points of congruence between ancient Celticism and Indian Hinduism. For instance, reincarnation is famously a central tenet to both systems and Lethbridge feels that the Druids appear very like the Indian Brahmins. As a devotee of *Krishna Consciousness*, I am struck by how closely the Hindu kirtan resembles modern pagan ritual—down to the consecration of the four elements and the communal raising of energy through *drumming, chanting, and ecstatic dancing*. Hinduism is, of course, a pagan (polytheistic) religion—paganism expressed in Eastern terms and paganism that has existed for centuries free of the interference of Christianity.

Another Roman altar from Reims, France, depicts the horned man as god of abundance. He is again cross-legged, seated between Apollo and Mercury. A bag on the god's lap pours forth grain, consumed by a bull and a stag. The god wears a torq. A British-Roman coin, dating from the first century CE, found at Petersfield in Hampshire, shows an antlered being with the solar wheel between his horns.[86]

The horned figure is most popular in north-central Gaul, in the Charente region of western France, at Saintes, and in Britain. He is sometimes (as at Nuits-Saint-Georges) triple-faced (in the manner of other Celtic deities); at other places, he is associated with *triplism* in other ways. Sometimes (such as Haute-Marne), the relief of the god has holes in his head, for the addition or removal of real or metal horns. This may "reflect seasonal ritual, where the antlers were inserted or removed in imitation of spring growth and autumn shedding of antlers on a stag."[87] He is depicted as a god of abundance, replete with cornucopiae, fruit, bowls and bags of grain or money. He is shown as a god of fertility, associated with either penises or with snakes (especially ram-horned snakes; snakes, to the Celts, were symbols of renewal). His identification with the graceful power and animal virility of the stag is shown by his ant-

---

86 *Dictionary of Celtic Myth and Legend*, p. 60
87 *Dictionary of Celtic Myth and Legend*, p. 60

lers and his sometimes "cervine ears or hooves." Miranda Greene notes that Cernunnos is "one of the most striking examples of a semi-zoomorphic Celtic god." She concludes from this that Cernunnos the Horned One may have represented one of those shamanic Celtic "beings who regularly underwent transmogrification or shape-shifting from human to animal form, mentioned so frequently in the vernacular literature."[88]

Herla
Both Celtic and Teutonic Europe mythologize processions of the dead. In Celtic Europe, this is seen in the pageant of spirits who are wont to travel with a maternal goddess. In German and Scandinavian Europe, this image becomes somewhat more robust. An out-of-control Horde swoops across the land, occasionally leaving havoc and wreck in its wake. King Arthur and Charlemagne were said to lead the Hunt, as was Odinn or Wuotan. At other times, in other places, the Hunt was led by *Herla the King*, by *Herne the Hunter*, by *Herlechin, Herlequin, Harlequin, Hellequin*, or *Hillikin*. The myth of the *Horned One* includes several *Wild Hunt* leaders, identified by the distinctive *"H-RN"* prefix—which, like the *"C-RN"* prefix of "Cernunnos," is associated in Celtic languages with horned beings.

Herla is an ancient British king who led his men in a Wild Hunt after attending a wedding feast hosted by the Dwarf King. Walter Map, the twelfth-century writer, gives a vivid account of Herla's Ride, also providing one of the stories which describe the variation in time between the Otherworld and our own. Herla and his men travel deep within a mountain, to celebrate a wedding-feast of the dwarf-tribe. Although they thought that they had tarried a mere afternoon, when they get home, they find (Rip Van Winkle-like) that they had been gone two hundred years. When one of the men dismounts, he crumples to dust. So there is nothing to do but to ride on and on, *"across the Moors of the West Country and the fells of the North, round the lakes between the mountains in Wales and through the Yorkshire dales."*[89] Anybody who sees Herla and his Host must expect either calamity or death.

---

88 *Dictionary of Celtic Myth and Legend*, p. 60
89 Sybil Marshall, *Everyman's Book of English Folktales* (London: J.M. Dent & Sons Ltd., 1981), p. 105

The story of the spectral horseman is an old favorite, with even American versions—think of Sleepy Hollow. *Another tale has a farmer returning home after dark, who encounters another rider on the dark road. The anonymous horseman tosses something to the farmer, who catches it. Because it is dark, the farmer cannot see what he has caught. He imagines that it is a rabbit, fresh from the hunt. When he gets home, his servant brings a lantern, and, to his dismay, he sees that he has been holding the body of his infant child. The shade vanishes at the instant that his servant tells him that the baby died about a half-hour before.*[90]

Herla was said to lead orgies in the cavern of the gnomes, something of which witches and heretics were accused throughout the Middle Ages.[91]

Harlequin

From *Herla the King* comes *Herlequin/Harlequin*. Map's twelfth-century account of King Herla roughly coincides with the 1091 report of the Ride of *Harlequinn*, called the Ride of the Dead, in Bonneval, France. The monk Ordericus Vitalis reported in his *Church History* a priest who was said to have witnessed a large procession one night, a crowd with people both on horses and on foot. In the fashion of the ecstasy traditions, the priest was said to recognize many of the recent dead. *"This is doubtless the troop of Harlechin, of which I have heard but never believed,"* the priest concluded.[92] At the head of this train was a giant with a club.

Hellequin/Hennequin is one of the most evocative archetypes ever—human, yet eerie and unworldly at the same time. He is the masked clown of the Middle Ages—the jester, the fool. He can be endearingly child-like—shy, quickly amused, easily distraught. Or he can be an erotic, mysterious lover with a semi-dangerous seduction.

As *arlecchino*, he is a character in Italian comedy and English pantomime, where he is a rival in the affections of Columbine. Tinkling bells (a Celtic touch) herald his approach. In equally Celtic manner, he is associated with *fayres* and with *Dame Habonde*. He wore the Fool's traditional forked cap, with its two drooping, *horn-like* appendages. Like the other Horned Gods, he is a mor-

---

90   *Everyman's Book of English Folktales*, p. 105
91   Russell, *Witchcraft in the Middle Ages*, p. 117
92   Ginzburg, *The Night Battles*, p. 48

tuary deity: the name *Hellequin* (also *Hielekin;* also *Karlequinte* in several thirteenth-century Hessian poems) is connected to the German *helle* (the underworld), in his case "personified and made masculine."[93] This identifies him as a *chthonic fertility-god*. It therefore makes sense that medieval theologians called him a demon; significantly, he appeared on stage in the *Jeu de la Feuillee* (1262), as both a comic devil and as the prince of faeries.[94]

Harlequin is one of the great medieval *Masters of Misrule*, who turned social custom upside down and reveled in a ribald, anarchic, carnival-like atmosphere of creative mayhem. His wonted masked face indicates his shamanic urges to slip between the worlds; he was the Lord of the masking occasions in which the Middle Ages delighted—and over which Puritan Reformists developed grave misgivings and directed much vitriol. Hellequin was the living spirit of Mardi Gras in the medieval world.

In his adventures of merriment and absurdity, *Herlekin* was attended in the same manner as the parading folk-goddesses—he was followed by a train of witches and *hide-covered creatures*. The witches indicate his connection with the spirits of the supernatural world; the hide-covered creatures are another example of the ritual *imitation of animals* by celebratory humans.

"Fool" originally had meanings beyond silliness; the French *folie* meant "madness" or "lunacy," and the *Feast of Fools* was an ecstatic celebration. Followers of Harlequin were called *sauvages, selvatici, selvaggi,* and *homines selvatici*—"wild men" (in keeping with the pagan tradition of ecstatic celebration), from the root *silvus*, meaning "forest."[95]

Hellekin is often imagined in the amorous pursuit of women. However—as with other European divinities (there are stories about Odinn and Loki)—Hellekin seems to have jumped a fence now and again. An associate of his is *Crokesos*, a shape-shifting elf akin to Puck. He, too, was thought to wear a multi-colored coat adorned with bells; an association with various French terms im-

---

93 Grimm, *Teutonic Mythology*, vol. III, p. 942

94 Francois Laroque, *Shakespeare's Festive World: Elizabethan Seasonal Entertainment and the Professional Stage* (New York: Cambridge University Press, 1991), p. 26

95 Arthur Evans, *Witchcraft and the Gay Counterculture* (Boston: Fag Rag Books, 1978), p. 70

plies a homoerotic identification, specifically involving the subject of anal penetration.[96]

Harlequin's ambiguous sexuality has enabled us to conceive him as both female and male. We remember Harlequin for his erotic aspects in the eponymous romance novels that are so very popular. In another well-known modern incarnation (DC Comics), Harlequin has gender-jumped into *Harley Quinn*, a female clown of crime, who is a partner to the psychotic Joker in *Batman*.

Horned Ones

Herla and *Herne* are variant spellings of the same word. The Romans incorporated their Latin religion into the native beliefs of the lands which they occupied. We therefore find syncretized systems of belief—Celtic gods, say, joined with Roman ones. The name of the horned god whose altar was buried beneath Notre Dame—*Cernunnos*—then represents the Latinized version of a Celtic name; the *-os* ending is the suffix added to masculine nouns in Greek and in Old Latin. The original version of the name, we then infer, is *Cernunn*. Now—the prefixes *Cer*—and *Her*—are interchangeable, both being Indo-European roots which mean "horn." *Cernunn* may thus be rendered as *Hernunn*. This, as Arthur Evans suspects, was "the original Celtic ancestor of Herne, which is one of the oldest names for the male figure we're dealing with."[97]

> *So was Helgi beside the chieftains like... the young stag, drenched in dew, who surpasses all other animals and whose horns glow against the sky itself.*
> —the Verse *Edda*[98]

The *Star Carr* settlement in Yorkshire, England, is a remarkable example of a prehistoric site. Dated c. 9000 BCE, it occupies a space on the timeline continuum roughly half-way between the Trois Freres Sorcerer and us. Their "stuff" reveals much about their society to us. A wooden paddle suggests that they possessed boats that they used on the nearby lake. Canine bones indicate that they

---

96 Randy P. Conner, *Blossom of Bone: Reclaiming the Connections between Homoeroticism and the Sacred* (HarperSan Francisco, 1993), p. 170
97 Evans, *Witchcraft and the Gay Counterculture*, p. 69
98 Larrington, *The Poetic Edda*, p. 139

THE HORNED GOD OF WYTCHES 35

had domesticated dogs. A huge number of "barbed points" reveals that they applied themselves with industry to the manufacture of spearheads. Remains demonstrate that they overwhelmingly killed stags when they hunted, presumably leaving hinds and fawns—making it likely that they practiced a form of animal-husbandry and deer-herd management.

Most fascinating of all is the presence of masks or head-gear fashioned from the skulls of deer. The head-pieces are made from the skull frontlets, leaving the antlers attached. Perforations indicate that they were worn; the interiors of the skulls have been hollowed, as if to make them lighter. It is possible that they were used as camouflage, to help the hunters invade the herd. More probably, they were used in some sort of magical ritual.[99]

The stag is well-represented in the animal masquerades of Europe. Hungarian minstrels sing of an astral stag, which holds the sun, the moon, and the stars in his antlers. This mystical deer announces himself as a messenger from God. Russia and the Slavic

---

99 John Manley, *Atlas of Prehistoric Britain* (New York: Oxford University Press, 1989), p. 27

countries are also familiar with the legend. "*A stag with a miraculous head Has a thousand ends to his horns; On these thousand ends burn a hundred thousand candles; They burn without being lit, They extinguish themselves.*"[100] Stags are often depicted in Celtic iconography, shown in a variety of representations and featured in the literature. Bronze and Iron Age carvings at Camonica Valley, in the Italian Alps, are fascinated with the stag. Naquane Rock (c. 700 BCE) shows an ithyphallic hunter with a creature half-man, half-stag.[101] Otherwise, the stag is depicted enclosed within a circle of praying and dancing humans. We like this image—*the stag depicted enclosed within a circle of praying and dancing humans*—because it is seemingly repeated centuries and centuries later, in the early seventeenth-century chapbook *Robin Goodfellow: His Mad Pranks and Merry Jests*, which shows Robin the Stag-God encircled by celebratory humans.

The Leinster epic of the *Ossianic* cycle is wholly dedicated to deer, describing a civilization of hunters who apparently developed something of a deer-cult. The Ossianic cycle is the Irish/Highlands saga of the forest-band, the *Fianna* or the *Feinn*, a group that apparently felt a deep, abiding connection with the cervine. The true name of the band's leader Finn/Fionn is *Demne* ("deer"); that of his son *Oisin/Ossian* is "fawn"; that of Finn's grandson *Oscar* is "he who loves deer." Ossian is so named because his mother, Sava, was turned into a doe by an evil Druid.[102]

The hunting of a deer could take on mystical overtones in a culture so inclined. The story of *Peredur* in the *Mabinogion* (the probable basis for the *Perceval* legend), demonstrates childhood precocity (in a method typical of Celtic stories) when Peredur drives two deer into the goat-house with his mother's goat herd. Otherwise, at the end of the story, he must attack and kill a great stag with only one, unicorn-like, antler in the middle of its forehead. In the Highlands poetic narrative *The Lay of the Great Fool* (Laoidh an Amadain Mhoir) the Great Fool slays a deer; in the prose opening to the *Lay*, the illicit son of a knight, raised in secret, precociously kills a deer; his foster-mother

---

100 Violet Alford, *The Hobby Horse and Other Animal Masks* (London: The Merlin Press, 1978), p. 142
101 Green, *Dictionary of Celtic Myth and Legend*, p. 198
102 Markale, *Merlin*, p. 162

makes him a dress of the deer's hide, a shamanic trophy of his heroic initiation.[103]

The deer-hunt takes on less mystical overtones, but remains a symbol of heroic accomplishment nonetheless, in the *Grail* story of Perceval (the Grail *Perceval* being very like the Welsh *Peredur*). In Gautier de Doulens's continuation of de Troyes's *Le Conte du Graal* (c. 1200), a damsel promises Perceval her charms if he will bring her the head of a stag which roams the castle park. Perceval succeeds, but the head is carried off by a Robber Knight and Perceval spends a great portion of the manuscript trying to recover it.[104] The *Didot Perceval* tells much the same story: a damsel will grant Perceval her favor only if he captures the white stag of the wood.[105]

The storyline of the deer-hunt as a mythic quest persists in the *Suite du Merlin*, a continuation of the *Vulgate Merlin*, when a white stag invades Arthur's wedding feast, followed by the pursuant Lady of the Lake.[106] Stags serve as portents in the *Morte d'Arthur:* a white hart interrupts the wedding feast of Guinevere and Arthur (III–V); Gawain undertakes the quest-journey of a chase. Otherwise, Arthur, Uriens, and Accolon have after a hart (IV–VI). When it is killed, they see a richly appointed, torch-lit boat. They board and are welcomed by twelve maidens.

Like the Welsh *Peredur,* the supreme wizard *Merlyn* is unquestionably Welsh and often associated with the stag. In the *Vita Merlini* (c. 1132), Merlyn, as the Madman of the forest, appears before his wife Guendoloena mounted on a stag (the Serbian *Vila* also rode a stag), driving before him a herd of deer (motif: Merlin the Sacred Madman, master of forest-animals). Merlyn tears an antler from the stag's head and hurls it when he sees the man Guendoloena is to marry.[107] In the *Merlin* of the *Vulgate Cycle*, a Wild Man appears before the Roman Emperor's court to prophesy. Before he leaves, he writes these words in Hebrew: *"Know that the great antlered stag who*

---

103 Alfred Nutt, *Studies on the Legends of the Holy Grail, With Especial Reference to the Hypothesis of its Celtic Origin* (New York: Cooper Square Publishers, 1965), p. 153–160

104 *Studies on the Legend of the Holy Grail*, p. 16

105 *Studies on the Legend of the Holy Grail*, p. 29

106 Richard Cavendish, *King Arthur and the Grail: the Arthurian Legends and their Meaning* (New York: Taplinger Publishers, 1978), p. 115

107 Markale, *Merlin*, p. 4

was hunted in Rome, as well as the Wild Man who interpreted the emperor's dream, was Merlin, the prime councillor of King Arthur of Britain." Merlin then leaves Arthur's court for the Forest of Broceliande, *"full of does, stags, and deer."*[108] Here he meets a noblewoman named *Uiuiane* (Vivyan) by a fountain (motif: Celtic water-worship).

Keeper of Windsor

That the stag was a powerful creature in native European animal-worshipping mythology is demonstrated by nothing so well as the legend of *Herne,* an English variant on the Gallic *Cernunnos.* The best known tale of Herne goes as follows (please note that it is a Wild Hunt tale, with the same supernatural elements associated with the Hunt in Germany): *Herne is a forester (a "keeper"). Of course, he is the best forester there is; he lives as one with the forest and knows every single tree and animal as well as he knows himself. He is a master of the hunt and he enjoys the king's great favor. All the other king's men grow jealous of Herne and begin to meet in the woods at night to plot against him. Soon they treacherously implement a plan that leads noble Herne to a wicked and untimely death.*

Before you know it, though, a ghostly figure of dark vengeance begins to stalk the woods at night—a great, massive rider, upon a huge, sturdy steed, both rider and steed as black as blackest night. Most terrifying of all, the midnight specter is distinguished by an immense rack of antlers branching high above his head. *He haunts the king's men, forcing them to ride hard with him night after night until they are so tormented that they confess to the king and are each hung from* Herne's oak.

The idea of a vengeful god seems especially Celtic, the Celts being a people capable of enormous grudges and the same people who conceptualized war-goddesses such as *Badb* and *Morrighu* and the cursing *Macha.* Before we get all sanctimonious about the unenlightened primitiveness of Vengeance Gods, however, let us recall that the God of the Old Testament and Revelation looks to have had a pretty quick temper, too, ahem, ahem. Beings such as Herne and Macha do provide vehicles through which desires for hard justice may be directed—who of us has not felt keenly the sharp pang of injustice, either personally or out of an empathetic sympathy with someone else?

---

108 *Merlin,* p. 16

Herne may be seen as a pronounced mortuary figure—clearly another manifestation of the Hunt *Leader of souls*. His antlered head is clearly a stag-identification. He is sort of a personalized aspect of the hunted deer, who might, we imagine (if so able), resent being hunted cruelly to death. Herne's identification with an oak is notable, as the Celts worshipped trees; the word "Druid" is thought to derive from the Celtic word for "oak."

Many stories of Herne are markedly Odinn-like: they often describe someone's finding a hunting-horn at a spot associated with Herne; as with Odinn, blowing the hunting-horn can be a very big mistake, as it tends to draw the Wild Hunt to you.[109]

There is an old tale goes

A really famous reference to Herne occurs in Shakespeare's play *The Merry Wives of Windsor* (IV.iv.26–36), as Mistress Page relays the legend: *"There is an old tale goes that Herne the hunter, sometime a keeper here in Windsor forest, doth all the winter-time, at still midnight, walk round about an oak, with great ragg'd horns; and there he blasts the tree, and takes the cattle, and makes milch-kine yield blood, and shakes a chain in a most hideous and dreadful manner: you have heard of such a spirit; and well you know the superstitious idle-headed eld received, and did deliver to our age, this tale of Herne the hunter for a truth."* Note the process whereby, according to Mistress Page, these old myths survived the years— *"the superstitious idle-headed eld"* (*"eld"* meaning both "elders" and people of an older time) *"did deliver to our age"* these tales *"for a truth."* One can imagine many a young child (one of them perhaps named Will Shakespeare) attending to the ghostly legend of Herne by the fireside, with a nervous eye fixed outside the window at the dark woods of Stratford.

For the play's ultimate comic set-up, the eponymous merry wives (Mistresses Page and Ford) convince Falstaff to meet them at night near the famous Oak of Herne. He thinks he is arranging a romantic assignation and shows up wearing a pair of deer-horns (symbolic of beast-like pagan virility), in anticipation of the impassioned three-way that he thinks will ensue. Essentially Falstaff costumes himself as Herne; he means to say, "I am the Horned One."

Little does he know that everyone else is dressing up like feyries and hobgoblins, to surprise Falstaff by making him think that

---

109 Briggs, *Encyclopedia of Fairies*, p. 220

the Faerey Ride is breaking out upon him; this will freak him out and humiliate him, which will be really funny, because Falstaff is such a lying con-man. (Essentially Falstaff is getting *punked* at the end of *Merry Wives*.) After everyone has had their fun laughing at Falstaff's fear and embarrassment, they are going to dance a customary round at Herne's oak—at midnight.

Scholars agree that it is possible that some kind of Mummer's Play enacting some sort of ritual concerning Herne (a pagan Passion Play or something) might have been preserved at Windsor during the time of Shakespeare, inspiring the ending to *Merry Wives*. Russell reminds that varieties of Morris Dance maintained in isolated villages even until the twentieth century reveal survivals of folk-custom similar to that seemingly alluded to in *MWW*.[110] At any rate—the identification of a group of *Elizabethans* faring into the *woods* at *night*, dressed up as *spirits of the otherworld*, to *dance around* a haunted *oak tree* at midnight—in the company and in the honor of a *pagan horned deity*—is a very pagan circumstance for the late sixteenth century. It also smacks more than a little of a witches' Sabbat or a meeting of Night Women—at the time of *Merry Wives* (late 1590s), people are getting set on fire on the Continent over allegations not dramatically dissimilar to these. (Incidentally— there are apparently several ancient oaks in Windsor Park that are known as "Herne's Oak.")

Herne is a stud god. His horns are those of the rampant stag; he is connected with the cosmic powers of renewal and the vital sex-force of the forest. Since the ancient Europeans associated death with sex, and they associated both death and sex with deer, Herne has a certain sexy Plutonian quality. *The "connection of fertility gods with the earth and hence with the underworld of ghosts and... spirits was a venerable tradition in both Mediterranean and Northern cultures."*[111]

By this connection, the pagans saw in both death and sex the powers of the universe—the power of creation and the power of extinction. That which is born is that which is destined to die. Each glimpse of eternity is a glimpse of death. The world blooms, and the world dies, but we keep on having sex, and orgasm means "little death," and through the blood and the pain of labor the child is born and hopefully will live to grow up and help out on the farm. Death and sex.

---

110 Russell, *Witchcraft in the Middle Ages*, p. 300, n.4
111 *Witchcraft in the Middle Ages*, p. 47

Herne is a complicated business. On the one hand he is a very dark and brooding god; his is an understanding that that life can be harsh, that fate can be grim. This does not make him evil; it makes him *chthonic*, or "underworld-like" (subtle distinction). *Chthonic* means deep and deep means wise. Herne represents a fearsome universe. This is something that the ancients recognized; Indo-European and Eurasian shamans said that only through the descent into the underworld, through the ecstatic voyage of the *living into the world of the dead,* does wisdom and enlightenment come.

Tom Cowan's thoughts about the supernatural Herne are germane: "Here we find another example of the paradox known to shamans. Behind the mysteries of nature sits an intelligence who is sometimes fierce, sometimes gentle, but to those who know how to speak the secret language of the animals, is always attentive and eager to communicate. Like the Eskimo spirit Sila, Herne may say to us, 'Be not afraid of the universe.'"[112]

It is worthwhile to reflect upon Herne's resemblance to another dark, brooding hero, a man undeniably associated with the night, a man angered by injustice, a man likewise associated with horn-like appendages. But however dark and brooding he is, *Batman* is also very sexy and very good.

Herne and other such supernatural pagan phenomena seem to occupy the same place in the English cultural mind that ghost-sightings and UFOs occupy here in America. Herne (who may perhaps be thought of as the Ghost of Windsor) is said to be a sort of Protector Deity, who will appear should England or the royal family ever need him. Witnesses claimed sightings of the Horned One before the Second World War, as they did with the Wild Ride and Drake's Drum and the Devil's Dandy Dogs and other unearthly phenomena; people living near Windsor have, apparently in our own modern times, reported a wild yelping of hounds as occurring periodically. Presumably reported in much the same manner as other such occurrence is reported: "You're going to think I'm crazy, but I *swear*—"

Katharine Briggs recalls that, when a schoolgirl in Edinburgh in 1915, her teacher told Katharine that her (the teacher's) father was a retired colonel with apartments in Windsor Castle. On

---

112 Tom Cowan, *Fire in the Head: Shamanism and the Celtic Spirit* (HarperSanFrancisco, 1993), p. 121

moonlit nights, he told his daughter the teacher, he saw Herne standing under his oak.[113] And the story is told of a present-day royal guard who was found passed out on the grounds. When revived, he seemed to have suffered a shock and kept repeating something about "a statue that came to life"—which would probably knock anybody out. What fascinates though is—*it doesn't matter if the story is true or not. Even if it is just one of those strange "modern myths" which is told as if it were true*, it still is a twentieth-century version of the same phenomenon which has been described in the folklore since at least Ginzburg's benadenti: *a vision, of a pagan figure, seen by someone who has fallen into an unconscious (ecstatic) state in consequence!*

Alexandrian Traditionalists Janet and Stewart Farrar represent the "second generation" of witchcraft, after the death of Gardner in 1964. Their many books (including *What Witches Do* and *The Witches' Way*) dominated the "witch scene" during the late 1960s and 1970s. In *The Witches' God*, they pass on an interesting theory about how the horned god's name came to be.[114] The hind, when she wants the company of a stag, calls to him. The Farrars assure us that anyone who has ever been in a still forest and heard the rich, throaty call *"Hh-errrn! Hh-errrn! Hh-errrn!"* reverberate throughout will not forget the thrill. It is likely that our forebears were equally awed by the exciting sound and fixed upon the hind's call as the name of the stag-god. At the time, the Farrars made their home in Ireland near a medieval market cross and a churchyard stone, both of which featured the horned god. Several places in England incorporate "Herne" or "Hern" in their names, implying that such places were once dedicated to the forest-god. One such example is *Herne Hill* in South London. This name is often interpreted as being originally *Heron Hill;* but, as the Farrars point out, "since when did herons, which are river-fishers, live on hills?"

Other horned beings

As with "Herla" and "Herne," the names of other folkloric figures reflect the H-RN, or K-RN, root that denotes the Horned One.

The *Cerne Abbas Giant* resides above the village of Cerne Abbas in Dorset, England. The turf has been cut away to the chalk be-

---

113 Briggs, *Encyclopedia of Fairies*, p. 220

114 Janet and Stewart Farrar, *The Witches' God* (Custer, Washington: Phoenix Publishing, 1989), p. 99

neath, outlining a 180-foot-high giant carved into the hillside. He is a naked man (very Celtic), with a notable penis (he is sometimes called "the rude man" for this), holding aloft a club in his hand. It is "very probable" that the giant was carved during the Roman period, thus dating to the late second century CE, and it is "quite likely that [the giant represents] a Celtic fertility god."[115] Remarkable is the fact that the Rude Man (in all his rudeness) has been preserved over the centuries of Puritanism and Victorianism—testament to how thoroughly "of the landscape" and "of the locality" he appears to be.

An abbey was founded at the spot in 987 CE, possibly as a "countermeasure against the paganism represented by the giant."[116] Periodic scouring prevents the grass growing back over the giant (the village church has a 1694 record of *"repaires"* made to *"ye Giant"*) and the day came to be considered a holiday. In a custom first recorded in the early 1900s, a Maypole is traditionally erected above the giant's head on the first of May and danced around, "in a fertility ritual which was presumably stimulated by the presence of the overtly virile image." It is possible that the May ritual postdates the carving, perhaps by a significant amount of time; at the same time, "it may reflect a fertility cult which had been going on for centuries, perhaps for two millennia." Since May 1 was an important Celtic holiday, the "Cerne Abbas figure may well have been at the centre of such fertility ritual."[117]

Similar to the Giant of Cerne Abbas is the *Long Man of Wilmington*. A true giant at 231 feet in height, similarly carved into the earth, he holds two staffs or rods in his hands. Comment has been made that he resembles a man standing in a doorway, which is interesting as the megaliths of Stonehenge resemble gigantic doors. Otherwise it might be worth pointing out that both Celtic kings and Faerey kings bore staffs of office. Scholars agree that a prehistoric date for the Long Man seems likely. A sixth- or seventh-century artifact possibly connected with the Long Man is an Anglo-Saxon buckle from a burial in nearby Kent that depicts a nude man holding two staffs; the Long Man is first definitively established by a drawing attached to a 1710 land survey.

---

115 Green, *Dictionary of Celtic Myth and Legend,* p. 59
116 *Dictionary of Celtic Myth and Legend,* p. 58
117 *Dictionary of Celtic Myth and Legend,* p. 59

A very interesting theory to the mysterious Man is the observation that he could represent a prehistoric surveyor, with two sighting staffs. As a theory also circulates that many of England's prehistoric monuments lie in ley lines (lines of straight, undeviating latitude and longitude), this makes it possible to imagine the Long Man as the Prospero of the pre-Celtic Britons, directing the fashioning of the English countryside into a ritualistic landscape.

The universality of horned gods

In Sharon Caulder's brilliant book *Mark of Voodoo: Awakening to My African Spiritual Heritage*,[118] she includes in her photographs a contemporary statue of the Voodoo deity *Legba* in Ouidah, Benin. The statue depicts a seated man; his flat nose and mossy beard and hair identify him as African. He is further distinguished by two great horns sprouting from his head, a tail behind him, and a very obviously erect penis. This is a contemporary African sculpture; however, if it were possible to time-travel the work back to Celtic Europe in (say) 100 bce, I am sure that a Gallic Celt would identify the statue as Cernunn and a British Celt would call it Herne.

Daghda

Getting back to the club waved by the Cerne Abbas Giant: The father-god to the Celts was *the Daghda,* many Celtic tribes venerating some version of the Daghda as their own tribal ancestor. (The Daghda is primarily thought of as an Irish god, but can be traced back to Gaul, to judge from inscriptions and place-names of the Roman period.[119]) A rough, uncouth man, the Daghda was primitive even by Celtic standards. (The Daghda's son *Oghma,* inventor of the Celtic alphabet, may represent a more civilized version of the Daghda, as may gods such as Bel and Lugh.) Rough-hewn though he was, the Daghda was also credited as being *Eochaidh Ollathir,* the "Great Father," and *Ruadh Rofessa,* the "Lord of Perfect Knowledge."[120] Lethbridge finds it interesting that the Daghda's name resembles "Daddy," "Dad," and "Dadda."

---

118 Sharon Caulder, *Mark of Voodoo: Awakening to My African Spiritual Heritage* (Llewellyn Publications, 2002)

119 H. R. Ellis Davidson, *Myths and Symbols in Pagan Europe: Early Scandinavian and Celtic Religions* (Syracuse University Press, 1988), p. 207–8

120 *Myths and Symbols in Pagan Europe* p. 204–5

The Daghda, and other tribal Celtic god-guardians, are sometimes thought of as having bull's horns. (It has been imagined that the Cerne Abbas Giant, as his name would suggest, might have once had horns—if so, the turf has evidently been allowed to recover these especially pagan emblems.) The Daghda was thought to have immense sexual powers; his ritual mating with the local territorial-goddess guaranteed prosperity for the region. It is a fact that the Giant of Cerne Abbas shares many of the Daghda's attributes: *a mighty dick; to judge from his size, great power; and of course—a club.*

Like Thor with his hammer or Arthur with Excalibur, the Daghda was distinguished by his emblematic weapon. With one blow of his club, the Daghda could dispatch a man from life; with the other end, he could gently restore life to the man. Boundary ditches dug between provinces and around sacred enclosures were said to be marks left by the Daghda's club; the great mace carried about ceremonially in England's House of Commons possibly descends from the Daghda's club, as does, in all likelihood (thinks Lethbridge), the club held by William the Conqueror on the Bayeaux Tapestry.[121]

The thing of significance to arise from the tribe-protecting father-god the Daghda is the number of excessively primitive, rough-hewn characters who appear in later folklore—often identified by a very large club. In a monk's eleventh-century French account of the Troop of Harlechin, the parade of the dead is led by a *giant waving a club*. Likewise, in the Lutterworth Christmas Play, none other than Beelzebub himself joins the other folkloric characters in making a holiday appearance: *"In comes I, old Beelzebub; Over my shoulder I carry my club, and in my hand a frying pan, pleased to get all the money I can."*[122] I take it that the frying pan was to receive donations proffered for the actors; I can't think of any reason to outfit Beelzebub with a club, except that someone made a connection between the Devil and the Daghda, just as someone apparently made a connection between the Devil and giants, and the Devil and Odinn, and the Devil and Thor.

---

121 T.C. Lethbridge, *Witches: Investigating an Ancient Religion* (London: Routledge and Kegan Paul, 1962), p. 62

122 John Matthews Manly, *Specimens of the Pre-Shakespearean Drama* (New York: Dover Publishers, Inc., 1967), p. 295

The concept of the Devil as an evil adversary appears originally to have been missed by the pagans of Europe, who not-infrequently imagined the Master of Hell in terms of their own native deities. Therefore, since Beelzebub seems to have been recognized as another aspect of the paternal Daghda, here he is (in the Christmas play, no less) jovially bearing the Daghda's signature club; it might help the association if the Daghda is imagined in this instance as horned, as the Devil was said to be. The situation might be comparable to that found in another mummers' play, *A Christmas Mumming: the Play of St. George*, in which it is Father Christmas who walks in, swinging a mighty club.[123] The Daghda-istic qualities of paternalism are (in this case) transferred via the club to that Jolly Old Elf, St. Nick.

Atavistic creatures

Other *giants with clubs* are found. In the Arthurian writer Chretien de Troyes's *Yvain* (c. 1170), the protagonist meets a churl (Vv. 269–580): *"I saw sitting upon a stump, with a great club in his hand, a rustic lout, as black as a mulberry, indescribably big and hideous . . .* [the fellow is compared to various animals] *There he stood, leaning upon his club and accoutred in a strange garb, consisting… of the hides recently flayed from two bulls or two beeves: these he wore hanging from his neck."*[124] The Daghda is identified in such situations by his club, and by his second distinguishing characteristic, the atavistic *wearing of skins*.

Notably similar is Map's twelfth-century account of the dwarf-king in his story of Herla: *"a pigmy no bigger than an ape, and of less than half human stature. He rode on a large goat; indeed, he himself might have been compared to Pan. He had a large head, glowing face, and a long red beard, while his breast was conspicuous for a spotted fawnskin which he wore on it. The lower part of his body was rough and hairy, and his legs ended in goats' hooves."*[125]

All of these elements of primitivism are intended to denote characters older than civilized time. It is worth observing that the

---

123 John Gassner, ed. *Medieval and Tudor Drama* (New York: Applause Books, 1987), p. 30
124 *Chretien de Troyes: Arthurian Romances*, W.W. Comfort, trans. (Dutton, New York: Everyman's Library, 1978 ed.), p. 184
125 Briggs, *Encyclopedia of Fairies*, p. 247

King of Dwarfs rides a goat, as many witches ride goats across the sky in illustrations to anti-witch books. The pagan circumstance of riding the pagan animal, a *goat,* will connect witches to the pagan creature, the Dwarf-King (meant to symbolize an existential orientation pre-dating recordable memory). The idea of ancient dwarfs (comparable to fays in European paganism) crawling into our consciousness out of subterranean caves and tunnels is very suggestive, in a Jungian and Freudian kind of way, as caves so readily intimate regression into the past. The fawn's skin worn by the Dwarf is another reference to the cult of the mythic deer; other significant details that denote an animalistic, "living with nature" nature are the fact that his bottom half is hairy (like a forest-beast) and—most notable of all—*his feet are the* cloven hoofs *of a horned animal.* In all of his significant attributes—his *goat-riding* and *skin-wearing,* the fact that his bottom-half is *hairy* and his feet *cloven-hoofed*—the Dwarf King signals an avenue of return into the lost ages of prehistoric (and heathenistic) religion. The Anglo-Saxon comparison by Map of the Dwarf-King to the classical woodlands-god *Pan* should be marked.

In the Charlemagne Romances (according to *Bulfinch's Mythology*), atavistic creatures guard sacred places (and therefore the sacred secrets that they keep): a *club-wielding giant* opposes Rinaldo at the mouth of the cave where the magical horse Rabican is kept; and Rogero is challenged at the entrance to Alcina's castle by hordes of hobgoblins, half-animal, half-human, clad in skins. In the Irish tale of *Tom o' the Goat-skin,* the hero comes to the court of the King of Dublin, clad in skins and armed with a club.[126]

The Daghda-esque character in *Yvain* tends beasts—like the mythic motif of "the Lord of Animals," comparable to the Ancient World depictions of the Mother-Goddess imagined as "the Mistress of Animals." A prehistoric seal from Mohenjodaro, India, equally depicts the mighty god *Shiva* surrounded by beasts, as "Lord of Animals." Tending beasts is another indication that the tender is a Celtic god-figure; paternal Celtic gods such as Cernunn and the Daghda are associated with animals and plenty. The Daghda stand-in of *Yvain* presides over a (symbolic and literal) crossroads in the story's advance and gives directions to a magical spring and basin (motif: Celtic water-worship). This is identical to a situation

---

126 Nutt, *Studies on the Legend of the Holy Grail,* p. 134

in the pagan Welsh *Mabinogion* story of *Owein*, whereby Kynon encounters a *huge black man*, surrounded by *animals*, who likewise directs him to the *enchanted fountain*. The motif is the same: *the huge, alarming men serve as guardians of a sacred site and as the keepers of the site's wisdom.*

Black of face

Another clue to the inordinate past of the Primitive Churl (in addition to skin-wearing) is the fact that he is often *black*—like the black-faced old hags of Celtic legend, such as *Caillech Bheur* and the many hag-faced daughters she produced. In Chretien de Troyes's *Conte du Graal*, the loathly damsel who upbraids Perceval is *"blacker... than the blackest iron covered with pitch."*[127] The idea of "black-facedness" as being indicative of "ancientness" perhaps accounts for the number of *Black Madonnas* found throughout Europe—the Christian Mother of God married to really old *cults of Fertility-Goddess* worship. It seems all the more significant, given that these figures who serve as guides and instructors in the course of a quest are all identified as black, that the Devil so often appears in witch-stories as a *Man in Black*.

A woman tried in Geneva in 1401 said that the Devil used to appear at her call, as a man dressed in a *black tunic.*[128] The witches of Dauphine worshipped the Devil in the form of a terrible knight dressed in *black armor* (this is also the symbolic image of *Edward the Black Prince*, legendary hero-son to Edward III, known for his ebony battle-suit). Otherwise the Dauphine Devil would be dressed in *black garments* with a crown atop his head. The Somerset witches described by Glanville (subjects of the last major witch-case in England) visited with a *black-garbed* Satan. Just as *animal-skins* and *cloven hoofs* and (sometimes) a *club* signify that *the Devil* was assimilated to *pagan beings*, so too seems the fact of the Devil's *blackness*.

Dressing-up rituals

Effort was made in the many popular seasonal "dressing up" rituals which continued throughout Europe to turn people into representations of the *spirits of the dead,* and to imitate the behavior of the *wild dead* as much as possible. We thus find customs whereby peo-

---

127 *Studies on the Legend of the Holy Grail*, p. 136
128 Russell, *Witchcraft in the Middle Ages*, p. 209

ple *invade the homes of others,* or demand some sort of *edible or monetary offering* as propitiation, or are permitted to indulge in *light theft or prankster hijinks.* (These will be noted as on-going *Halloween customs.*) Such customs, which in the Middle Ages often involved *drag* and the ceremonial display of *ritual animals,* could entail *blackening the face* as well. In Germany, the White Horse made his appearance on St. Nicholas's Day accompanied by the Feen (fayryes), which were men dressed as old women with their faces darkened.[129] The Padstow Old Hoss used to dip his hands into oil and soot, in order to blacken folks caught in his route; this was understood to impart fertility to the victims.[130] French bears in Roussillon likewise blackened Carnival victims with fertility-magic, before being captured by cross-dressed brides, who disappeared with the bears down the street in a wild gallop.[131] In the Swiss Alps, guiser bridal couples were accompanied by *Schnabelgeissen* (goats' heads carried on sticks) and an accordionist who had sooted his face. Otherwise, a guiser group was made up of a pretend-bride and groom, accompanied by a black-face devil.[132] Chimney-sweeps often accompany wedding parties in England, Hungary, and elsewhere, blackening being so thoroughly understood as a fertility-ritual.[133]

Names

The names of folkloric notables (such as the Ulster hero *Conall Cernach* for instance, or various *medieval saints*) continue to reflect the H-RN, or K-RN, root of the Horned One.

St. Kieran of Clonmacnoise had a tame fox that carried his writings for him (Lord of the Animals motif); when he died, the saint asked for his bones to be left atop a hill *"like a stag."*[134] St. Kieran of Saighir lived in his hermit's cell with a boar, a fox, a badger, a wolf, and a stag (Lord of the Animals motif). Another Irish saint, *Cainnech,* was acquainted with a stag (Celtic stag-worship), who allowed the good man to use his antlers as a book-rest.[135] The

---

129 Alford, *The Hobby Horse,* p. 116
130 *The Hobby Horse,* p. 40
131 *The Hobby Horse,* p. 95
132 *The Hobby Horse,* p. 128
133 *The Hobby Horse,* p. 141
134 Farrar, *The Witches' God,* p. 98
135 *The Witches' God,* p. 98

French seaside village of *Carnac* is an area known for its majestic avenues of *stone alignments*. A *bull-cult* of some kind seems evident, to judge from the *cattle bones* found in nearby *preherstoric burials* and the statue of a bull taken from the remains of a Roman villa.[136] A church painting is still seen of Carnac's patron saint *Cornely* blessing bulls, surrounded by *dolmens* (hanging stones) and *menhirs* (standing stones).[137] A local custom has always been to drive the cows through the streets on Cornely's *equinoctial feast day* of September 13, after the cows have been blessed at the church.

Horned women

The "horned" motif occasionally gender-jumps to the female, as the Briggs tale of *The Horned Women* demonstrates:

> *A woman is sitting carding and spinning* [so this story was probably devised by some woman, as she went about the tedious chore of her carding and spinning] *when there is a knock at the door. "I am the Witch of One Horn," announces the visitor, as she comes in (a great, towering woman). She sits and begins to card. "The women tarry long," the stranger observes, when there is another knock. "I am the Witch of Two Horns," and she sits and starts spinning. Finally there are twelve horned women, sitting about the fire working. "Rise and bake us a cake," they demand of their hostess. So this good lady goes to fetch water. "Carry it in a sieve," they command. She tries, but the water falls out. Suddenly—a voice in the air: "Bind it with moss and clam it with clay!" The voice continues: "When you get to the north side of the house, cry aloud three times, 'The mountain of the Fenian women and all the sky above it is on fire!'"*

It is kind of fascinating that the horned women are the "Fenians," because of course the Fenians are the same as the *Fian/Fianna*—the mythic Celtic forest-band heavily identified with the

---

136 John Michell, *Megalithomania: Artists, Antiquarians, and Archaeologists at the Old Stone Monuments* (Ithaca, New York: Cornell University Press, 1982), p. 65

137 *Megalithomania*, p. 65

Robin Hood/George a Green woodlands mythology—named for its shaman-warrior leader *Finn mac Cumhaill*.

> So the woman does as the voice directs and as she cries, out come flying the twelve horned women, who pound off to save their stuff from fire. Now that the women are distracted and gone (but soon to realize their deception), the very-helpful voice speaks yet again and the woman rushes about frantically fulfilling its instructions. She spills the foot water out of the house; jams a wooden bar over the door; breaks up a meal cake that has been baking on the fire (made with a bit of blood drawn from each member of the household); and she slips a piece into the mouths of each of her children. Lastly, she locks up the witches' web (the cloth that they had been working upon) into a chest. Just in time—for at that instant!

> "Open, open, feet water!" the horned wytches command. "I cannot, I cannot, for I am scattered," answers the foot water. "Open, open, wood and tree and beam!" "I cannot, I cannot, for I am fixed athwart the door." "Open, open, cake mixed with blood!" "I cannot, I cannot, for I am broken into pieces and my blood is on the lips of the children." The witches curse to themselves and leave.[138]

Andro Man

As example of how all this deer-worship mythology played out in the mortal realm of physical life:

In 1597 *Andro Man* was swept up in the Aberdeen witch-scare in Scotland. It was every bit as characteristic of Scots witches as it was for the Italian benadenti or for Central European nightwanderers to relate vivid personal histories, thoroughly invested with the native mythologies of their period; they sound as if they had very rich and imaginative interior lives. We possess these oral histories because they were transcribed in the course of witchcraft investigations (thereby inadvertently opening a window into late-medieval folk-culture). The Aberdeen witch-scare inaugurates the bloodiest witch-hunts in Scotland to that date.

---

138 Briggs, *Anatomy of Puck*, p. 227

Andro Man's story commences with a birth (of the Fay Queen's baby) and a death (of Andro's cow, on Ferye Hill). According to the record which is presumably based on his testimony and which is apparently being read back to him for his consenting agreement, the Queen of Elfame (Scottish witch-story is very preoccupied with the doings of the Queen of Elphame or the Fayrey Queen; a number of Scots wytchis claimed personal relationships with the Fee Queen) *"came to thy mother's house, in the likeness and shape of a woman... and was delivered of a bairn, as appeared to thee there, at which time thou being but a young boy, bringing in water, the Queen of Elphen promised to thee, that thou should know all things, and should help and cure all sorts of sickness, except stone dead, and that thou should be well entertained, but would seek thy meat or thow deit, as Thomas Rymour did."*

This is a very typical circumstance in European paganism— an individual claims to have been singled out for greatness by some sort of divine experience with a supernatural being, quite often imagined in Scotland as the Queen of Elves. To judge from Andro's story, the Queen had come to his house once when he had been a boy and had delivered a baby there (the delivery of babies was a big deal in Celtic folklore). Andro apparently came upon this private moment suddenly, in the course of fulfilling his chores by fetching in water. As a consequence, she bestows upon him her favor—he will "know" things and be able to cure any infirmity. The only thing blocked to him is the stepping-stone to divinity— he can not restore life to the dead. There is a reference to *Thomas Rhymer*, a legendary figure from some centuries previous, a mortal man who equally enchanted the Ferey Queen and who was gifted with extra-normal powers.

When he grows up, Andro's healing abilities begin to manifest. He is able to free one woman from the falling sickness and another from the misfortune of *"being heavily diseased with a furiosity and madness."* Like the benandanti and the night-wanderers (and like many characters in popular fare today, such as *The Sixth Sense* kid and the stars of TV's *Medium* and *Ghost Whisperer*), Andro has paranormal perception of the dead; of the fays, he *"kens* [perceives] *sundry dead men in their company."*[139]

Once he has started his career tending to the sick and the

---

139 Purkiss, *At the Bottom of the Garden*, p. 106

mad, his relationship with the Queen takes a notable turn. After *"the space of thirty-two years since or th*[ereabouts], *thou* [began] *to have carnal deal*[ings] *with... the Queen of Elphen, on whom thou begat diverse bairns, whom thou has seen since; and that at her first coming, she caused one of thy cattle die upon an hillock called the Elphillok, but promised to do him good thereafter."[140] Andro begins to have interludes of romantic intimacy with the Elphin Queen, who bears children conceived by him. This is a very Celtic occurrence—Cuchulaidh's mother conceived him with the sun-god Lugh, as Merlyn's mother did likewise with a otherworld spirit later said to have been the Devil. The Queen is apparently capricious, killing off one of Andro's cows on Elf Hill, but then repenting of her action and renewing her promise to do well by Andro. (It is interesting to find elves still associated with hills in Scotland on the cusp of the seventeenth century.)

The true reason that Andro might have been implicated in the witch-scandal comes out: it seems that he might have been arrested less for the suspicion that he trafficked with the Devil than perhaps simply for the fact that he engaged in unpopular political activity.

Andro Man starts to seem like an activist or something. A major source of social friction at the time was the closing off of "common" grounds for private or restricted use. Andro apparently had been "acting up" to preserve ancient grazing rights upon local commons. *"Thow has meted and measured diverse pieces of land... to the hind knight whom thou confessis to be a spreit, and put four stones in the four nooks of the ward, and charmes for the same, and... thow forbids to cast* [soil] *or divet theron, or put ploughs therein; and this thou did in the Manids of Innes, in the Manis of Caddell, and in diverse other places, which thou confesses thyself, and cannot deny the same."*[141]

Man measured out numerous parcels of real estate, apparently dedicating or re-dedicating them to the "hind knight." I'm not terribly sure who or what the hind knight was—"hind" is a female deer, so possibly Andro sees the "hind knight" as being a guardian of nature somehow; "hind" is also an archaic word for "worker" or "laborer," and "hind" can also mean "behind." Whoever or whatever the hind knight, he was apparently incorporeal—Andro con-

---

140 *At the Bottom of the Garden*, p. 135
141 *At the Bottom of the Garden*, p. 136

fesses him to be a "spirit." This is important, as Scots authorities at the time do not recognize any "spirits" other than devils.

Andro apparently blesses or charms the land-sections that he designates, in a manner familiar both to the medieval schools of ceremonial magic and to modern-day witches and neo-pagans. He puts stones and charms in the four "nooks"; essentially he consecrates each parcel to the four directions. He then forbids anyone else to dig or disturb the plots.

What Andro is actually doing is insisting upon the observance of an old Scottish custom, called the *"Gudeman's Croft,"* commented upon by Walter Scott in the 1820s. The Croft was a section of field which was never plowed or cultivated, but allowed to run wild in a sort of concession to the unruly qualities of nature, and an apology for imposing mortal restrictions upon her free spirit. Scott recalls "within our own memory" many such places, "sanctified to barrenness," in Wales, Ireland, and Scotland.[142] Andro Man may have thought that he was standing up for the little man or taking a stand for time-honored principle or appointing himself a defender of the untamed wild-lands. Whatever he did or thought he was doing, it was apparently interpreted as being a nuisance.

Andro relays an experience which perhaps—back in the Celtic day—might have been considered a deeply religious one. He describes what a modern wicche might call a vision of the God and Goddess—he sees a stag come out of the snow, whom he calls *Christonday*. With the stag is the Queen of the Elphen. *"Upon the Ruidday* [Rood-day] *in harvest, in this present yeir, . . . thow saw Christsonday cum owt of the snaw in likenes of a staig, and that the Quene of Elphen was their. . ."*[143] *"Upon the Rood-day in harvest, in this present year, which fell on a Wednesday, thou confesses and affirms, thou saw Christonday come out of the snow in likeness of a stag, and that the Quene of Elphen was there, and others with her, riding upon white hackneys, and that they came to the Binhill, and Binlocht, where they use*[d] *commonly to convene."*[144]

In one of the ecstatic, visionary testimonies that distinguish

---

142 Walter Scott, *Letters on Demonology and Witchcraft* (New York: Bell Publishing, 1970 reprint of 2nd ed.), p. 87

143 Margaret Murray, *The Witch-Cult in Western Europe* (Oxford: The Clarendon Press, 1962 ed.), p. 242

144 Purkiss, *At the Bottom of the Garden*, p. 138

Scots witch trials, Andro Man says that he had a vision of the Queen riding with her court upon white horses ("hackneys"); they repair to spots where they been accustomed to meet before (presumably before Scotland turned Christian). Andro sees Christonday—a stag.

Andro elaborates further of the Queen: *"the quene is verray plesand, and wilbe auld and young quhen scho pleissis: scho mackis any kyng quhom scho pleisis, and lyis with any scho lykis..."*[145] This description *("she is very pleasant and will be old and young when she pleases; she makes any king whom she pleases, and lies with any she likes...")* is wholly consistent with ancient Celtic folklore; this could serve as an admirable definition, for instance, of the Irish Queen-Goddess Medb, in the Celtic epic *The Tain*.

"*The said Andro confesses that Chrystonday rydis all the tyme that he is in thair cumpanie... Supposes to be an angel and God's godson... Suchlike thou affirms that the Queen of Elphin has a grip of all the craft, but Christsunday is the goodman, and has all power under God.*"[146]

Man connects Christonday with riding, that old pagan theme, and says that Christonday "rides" all the time that he is "in their company," meaning all the time that he is with the Fay Court. Andro attributes god-like status to Christonday (imagining him to be an "angel" and "God's godson"). This may have been an attempt on Andro's part to express the sacredness that he must have felt Christonday represented. However, as elevating a stag to the position of God's godson (although flattering in a pagan-reverential way), has to fall into the category of blasphemy (as viewed from the Christian Calvinist perspective), this cannot have pleased Andro's examiners.

Andro goes on—"*the Quene of Elphen has a grip of all the craft, but Christonday is the goodman, and has all power under God.*" This seems to be Andro's coming-to-terms with the relationship that he perceives between Christonday (who has "all power under God") and the Elfin Queen (who has a "grip of all the craft"). Like the untouched Croft of the fields, Christonday is the "Goodman."

From the perspective of heathen spirituality, this is all a very impressive account of a lifetime's pursuit of visionary revelation. From the harsh view-point of Scots Puritans and Reformists, this counts as Satanism. Undoubtedly as a result of the torture to which

---

145 Murray, *The Witch-Cult in Western Europe*, p. 242

146 *The Witch-Cult in Western Europe*, p. 242

he was assuredly subjected, Andro Man comes to agree that all the "spirits" that populate his belief-system—the Fay Queen, the hind knight, the miraculous stag that rides with the Elphame Court—are all "devilish." Those who confess to demonolatry in sixteenth-century Scottish witch-trials get burned at stakes.

This seems to me to illustrate the basic unfairness of witch-hunts. This dude has a vision of a stag that seems to him a vision of God. Others go, "Nope, heresy," and set the dude on fire.

Murray supposes that the evocative name *Christonday* is derived from some confused understanding of *Christus Filius Dei,* "Christ, Son of God." The stag is well-known in medieval iconography as a sacrificial figure, the holy victim whose shed blood becomes sacramental, as it leads to subsistence for those who hunt the animal. In the *Lay of the Great Fool,* the knight's son, when he first sees deer, asks what creatures they are. Animals *"on which were meat and clothing 'twas answered—it were the better he would catch them."* [147] In the magical vision conjured for Aurelius in Chaucer's *The Franklin's Tale* (518–33), he sees deer with high horns, and deer wounded by arrows and hounds. Likewise the ballad of *The Three Ravens* describes in reverent terms a dying deer. Certain stories of English King William Rufus describe him dreaming of turning into a slain deer, as he lies on the altar of a chapel.

Faerey-bandits

Another example of pagan deer/faerey mythology adopted as a symbolic guise by early-era political activists:

By the fifteenth century, the process of depriving people of access to lands that had been thought of as "public" was underway. Nobles were increasingly closing off lands into huge private estates and "parks," making it a crime for anyone else to hunt or "poach" the deer therein. This resulted in much hardship and public anger.

A band of yeomen, husbandmen, and tradesmen were indicted at Tonbridge in June 1451, for stealing deer from the deer-park of the Duke of Buckingham, at Penshurst, Kent. (This followed a similar action in January 1450 and an uprising in April 1451.) The raid had been conspiratorial; reference was made to *"others unknown to the number of one hundred men"* who also participated. Clearly they had been serious in their intentions. They had *"paint-*

---

147 Nutt, *Studies on the Legend of the Holy Grail,* p. 152

ed on their faces with black charcoal" and "in riotous manner and arrayed for war," had "chased, killed and took way from the said park 10 bucks, 12 [juvenile bucks] and 80 does belonging to the said duke, against the king's peace." In all instances, the perps exalted their cause of defiance and equality in a highly symbolic and inspirational way: they identified themselves as "servants of the queen of the fairies."[148] Without doubt, their painting their faces with charcoal was meant as an identity-disguise. However, given the context of their culture, it cannot have escaped their attention that they also guising themselves to represent the spectral riders of the Fay Court or the Wild Hunt.

The fifteenth century was one of marked protest—this is the era of Jack Cade, who led a rebellion in favor of the rights of common people, a trend that will continue through the English Civil War, the American Revolution, the French Revolution, the American Civil War, and finally the Russian Revolution in the twentieth century.

Puck and Robin Goodfellow

The Horned God of Europe is a little like a magic box that has a portrait of the Horned One on each side. Yet no matter how many times you turn it, a new picture always turns up.

The next manifestation of the god of witches to evolve is arguably the favorite character in medieval folklore—the composite figure *Puck/Robin Goodfellow*. Robin being the *Anglo-Saxon* incarnation of this being, and Puck representing his *Celtic* conceptualization, it appears that when the Anglo-Saxons met the Celts, such a perfect synchronicity was discerned that Robin Goodfellow and Puck became instantly intertwined forever (in the last speech of *A Midsummer Night's Dream,* the character refers to himself as both "Puck" and "Robin.")

Kind of their cultural Bugs Bunny and Santa Claus at the same time, *Puck/Robin* (like Bugs) is infuriated by injustice or unfairness and is a passionate defender of the underdog; his sense of mischief is good-hearted and only directed seriously against those who abuse power. Like Good St. Nick, *Puck/Robin* can be the very essence of generosity and magnanimity (provided one has proved oneself worthy). The widespread popularity of the char-

---

148 Purkiss, *At the Bottom of the Garden*, p. 67

acter may be seen in the many period references to him, both in the oral culture and through the literary world of published ballads, broadsides, and chapbooks. The most pertinent may be the seventeenth-century proto-novel *Robin Goodfellow: his Mad Prankes and Merry Jests*, wherein he asserts for all time his absolute devotion to good:

> *But to the good I ne'ere was foe:*
> *The bad I hate and will doe ever,*
> *Till they from ill themselves doe sever.*
> *To helpe the good Ile run and goe,*
> *The bad no good from me shall know!* [149]

Robin, like Puck, pretty much serves folklore as the uber-faerie or as the universal stand-in for all fays. In *Terrors of the Night* (1594), Thomas Nashe manages both to sum up nicely within a paragraph virtually the age's entire store of ferey-belief and to include elves, fayries, and hobgoblins behind the blanket-term *"Robbin-good-fellowes"*: *"The Robbin-good-fellowes, Elfes, Fairies, Hobgoblins of our latter age, which idolatrous former daies and the fantasticall world of Greece ycleaped Fawnes, Satyres, Dryades, & Hamadryades, did most of their merry prankes in the Night. Then ground they malt, and had hempen shirts for their labours, daunst in rounds in greene meadowes, pincht maids in their sleep that swept not their houses cleane, and led poore Travellers out of their way notoriously."* [150]

Nashe identifies fearey-mythology as being night-oriented; he also makes a connection between current Celtic-Anglo-Saxon faerie-mythology and the nature-spirits of Classical mythology— *"Robbin-good-fellowes,"* elves, faeries, and hobgoblins are the same creatures that the "fantasticall" world of Greece "ycleaped" (called, named) *"Fawns, Satyrs, Dryads and Hamadryads,"* in *"idolatrous former days."*

Nashe refers to the very friendly habit of the fee-folk, of "grinding malt" at night, which activity Nashe uses as a catch-all for all manner of domestic chores that the industrious citizens of the night would perform whilst muggles and mortals slept.

---

149 Briggs, *Anatomy of Puck*, p. 41
150 *Anatomy of Puck*, p. 23

The Pranks of Puck *(sometimes attributed to Jonson)*
Yet now and then, the maids to please,
I card (at midnight) up their wool;
And while they sleep and take their ease,
With wheel to thread their flax I pull.
I grind at mill
Their malt up still,
I dress their hemp, I spin their tow.
If any wake,
And would me take,
I wend me laughing's ho! ho! ho![151]

Robert Burton, discussing fays in general: *"a bigger kinde there is of them, called with us Hobgoblins, and robin goodfellows, that would in those superstitious times grind corne for a mess of milk, cut wood, or does any manner of drudgery work."*[152] Burton tells us of the superstition that Hobgoblins and Robin Goodfellows (who appear sort of one-and-the-same) will do "any manner" of drudgery, in exchange for a bowl ("mess") of milk. Like hobgoblins and Robin, genial brownies would occasionally do one's housework, as would the *phouka* (Puck). "The Phooka of Kildare," in the folk-story, describes itself as a ghost and takes the animal-form of an ass, but nonetheless cleans the kitchen at night like a brownie. Lady Wilde, in *Ancient Legends of Ireland*, tells the story of the miller and his son, who watched while a helpful band of phoukas thrashed the miller's corn.[153] Lobs would otherwise do house-chores at night; the First Fayry, in *A Midsummer Night's Dream* (II.i.16), bids Puck good-bye with *"Farewell, thou lob of spirits!"*

According to Nashe, fees also: collect hemp shirts as thanks for their help (it was imagined that fays most generally went about nude, being unself-conscious wild creatures); punished poor housekeeping (those that "swept not" their houses); pinched maids as they slept (a very suggestive bit of fay folklore); and most famously—danced in rounds at night, when not vexing night-wanderers by mixing them up in the darkness. All of these elements will be repeated again and again in the context of their folk-culture.

---

151 Purkiss, *At the Bottom of the Garden*, p. 174
152 *At the Bottom of the Garden*, p. 163
153 Briggs, *Encyclopedia of Fairies*, p. 326

Merry pranks

The ballad *"The Merry Pranks of Robin-Goodfellow: very pleasant and witty"* offers an "origin-story" for Robin, who—it is revealed—was fathered by Oberon, siring him with a mortal woman, thereby adding Robin Goodfellow to the list of folkloric figures who had a mortal mom and a supernatural dad. It also places Oberon into the category of "fay-kings who lust for pretty mortal girls sometimes."

> *In time of old, when fayries us'd*
> *To wander in the night,*
> *And through key-holes swiftly glide,*
> *Now marke my story right,*
> *Among these pretty fairy elves*
> *Was Oberon, their king,*
> *Who us'd to keep their company*
> *Still at their revelling.*
> *And sundry houses they did use,*
> *But one above all the rest,*
> *Wherein a comely lass did dwell,*
> *That pleas'd King Oberon best.*
> *This lovely damsell, neat and faire,*
> *So courteous, meek and mild,*
> *As sayes my booke, by Oberon*
> *She was begot with-child.*[154]

As the Feyrie King led his court in their nightly wandering revels, during which they visited various houses (motif), Oberon takes a fancy to one lass in particular, with the result that she bears the infant Robin Goodfellow. The midwife soon figures out that the child is of the sidhe (pronounced "shee"), and Oberon honors his paternal duties by sending the new mother delicacies and linens for the baby. Soon, however, the neighbors are complaining about the child's naughtiness (imagine living next-door to Robin Goodfellow during either the Terrible Twos or adolescence) and his mom tells the fayrey-lad he has to go off on his own. This is the starting point for many faerie-tales, *Jack and the Beanstalk* for one; Diane Purkiss points out that this mirrors the experience of mid-

---

154 Purkiss, *At the Bottom of the Garden*, p. 171

dling and lower-class boys—at a certain age, they are sent away to be apprenticed to a master.

Rich humor ensues when Robin is taken on by a tailor (like Shakespeare's Robin Starveling in *Midsummer*, who may have been named for the Goodfellow). Told to whip the sleeves of a gown, Robin whales at them with ferocity. In the manner of heroes who set off to have adventures in the world, Robin finds his identity—he meets his father and discovers his true nature. This is expressed in terms of a talent to turn himself into animals, confirming his link with the carnivalesque, his intractability, and his "endless capacity to disobey." [155]

As he will in *Midsummer*, Robin/Puck functions as Eros/Cupid in *"The Merry Pranks of Robin-Goodfellow: very pleasant and witty"* when he foils a lecherous old guy who is hot for his pretty young niece; Robin arranges the girl's marriage to a buff young dude instead. (Likewise, in *Tell-truth's New Year's Gift*, he helps young lovers escape parental tyranny, which is the general circumstance of *Midsummer* as well.) A "kind of spirit of stage comedy," Robin/Puck stands "both for good and tidy order and for the pleasures of emotional liberty." [156]

Knave in a white sheet

Country gentleman of a good family, Reginald Scot grew grave and concerned over the popular folklore of Robin Goodfellow. Scot had discovered a life's work and decried what he saw as horrendous abuses committed in the climate of hysterical witch-hunting that galed about him. In his book *Discoverie of Witchcraft* (1584), Scot argues passionately against what he considered to be foolish superstitions that unreasonably made people fearful. He places both witchcraft and faery-faith into this category, bemoaning, say, children's nurses who frighten them with tales of Robin Goodfellow and such. The result (says Scot) is that people grow up afraid of nonsense and get jumpy and freaky at night because of old-fashioned ridiculousness. Scot interestingly implicitly includes the Christian Church in his disapproval, charging that the Christians' terrifying people with the fool's tale of a Devil are as bad as flighty nurse-maids. Diane Purkiss notes that Robert Louis

---

155 *At the Bottom of the Garden*, p. 172
156 *At the Bottom of the Garden*, p. 173

Stevenson was traumatized by his nanny's tales of her monstrous Calvinist Devil.

Scot's most famous passage devolves into a very handy list of English feyrey-tale characters of the time (famous among folklorists): *"Certainly, some one knave in a white sheet hath cozened and abused many thousands, especially when Robin Goodfellow kept such a coil in the country. But in our childhood our mothers maids have so terrified us with an ugly devil having horns on his head, fire in his mouth, and a tail in his breech, eyes like a bason, fangs like a dog, claws like a bear, a skin like a niger* [black person, a super-early version of the infamous racial slur], *and a voice roaring like a lion, whereby we start and are afraid when we hear one cry Bough* [Boo]; *and they have so fraid us with bull beggars, spirits, witches, urchins, elves, hags, fairies, satyrs, pans, fauns, syl[v]ans, kit with the cansticke* [candlestick], *tritons, centaurs, dwarfes, giants, imps, calcars, conjurors, nymphs, changelings, Incubus, Robin Good-fellowe, the spoorne, the mare, the man in the oak, the hellwain, the firedrake, the puckle, Tom Thumb, Hobgoblin, Tom Tumbler, Boneless, and other such bugs, that we are afraid of our own shadows; in so much as some never fear the devil, but in a dark night; and then a polled sheep is a perilous beaste, and many times is taken for our fathers soul, specially in a churchyard, where a right hardy man heretofore scarce durst pass by night, but his hair would stand upright. For right grave writers report, that spirits most often and specially take the shape of women appearing to monks &c; and of beasts, dogs, swine, horses, goats, cats, hairs* [hares]; *of fowls, as crowes, night owls, and shriek owles; but they delight most in the likeness of snakes and dragons. Well, thanks be to God, this wretched and cowardly infidelity, since preaching of the Gospel, is in part forgotten."*[157]

Scot plainly felt that a great achievement of his time was the discarding of such harmful traditions of the past; again he makes a (very Protestant) connection between Celtic fayrey-faith and the tenets of Catholicism, musing with contentment that the *"great and ancient bulbegger"* Robin Goodfellow *"ceaseth now to be much feared, and poperie is sufficiently discovered."*[158] Briggs points out that this echoes Chaucer and anticipates Corbet, and remarks that, towards the end of the seventeenth century, belief in the feyries actually seems to have grown stronger.

---

157 *At the Bottom of the Garden*, p. 160

158 Briggs, *Anatomy of Puck*, p. 22

In some ways, his list is a display of erudition rather than folk-knowledge (satyrs, pans, fauns, and nymphs are not English conceptions) but Katharine Briggs assures us that "our native folk-lore...can supply an equivalent to most of these creatures." Shaggy lobs may reasonably be identified as satyrs, the Brown Man of the Muirs for Pan, mermen and merrows for tritons, Nuckelavee (a folkloric creature, half-man and half-horse) for a centaur, and "the innumerable white ladies and female fairies" for nymphs.

Others, the Man in the Oak, the Spoorn, Tom Tumbler (who may possibly be a poltergeist) and Boneless, have not survived until our time, although the Man i' the Oak seems reasonably like part of the tree-dwelling spirits/Green Man mythology. Calcars, sorcerers, hags, dwarfs, giants, and elfs all stem from Teutonic traditions; *Mare* is from the Anglo-Saxon *Mara,* a spirit who troubled dreams, seen in the *Nightmare* and *Mare's nest;* the Scandinavian *Alp* and the German *Mahrte* and *Drach* are of same nature, as is the medieval incubus. The *Hell-wain* is the wagon of the dead found in Wales and western England, surviving in English tales of ghostly carriages driven by headless horses and coachmen.[159]

Scot, in many ways, pre-dates the Age of Reason in his rejection of supernatural phenomena, anticipating the day when witchcraft would be as discredited as were faeries: *"And know you this by the way, that heretofore Robin Goodfellow, and Hobgoblin were as terible, and also as credible to the people, as hags and witches be now: and in time to come, a witch will be as much derided and contemned, and as plainly perceived, as the illusion and knaverie of Robin goodfellow. And in truth they that maintaine walking spirits, with their transformation, &c, have no reason to deny Robin Goodfellow, upon whom there hath gone as many, and as credible tales, as upon witches; saying that it hath not pleased the translators of the Bible, to call spirits by the name of Robin Goodfellow, as they have termed diviners, soothsayers, poisoners, and cozeners, by the name of witches."*[160]

Scot, in his torrents of disdain for superstitious faerey-culture, also comments upon the many traditions involving the fays (exemplified as Robin Goodfellow): *"In deede your grandams maids were wont to set a bowl of milke before him* [fays in general] *and his cousin Robin Good-fellow, for grinding of malt or mustard, and sweeping the*

---

159 *Anatomy of Puck*, p. 20
160 Purkiss, *At the Bottom of the Garden*, p. 162

house at midnight: and you have also heard that he would chafe exceedingly, if the maid or goodwife of the house, having compassion of his nakedness, laid any clothes for him, besides his messe of white bread and milk, which was his standing fee. For in that case he saith; What have we here? Hemton hamten here will I never more tread or stampen."[161] According to Scot, it had been customary a scant two generations before to lay out a bowl of milk for the fay-folk, observing the fiction that the fays would do all the housework at night. The capriciousness and the primitive nature of house-spirits become apparent when we discover that they go about naked, growing snippy and spiteful if presented with clothes. Scot finishes by quoting a popular saying attributed to pissed-off fayres—*"Hemton hamten here will I never more tread or stampen,"* meaning, "That's it, I'm not doing your work any more."

Merry wanderer of the night

> *"Either I mistake your shape and making quite, or else you are that shrewd and knavish spright call'd* Robin Goodfellow: *are not you he that frights the maidens of the villagery; skim milk, and sometimes labour in the quern, and bootless make the breathless housewife churn; and sometime make the drink to bear no barm; mislead night-wanderers, laughing at their harm? Those that* Hobgoblin *call you, and sweet* Puck, *you do their work and they shall have good luck: Are not you he?"*
>
> *"Thou speak'st aright; I am that merry wanderer of the night."*
>
> —So is Puck introduced in *A Midsummer Night's Dream* (II.i.32–43) (c. 1595)

The Celtic *Pouk:* known in Cornish as *Bucca;* in Welsh as *Bwcca* or *Pwcca;* in Irish as *phuka* or *pookha;* in English, as *Puck*. Related is the Danish *pog,* for "boy."[162] "Pouk" is otherwise a name given to the Devil; Langland speaks of *Pouk's Pinfold,* meaning hell.[163] Nationalist Welsh legend claims that Shakespeare borrowed his char-

---

161 *At the Bottom of the Garden,* p. 162
162 Grimm, *Teutonic Mythology,* vol. II, p. 500
163 Briggs, *Encyclopedia of Fairies,* p. 333

acterization of Puck from stories told him by a friend, who used to live near *Cwm Pwca*, a favorite haunt of the Welsh *pwcca*.

Puck is typically a character who needs little introduction. He is, in many ways, the quintessence of the folkloric spirit—the Bogey Beast, the Brag, the Grant—the boggarts, brashes, bogles, bugs, bug-a-boos, and other poltergeist-like spirits who torment humanity in general. He is their leader.

Like the British spirits *Dunnie*, and the *Hedley Kow*, Puck is a shape-changer who assumes a variety of forms, but favors the horse. This, of course, is another way to cause distress—"Many a wild ride has been suffered on the Phouka's back."[164] In *A Midsummer Night's Dream*, he shifts-shape variously into a horse, a headless bear, a three-legged stool, and a roasted crab-apple; one of the more delightful moments in the 1930s Warner Brothers movie of *Midsummer* is Puck's chasing the mechanicals through the woods, as we can see Puck's transformations on film, whereas we must imagine them in the play. *"I'll follow you, I'll lead you about a round, through bog, through brush, through brake, through brier: sometime a horse I'll be, sometime a hound, a hog, a headless bear, sometime a fire; and neigh, and bark, and grunt, and roar, and burn, like horse, hound, hog, bear, fire, at every turn."* (III.i.103–108)

> *This* Puck *seemes but a dreaming dolt,*
> *Still walking like a ragged Colt,*
> *And oft out of a Bush doth bolt,*
> *Of purpose to deceive us.*
> *And leading us makes us to stray,*
> *Long Winters nights out of the way,*
> *And when we stick in mire and clay,*
> Hob *doth with laughter leave us.*
> —Drayton, *Nimphidia*[165]

Like the Picktree Brag and the Bogy Beast, Puck enjoys himself by playing pranks; he turns himself into a stool in *Midsummer* so he can unseat an old matron and he makes himself into a roasted crab-apple so he can splash her when she sips her soup. According to Thomas Harman, Puck steals the bedcovers: *"I verily suppose that*

---

164 *Encyclopedia of Fairies*, p. 326
165 *Encyclopedia of Fairies*, p. 100

when they wer wel waked with cold, they suerly thought that Robin Goodfellow (according to the old saying) had bene with them that night."[166]

Even more fun than these amusing diversions is Puck's habit of misleading people in the dark. It was said that, if one got turned around in the woods and lost one's place, one had run afoul of either Puck or the faeries. *"... And so likewise those which* Mizaldus calls Ambulones, *that walk about midnight on great Heaths and desart places, which (saith* Lavater) *draw men out of the way, and lead them all night a by-way, or quite bar them of their way; these have several names in several places; we commonly call them Pucks."*[167] This disorientation is otherwise called being *Pouk-ledden, Pixy-led,* or *Mab-led.* Burton refers to it: *"As he (they say) that is led round about an heath with a Puck in the night."*[168] The superstition was so ingrained that William Tyndale uses it in 1531 as a metaphor for those who do not study the Good Book: *"The Scripture... is become a maze to them, in which they wander as in a mist, (as we say) led by Robin Goodfellow... they cannot come in the right way."*[169]

(Words of folk-wisdom: should you become hopelessly "Puckled" or "Mab-scrambled" some night, faerey lore promises that you will never find your way until you take off your coat and put it on again, turned inside-out. This is the only way to break the feyreys' spell.)

Puck is often associated with the will-o'-the-wisp, also called in German *feurig gehn, das irreding* (ghost), and *vafr-logi* (associated with graves, and treasure in graves).[170] These phosphorescent lights were supposed to be souls who had not gotten into heaven, roaming the earth in fiery shapes. They were otherwise described as spirit-children with firebrands, *"fire-men and frisking goats,"* the *irlicht* (err-light), sometimes *elf-licht*.[171] Imitation of the will-o'-the-wisp is responsible for the Jack-o'-Lantern.

---

166 Purkiss, *At the Bottom of the Garden*, p. 159
167 Katharine Briggs, *Pale Hecate's Team: An Examination of the Beliefs on Witchcraft and Magic among Shakespeare's Contemporaries and His Immediate Successors* (New York: The Humanities Press, 1962), p. 51
168 Briggs, *Anatomy of Puck*, p. 26
169 Purkiss, *At the Bottom of the Garden*, p. 159
170 Grimm, *Teutonic Mythology*, vol. IV, p. 1586
171 *Teutonic Mythology*, vol. III, p. 916

Puck plays

> *Captain of our fairy band, Helena is here at hand; and the youth, mistook by me, pleading for a lover's fee! Shall we their fond pageant see? Lord, what fools these mortals be!*
> —A Midsummer Night's Dream (III.ii.110–115)

Puck (Robin) is such a popular character there is a smallish sub-genre in the annals of Elizabethan drama that might be called "Puck plays" (as compared to Revenge Plays or History Plays or even Witch Plays). *A Midsummer Night's Dream* is the show we automatically identify with Puck, but he also stars (as Robin) in the comedies *Wily Beguiled* and *Grim, the Collier of Croydon,* suggesting an audience as eager for the stage antics of Puck as later ones would be for—say—Charlie Chaplin or Douglas Fairbanks.

Puck's role, like Oberon's for much of *Midsummer,* is to look upon the silly Athenians with amusement. Although "like all hobgoblins," Puck has his softer moments, "human follies are his perpetual entertainment." [172] Much as he gets considerable kicks out of tormenting the rude mechanicals and the young lovers, the upside-down reality that Puck creates for them results in the young lovers being able to marry the partner of their choice, rather than the mate their parents selected for them. In *Midsummer,* then, as elsewhere, Puck serves as "a force for social order against those who would disrupt it by too much authority." [173]

As the guy says at the beginning of *Midsummer:* "*The course of true love never did run smooth.*" (I.i.134) Puck and Oberon serve sort of as demented Masters of Ceremonies in the nighttime woodlands antics that they (wittingly and not) inflict upon the two sets of eloping lovers. Yet the maze of confusions and trials that the mortal lovers suffer at the hands of the fays affirm the rightness of their choices for marital partners; they undergo a *trial-test* in the midsummer woods and (as is the way with these things) emerge in the morning with the validation that had been lacking the evening before.

Oberon greets Puck in *Midsummer* (III.ii.4–5): "*How now, mad spirit! What night-rule now about this haunted grove?*" This single line emphasizes the thrilling quality of the "haunting" fees; the "night-rule" that up-ends the rationality of daytime and sets the stage for

---

172 Briggs, *Encyclopedia of Fairies,* p. 337
173 Purkiss, *At the Bottom of the Garden,* p. 173

joyful bouts of anarchy; and Puck (who presides over the night-madness of the Midsummer season) as the "mad spirit" ruling the festivities.

I guess medieval winters were long and depressing; it looks as if folks were bursting at the seams by the time summer rolled around, and the summer holydays appear to have been pursued with intensity and vigor. Seasonal festivities were observed with the appointment of a Lord of Misrule, whose antics helped create the desired atmosphere of joyful chaos so admired in the Middle Ages. Puck serves as the Lord of Misrule in *Midsummer*, spreading confusion among the mortals.

> *There's not a hag*
> *Nor ghost shall wag,*
> *Nor cry, ware Goblin! where I go;*
> *But Robin I*
> *His feats will spy,*
> *And send him home, with ho! ho! ho!*
> —From the broadside *The Pranks of Puck*,
> beginning *"From Oberon in Faeryland"*[174]

The lovers in *Midsummer* are chased, harassed, and tormented by Puck. *"Up and down, up and down, I will lead them up and down: I am fear'd in field and town: Goblin, lead them up and down!"* (III.ii.396–399) Puck then abandons them with his characteristic *"Ho, ho, ho!"* This phrase is heavily associated with Puck, appearing in every *Puck* or *Robin Goodfellow* play of the period. It is interesting that it is now Santa Claus to whom the phrase belongs; we wonder if he did not inherit it from Puck, although we imagine Santa's "ho, ho, ho" as being delivered in a heartier, chucklier baritone. Bugs Bunny's delivery of "ho, ho, ho" would mimic Puck's, I believe.

> *From Oberon, in fairyland,*
> *The king of ghosts and shadows there,*
> *Mad Robin, I at his command,*
> *Am sent to view the night-sports here;*
> *What revel-rout*

---

[174] Briggs, *Anatomy of Puck*, p. 41

*Is kept about
In every corner where I go,
I will o'ersee,
And merry be,
And make good sport, with ho, ho, ho!*[175]

Puck serves the Farie King Oberon, performing his bidding and zipping off on errands: *"I'll put a girdle round about the earth in forty minutes."* (II.i.176) *"I go, I go; look how I go, swifter than arrow from the Tartar's bow!"* (III.ii.100–101) The relationship between Oberon and Puck resembles that between Prospero and Ariel, and Lear and the Fool. (It is interesting to reflect that all three parts—Puck, Ariel, and the Fool—are sexually ambiguous and may be played by either men or women.) Puck also resembles Cupid more than somewhat in *Midsummer*. Cupid is invoked in the speech about the begetting of the flower Love-in-Idleness (II.i.155–169); portions of *Midsummer* may well have been inspired by Seneca's *Hippolytus* (where Cupid flies *"through the heavens"* with *"wanton weapons in his boyish hands,"* much like Puck girdles the earth), as well as by the *Anacreontea*, translated in 1554, and featuring evocations of seasonal festivities, wedding celebrations, and Eros/Cupid leading Anacreon through the woods to love.[176]

Like the *witch*, Puck appears with a *broom* at the end of Shakespeare's play. A reference is made to the traveling night-women, who like tidy homes; Puck explains that he has been *"sent with broom before, to sweep the dust behind the door."* (V.i.377–378) The night-time visits of the fayries and the night-women were supposed to bring blessings, and Puck alludes to this in his closing speech. *"If we shadows have offended, think but this, and all is mended—that you have but slumber'd here, while these visions did appear—and this weak and idle theme, no more yielding but a dream. Gentles, do not reprehend: if you pardon, we will mend. And, as I am an honest Puck, if we have unearned luck now to scape the serpent's tongue, we will make amends ere long; else the Puck a liar call: so, good-night unto you all. Give me your hands, if we be friends, and Robin shall restore amends."*

Puck was such a beloved being that his shows and ballads and

---

175 Briggs, *Encyclopedia of Fairies*, p. 238
176 Purkiss, *At the Bottom of the Garden*, p. 167

whatnot often end with a re-affirmation of his goodness and urge to helpfulness.

> *Thus having told my dreame at full I'le bid you all farewell.*
> *If you applaud mad Robin's prankes, may be ere long I'le tell*
> *Some other stories to your cares, which shall contentment give.*
> *To gain your favours I will seeke the longest day I live.*[177]
>
> —*The Pranks of Puck*
> (sometimes attributed to Jonson)

Puck has so much in common with other folkloric beings he seems to belong to a wide family of helpful spooks. Katharine Briggs feels that he must be related to *Billy Blind*, the friendly domestic sprite of the Border Country, who advises and helps Burd Isobel in the *Ballad of Young Bekie*. Ben Jonson's 1603 *Entertainment at Althorpe* utilizes a *Satyre* named "Pug," who is "essentially the same" as Robin Goodfellow.[178]

Folklore continues undecided as to whether or not *Robin Hood* was a real or a mythic person; arguing in favor of the mythic is the fact that Robin Hood's stubborn altruism and intransigent sense of fair-play resembles that of Robin Goodfellow, and that the name "Robin" is so woven throughout Brits folk-culture. Assuming that Robin Hood is a spirit, he might be another version of the Puck-like spirit *Auld Hoodie*.[179] From the "Rob" in "Robin" comes *"Hob,"* another name for the Goodfellow. In the manner of Robin Hood, a period-reference mentions *"Hobbe the Robber."* Children with the whooping cough at Brunswick Bay were taken to the *Hobhole,* so that the Hob could cure them. Their parents would call into the hole, *"Hobhole Hob! Hobhole Hob! My bairn's got kincough. Tak't off! Tak't off!"*[180] Briggs feels that the Hob, in this context, sounds not unlike the *woodmare,* the Anglo-Saxon echo.

Goat-games

According to Violet Alford, Scandinavia tends to favor the

---

177 *At the Bottom of the Garden*, p. 174
178 Briggs, *Anatomy of Puck*, p. 84
179 Briggs, *Anatomy of Puck*, p. 185
180 *Anatomy of Puck*, p. 190

goat as the object of seasonal animal-masquerades. This may not be surprising, as the goat is the sacred beast of *Thor/Donar/Thunor*, of whom is told the shamanic story of the god killing a goat, then resurrecting it. In *Norway*, down to this just-past century, maskers dressed as the *Julbukke*, or Yule-goats. They were received in homes and hospitably given cakes, an example of the traditional "alms-offering" which frequently accompanies this sort of ritual. Up until the end of the nineteenth century, goat guisers often appeared at weddings. One was understood to be a woman, but was really a man in drag; his partner, understood to be male, was the shorter of the two. Both wore goats' horns; the "woman" carried a club and a sack.[181] Otherwise goats' heads were held on sticks, a reminder at festive occasions of the spirits. *Sweden* is likewise fond of Yule-goats, usually as a carved head mounted on a stick,

---

181 Alford, *The Hobby Horse*, p. 119

born by a man dressed in hide. At Braunligen, in Thuringia, the *Braunliger Bock,* a "tourney-goat" with a great mane and curved horns, appears at important functions; elsewhere in Germany, at Yule, Carnival, and at weddings, the goat and the bear alternate with the *Schimmel,* or the White Horse.[182]

A strong connection exists between goats and Puck. Puck is traditionally depicted with small goats' horns, and Puck may possess goats' feet as well. The identification may derive through the French word for "goat," *bouc;* also related is *bucca,* or "buck," meaning a male stag, hare, or goat.[183] Grahn theorizes that the homo word "butch" (meaning "super-masculine," whether applied to a woman or a man) so derives as well; her thinking is that originally the tough-ass person who made the sacrifice of the buck or the goat would have been the "butch," subsequently wearing the leather of the sacrificial animal.

The connection between Puck and goats may be further seen in the case of the famous *Puck Fairs,* held throughout southern Ireland in mid-August. The most famous is the Fair of Killorglin, held in Kerry. The "ceremonies belonging" have elements in common with the winter-tide Feast of Fools celebrations, in which either a mock-king or a sacrificial animal is elected and crowned to reign over the proceedings. The designated goat is raised high above the crowd on a platform, where he is combed and decorated. (Murray includes a 1930s photo in her book *The God of the Witches* which shows a girl solemnly crowning the Puck-goat.) Bands play and dancing goes on for three days. At the end, the "Puck" is returned to his owner; if there ever was a killing attached to the Puck Fairs, it is no longer remembered.[184] (Alford remarks that the affair is oddly reminiscent of the prohibition from the 1240 Synod of Worcester, which ordered people not to *"raise up rams on high."*) Other goat ceremonies, or goat-impersonations, took place throughout Europe at various intervals. Catalonian shepherds, for instance, used to dance about a goat, a bell ringing from her neck.

---

182 *The Hobby Horse*, p. 116

183 Judy Grahn, *Another Mother Tongue: Gay words, Gay Worlds* (Boston: Beacon Press, 1984), p. 146

184 Alford, *The Hobby Horse*, p. 22

Mad Pranks and Merry Jests

> "Once upon a time, a great while ago... about that time (when so ere it was) there was wont to walk many harmless Spirits called Fairies, dancing in brave order in Fairy rings upon green hills [motif] ... (sometimes invisible) in divers shapes; many mad pranks would they play, as pinching of sluts ["housemaids" or "domestic wenches"] black and blue, and misplacing things in ill-ordered houses, but lovingly would they use wenches that cleanly were, giving them silver and other pretty toys."[185]
> —*The Mad Prankes and Merry Jests of Robin Goodfellow* (1628)

Mad Prankes and Merry Jests counts as a forerunner to the novel: a written narrative about a fictional protagonist, with a beginning, middle, and end. An account of current traditions associated with Goodfellow, the pamphlet was reprinted by Halliwell as *The Life of Robin Goodfellow*.[186]

Nutt considers *Robin Goodfellow: his Mad Prankes and Merry Jests* to be the last broken-down version of the pagan Welsh story of *Manannon mac Lir* (Manannon, the son of Lyr). Being the son of mortal woman and a supernatural being (in this case, Oberon) makes Robin like Manannon—and Merlin and Macbeth and Mother Shipton. His immortal paternity confers on him the power of shape-shifting; his characteristic love of impish mischief, feyry amorousness, and fay sense of justice are in evidence. He takes the form of the Will-o'-the-wisp and plays bogey-beast tricks, such as turning into a horse. Many other fay-celebrities join him at the end, including Faery Patch, who supervises farm and beasts, and the ghostly Church Grim: *"My nightly business have I told, To play these trickes I use of old; When candles burne both blue and dim, Old folkes say, Here's Faery Grim."*[187]

The *Lay of Grimnir* ("Sayings of the Masked One"), in the Verse *Edda*, is a sort of monologue of Odinn's, wherein he describes

---

185 Purkiss, *At the Bottom of the Garden*, p. 164
186 Briggs, *Encyclopedia of Fairies*, p. 268
187 *Encyclopedia of Fairies*, p. 206

himself (46–8). *"I am called Mask, I am called Wanderer...Flame-eyed...Mask and Masked One, Maddener and Much-wise; Broadhat, Broadbeard, War-father...Father of All, Father of the Slain...by one name I have never been known since I went among the people. Grimnir* [Masked One] *they called me..."*[188]

Many of the preherstoric earthworks of southern England are known subsequently as *Grimsdyke;* as Branston points out, these not only attest to the awe in which Wode was held, that his Anglo-Saxon worshippers were so impressed by the vast earthen mounds that they thought only Odinn capable of erecting them, this also testifies to the popular nature of Wod's worship, since he was known by a familiar nickname.

This identification assumes a mortuary hue when it attaches itself to the *church grim*—a spirit (often imagined as a spectral black dog, comparable to other ghostly dogs of the British Isles) who is supposed to have guarded churchyards from the Devil. Faerey Grim sometimes takes this form: *"I walke with the owle, and make many to cry as loud as she doth hollow. Sometimes I doe affright many simple people, for which some have termed me the Blacke Dog of Newgate."*[189] The legend of these extra-worldly creatures (otherwise thought of as death-portents) is attributed to old memories of foundation sacrifices. Folklore says that the first human buried in a graveyard has the responsibility of protecting it from witches and goblins, so a black dog is sacrificed first, to take care of the job. Comparable to the English church grims are the *fossegrim* of Norway and the *kirkegrimm* of Sweden.[190] The Swedish kyrkogrim is said to appear as a lamb because, in the early days in Sweden, lambs were buried under the altar; the kirkegrim in Denmark appears as a "grave-sow." Many beliefs and superstitious customs surround these supernatural animals, sacrificial guardians of the dead, who are also associated with the Teutonic All-Father, *Grimr the Terrible One.*

A very nice thing about *Robin Goodfellow: his Mad Prankes and Merry Jests* is the fact that it is preceded by a wonderful cover-illustration of Robin. Therefore—unique of all the texts that we have

---

188 Larrington, *The Poetic Edda*, p. 58
189 Briggs, *Encyclopedia of Fairies*, p. 205
190 *Encyclopedia of Fairies*, p. 205

reviewed so far—we can *see* what the seventeenth century imagined Robin to look like—and get an idea of how they expected him to look when they saw him on the stage.

How does he look? First of all, he is a naked man, his dick (which resembles a turnip) and balls swinging blatantly between his thighs. As nudity was not a Jacobean virtue, and as precious few other figures were publicly presented nude, Robin's free-spirited naturism must indicate how totally wild-natured he was thought to be; his unihibitedness also reminds us how disrespectful it was held to be, to presume to cover his ecstatic nudity.

He wears a necklace and waves a broom (the witches' symbol) and a candle (which otherwise might be taken for a wand or a magical staff, topped by a mystical crystal).

He is dancing in the midst of a circle of people. A bird flies overhead and a dog looks to be jumping in excitement. A musician provides music with his pipe. The whole picture suggests celebration and merriment.

The most significant thing about Robin Goodfellow on the cover of *Robin Goodfellow: his Mad Prankes and Merry Jests* is his legs. He has the hairy thighs, slender shins, and cloven hoofs of a deer.

He looks like the Greek forest-god *Pan*. He also looks exactly like the Celtic deer-god Cernunnos; save for the fact that Robin has bull's horns instead of deer's antlers, he might as well be the figure on the Gundestrop Cauldron.

That by 1628 there was some precedent for Robin's appearance is seen in *Love Restored* (published in 1616), starring, *"ROBIN good-fellow, hee that sweepes the harth, and the house cleane."* Robin here is in shape-shifting mode, trying various disguises to get into court (this must have been fun for the audience). Eventually he comes onstage as himself: *"In this despaire, when all invention, and translation too, fayl'd me, I eene went backe, and stucke to this shape you see me in, of mine owne, with my broome, and my candles, and came on confidently, giving out, I was a part o' the device."*[191] Note the broom and candles.

Robin Goodfellow and Puck frequently appear as manifestations of the same being. However, there is a notable difference between the two. Just as Herne the Hunter shares many character-

---

191 Briggs, *Anatomy of Puck*, p. 85

istics with Batman—and as Batman is often shown in relation to a younger, smaller, more adolescent counter-part (named "Robin," no less)—Robin Goodfellow (who can be compared to Herne the Hunter) may be contrasted with Puck in terms of age.

There is something about Puck that is without question young. The most brilliant performance of Puck ever has to be Mickey Rooney in the 1935 Warner Brothers movie version of *A Midsummer Night's Dream*, when he was about thirteen. (Malcolm also has a go at Puck in the first season of *Malcolm in the Middle*, when the kids on that show were still kids.) Rooney is so good as Puck (a critic noted that his laughter manages to be both infectious and sinister, which is very Puckish) that, once you have seen him, adults no longer look right in the role. Playing opposite Rooney as Oberon is Victor Jory (otherwise known as the Yankee overseer in *Gone With the Wind*), wearing an awesome, antlered head-dress (very Horned God); Rooney and Malcolm both play Puck with goat's horns. The youth of Puck is further emphasized by the fact that—a few centuries later—he is surely reborn as Peter Pan.

As Celtic Goddesses could be both old and young, the God appears to have had two personae—a man and a boy. The man is Oberon—Herne—Robin Goodfellow. The boy is Puck. The relationship of Robin to Puck is the relationship of the adult stag to the adolescent goat.

Robin and Puck are unique folkloric figures in one other way—they can be specific and generic, singular and plural. There is Robin Goodfellow; there can be many robin goodfellows. There is Puck; there can be various pucks. The only other personage I can think of who can be both one and many (I kind of hate to say) is the Devil (there is the Devil; there are various devils).

Horn dances

Of all the characteristics of animals, none fascinate so as the ability of some select beasts to grow *horns* on their heads. Since humans are unable themselves to achieve horns, and since horns provide so dramatic an ornament, the symbology of horns has impressed whole groups of people throughout the herstory of humanity. The high incident of mythic European horned beings demonstrates the fascination horns held for the pagans of Europe. Likewise, the fact that the *hunt* was mythologized into a significant folkloric occurrence demonstrates the mythic power which the pursuit of an animal, and the victorious return with the kill, held for the early peoples of Europe.

Sir Gawain and the Green Knight (c. 1375) describes a festive return from a hunt: *"High horns and shrill set hounds a-baying, then merrily with their meat they make their way home, blowing on their bugles many a brave blast."* (1362–64) "High horns" refers to the bugles; it is explained that, during this Christmas season, they are not hunting the bucks, presumably wishing to have plenty of bucks to sire young deer upon does in the rutting spring. It is interesting, though, that the phrase sounds as if it refers to deer's horns held high into the air. There had to have been some significant element of ritual to the slaying of a deer. Nothing else would explain the nearly-a-page of verse that details the dismemberment of the hind in *Sir Gawain*: *"And next at the neck they neatly parted the weasand from the windpipe, and cast away the guts. At the shoulders with sharp blades they showed their skill…"* (1335–37) A different hunt is detailed every day that Sir Gawain stays at the lord's castle, waiting for New Year's Day and his appointment with the *Green Knight*, implying a ritualistic passage of time.

Ben Jonson's *The Sad Shepherd* opens with a prideful account of the hunt of a massive stag (an implicit foreshadowing of the horned woodlands-spirit *Puck-Hairy* who will appear later in the show). Hunting deer clearly was an important pastime for pagan Europeans, undoubtedly going all the way back to the Stone Age and for a very serious reason: leather to make stuff out of and meat for protein. The need to catch a deer encouraged the desire to think like a deer—this might well be the secret behind the enigmatic *Trois Freres Sorcerer,* painted on the wall of the Caverne des Trois Freres in Ariege, France. He has a deer's antlers on his head and may be wearing some sort of animal skin; his odd, hopping pose may be some sort of ritual dance. He may represent a Paleolithic deer-shaman calling the spirits of the deer to his tribes-people. Like those native to the North American continent, populations who depended upon hunting for livelihood tended to make mystical identifications with the animals which they hunted.

Shakespeare (he of the preserved folk-story) uses the successful return from a hunt as the cause for ritual festivity in the forest-play *As You Like It* (c.1600 [IV.ii]), implying ancient antecedent for the custom. The hunters have killed a deer and now must celebrate the event; this they do by performing what folklorists call a *horn dance*—they sing a ritual song and dance with the antlers of the deer. *Since Shakespeare reflects social custom in his plays, and since he obviously introduces the scene merely in order to interject a song (a not-untypical Elizabethan dramatic device), we may assume that his audience automatically associated killing a deer with joyful merriment.*

First, the man who took down the deer must be presented to the Duke *"like a Roman conqueror; and it would do well to set the deer's horns upon his head, for a branch of victory. Have you no song, forester, for this purpose?"* It is interesting, the apparent custom of wearing the horns of the slain deer ("setting" them upon the hunter's head "for a branch of victory"); this is an impersonation of the deer itself, the Trois Freres Sorcerer, and Herne the Hunter, all at once. *Marian, in* The Sad Shepherd, *makes her first entrance returning from the hunt, of which she was the victor. We wonder, then, does this mean that Marian is wearing the horns of the deer that she has killed? It would be very Artemis-like of her if she were.*

As You Like It, The Sad Shepherd, and The Merry Wives of Windsor, all "collect" folklore. A study of these plays is the study of pagan custom, retained as countryside custom. The victory song which the foresters sing in *AYLI* (IV.ii) is well-known to folklorists: *"What shall he have that kill'd the deer? His leathern skin and horns to wear! Then sing him home!"* This implies a tradition to the winning return from a hunt—the triumphant hunter's wearing *the skin and horns of the slain deer.* (Presumably it proved desirable to wear just the horns and not necessarily the skin, which would be inconveniently ooky, I would think, at least until the skin dried into leather, although the custom seems to have been remembered as wearing both.)

I find it very intriguing that Shakespeare presents a primitive and magically shamanic tradition as de rigueur for sixteenth-century huntsmen; many ritualistic practices among Native peoples of the Americas, Africa, and Polynesia stem from the belief that by manipulating the physical effects of one's vanquished foes, one gains magical control over their spirits. The Native American shamanic habit of aligning themselves with the spirits of the buffalo or the bear prior to a hunting expedition, by dressing and ritualistically imitating the beasts (seeking to become as *one* with the beasts), is well-known. By dressing in the skin of the killed deer and by making a fetishistic trophy of its antlers, the hunter does three things at once: he *demonstrates* to the universe his power over the deer; he *sets the stage* for the killing of more deer; and he effectively *celebrates* the life-force of the deer. By dressing himself as the deer—by *impersonating* the deer—the hunter causes the deer to *live again;* he presents himself as the Master and God of deer.

Abbot's Bromley

The horn dancers of Abbot's Bromley, in Staffordshire, England, are the subject of controversy. The Horn Dance is one of those folk customs which has become famous for still being performed. There are many examples on YouTube. The dance is singularly well-known; tourists come to photograph it and folklorists to study it. *It is equally well-known to modern witches and pagans, who like to claim it as proof of the preservation of European pagan customs through the centuries of Christianity.* This is both valid and not.

It is not certain that the Dance originated in the Dark or the Middle Ages—its first mention is in the seventeenth century. It is *like* a remnant pagan custom (as are countless other seasonal folk customs involving animal masquerades), but there is no guarantee that it *is* a remnant pagan custom. Moreover, it is possible that the Horn Dance was originally a festive occasion of another sort, into which horns were interjected. Festive dances and merry-making were a habitual medieval custom and the Abbot's Bromley dance may have started out as another sort of ritual occasion.

Apparently the Dance has gone through some permutations over the years, but elements about it suggest a one-time seasonal rite. It is inevitably compared to the hunting dance in Shakespeare's play; both seem to suggest antique ritual custom involving horns, although it is impossible to know exactly how the Abbot's Bromley Dance came about. Alford does not think that the dance is related to the *cervulus* (the animal-mask disguise) that came to people's doors at the January Kalends,[192] while others disagree that the dancers have no connection with the cervulus.[193] Horn Dances must once have been popular in England; at least sixteen

---

192 Alford, *The Hobby Horse*, p. 55
193 *The Hobby Horse*, p. xxiv

horned rituals are recorded as performed in the three western counties from 1600–1660.[194] As this was the most Puritanical of seasons, this perhaps gives hope of what might have been during more hospitable times.

The first mention of the Dance comes from Robert Plot, a seventeenth-century historian, in a chronicle of Staffordshire. *"They had, within memory, a sort of sport which they celebrated at Christmas, on New Year and Twelf Day, called the Hobby Horse Dance* [Plot describes a Hobby Horse, a man *"that carryed the image of a horse between his leggs";* this man is outfitted with a bow and arrow] ... *With this Man danced six others carrying on their shoulders as many Reindeer Heads, three of them painted white and three of them red ... while they danced the Hays and other Country Dasnces."*[195] Note that this description connects the Dance with the Hobby Horse (a fake ritual-horse) and not necessarily with the deer horns. It is an Animal-Masquerade—but not a Horn Dance.

An eighteenth-century account describes a *"Morrice"* (as in "Morris Dance"), as well as *"six Elkes Heads, in which is a Bow and Arrow, a Sword and a Pot-lid and a thing made in the shape of a Horse with Hoops and Cloathes."*[196] A nineteenth-century account of the Dance is found in a book titled *Old English Customs Extant at the Present Time: An Account of Local Observance, Festival Customs, and Ancient Ceremonies, yet Surviving in Great Britain* (1896):

> *The annual wakes at Abbot Bromley, a village on the borders of Neewood Forest, near Stafford, is celebrated by a curious survival from medieval times called the Horn-Dance. Six deer-skulls with antlers, mounted on short poles, are carried about by men grotesquely attired, who caper to a lively tune, and make the 'deer,' as the antlers are called, dance about. Another quaintly-dressed individual, mounted on a hobby-horse, is at hand with a whip, with which he lashes the deer every now and again in order to keep them moving. Meanwhile a sportsman with a bow and arrow makes believe*

---

194 David Underdown, *Revel, Riot, and Rebellion: Popular Politics and Culture in England: 1603–1660* (Oxford: Clarendon Press, 1985), p. 101

195 Alford, *The Hobby Horse*, p. xxx

196 *The Hobby Horse*, p. xxxi

> to shoot the deer. The horn-dance used to take place on certain Sunday mornings at the main entrance to the parish church, when a collection was made for the poor. At the present day the horns are the property of the vicar for the time being, and are kept, with a bow and arrow and the frame of the hobby-horse, in the church tower, together with a curious old pot for collecting money at the dance. It takes place now on the Monday after Wakes Sunday, which is the Sunday next to September 4th. Similar dances formerly took place in other places in the county of Stafford, notably at the county town and Seighford, where they lingered until the beginning of the century. The under-jaw of the hobby-horse is loose, and is worked by a string, so that it "clacks" against the upper-jaw in time with the music. The money is collected by a woman, probably Maid Marian; the archer is doubtless a representation of Robin Hood; and besides these characters there is a jester. Dr Cox has examined the horns and pronounced them reindeer horns.[197]

Needless to say, reindeer antlers are scarce now in England; the last that reindeer were heard of in the British Isles was in Caithness, Scotland, in the twelfth century. Carbon analysis on one set of antlers dates it to the eleventh century; it is proposed that perhaps the horns were brought into England by Norwegian settlers.[198] How the horns came to be in the hands of the ritual dancers at Abbot's Bromley is a mystery.

Margaret Murray includes an antique photo of the Horn Dancers in her book *The God of the Witches,* published in 1931—which picture is all the more quaint when compared with a modern photograph, the two pictures documenting but a small section of the long timeline of tradition continued (at least from the seventeenth century) in Staffordshire. It is not known whether the dancers ever wore animal-skins or a substitute; the first accounts describe the

---

197 Doreen Valiente, *Natural Magic* (Custer, Washington: Phoenix Publishing, 1975), p. 159

198 Prudence Jones and Nigel Pennick, *A History of Pagan Europe* (New York: Routledge, 1995), p. 159

dancers wearing pieces of cloth sewn onto their clothes, a common make-shift disguise across Europe. Quasi-medieval costumes were introduced in the nineteenth century, which have been updated since, reflecting the taste of various periods as well as romanticized attitudes about the past.

The general resemblance of the Abbot's Bromley Horn Dance to that performed in *As You Like It* makes it tempting to suppose that the Abbot's Bromley dance represents a real-life survival of the sort of magical hunting/fertility traditions at which Shakespeare's play hints. Such ritual celebration is very close in spirit to the Wild Hunt.

Whether through the genuine survival of an ancient hunting rite or the conceptualized recreation thereof—the Abbot's Bromley Dancers *impersonate* the deer-spirit object of the hunt.

Ritual impersonations of the God

There is a charming tradition that a patron of Shakespeare's acting company (George Carey, the second Lord Hunsdon) commissioned *The Merry Wives of Windsor* as a thank-you to Queen Elizabeth for his installation into the Knights-Elect of the Order of the Garter in May 1597—which august event took place at Windsor. *Merry Wives* appears to belong with the plays written in the latter 1590s; it is unique in the canon for being the only play set in Shakespeare's contemporary England.

⁓

Master Ford: *"Why yet there want not many that do fear in deep of night to walk by this Herne's oak: but what of this?"*

Mistress Ford: *"Marry, this is our device, that Falstaff at that oak shall meet with us, disguis'd like Herne, with huge horns on his head."* [Note: this line "disguis'd like Herne, with huge horns on his head" appears in the Quarto version of the play; not, however, the Folio.]

Mistress Page: *"Nan Page, my daughter, and my little son, and three or four more of their growth, we'll dress like urchins, ouphs, and fayries, green and white, with rounds of waxen tapers on their heads and rattles in their hands: upon a sudden, as Falstaff, she and I, are newly met, let them from forth a sawpit rush at once with some diffused song: upon their sight, we too in great amazement will fly: then let them all encircle him about, and fayrie-like to pinch the unclean knight; and ask him why that hour of fayrie-revel, in their so sacred paths, he dares to tread in shape profane."*

The Horned God of Wytches

Mistress Ford: *"And till he tell the truth, let the supposed fayries pinch him sound and burn him with their tapers* [candles]."

Mistress Page: *"The truth being known, we'll all present ourselves, dis-horn the spirit, and mock him home to Windsor... My Nan shall be the queen of all the fayries, finely attired in a robe of white."*

Evans: *"Let us about it, it is admirable pleasures and fery honest knaveries."* (IV.iv)

Merry Wives is one of about half the plays in the canon that exist in two versions—a quarto edition (meaning that it was published independently at some point, 1602 in the case of *MWW*) and the slightly reworked version of *MWW* seen in the Folio (the collection of Shakespeare's plays issued in 1623). The basic outline and much of the *MWW* text is the same in both quarto and folio: significant are the additions of longer, more poetic sequences apparently composed and inserted after the script was assembled. Falstaff's anticipatory wait in the forest is lengthened (the shorter quarto version clearly less satisfying). Mistress Page has just three lines mentioning Herne in the quarto, not the robust speech of the Folio. There is no Garter Speech in the quarto and the sequence after their joke is revealed to Falstaff has been completely reworked in the Folio. All of these changes improve the show, either stretching out comic suspense or adding lovely sequences of poetry, poetry that must have taken some little while to compose. Apparently the short date between the announcement of Hunsdon's honor and the event itself left little time for much beyond a sketchy, slap-dash sort of initial script.

Fenton: *"Hark, mine good host. Tonight at Herne's oak, just 'twixt twelve and one, must my sweet Nan present* [dress as] *the Fayrie Queen... they must all be mask'd and vizarded* [important motif, referring to wearing masks, disguises, costumes], *that quaint in green she shall be loose enrob'd* [loose, green robes will have feyrey-spirit overtones to them], *with ribands* [ribbons] *pendent, flaring 'bout her head."* (IV.vi)

[Elsewhere] Mistress Quickly: *"I'll provide you a chain and I'll do what I can to get you a pair of horns."*

Falstaff: *"How now, Master Brook?... Be you in the Park about mid-*

night, at Herne's oak, and you shall see wonders...Follow; strange things in hand, Master Brook! Follow." (V.i)

[Later] Shallow: *"It hath struck ten o'clock."*

Master Page: *"The night is dark, light and spirits will become it well. Heaven prosper our sport! No man means evil but the Devil and we shall know him by his horns.* [This is a joke upon the fact that Falstaff will be wearing horns in imitation of Herne the Hunter—but like the Devil as well] *Let's away; follow me."* (V.ii)

[At the site] Mistress Ford: *"Where is Nan now? and her troop of fayries? and the Welsh devil* [Evans]?"

Mistress Page: *"They are all crouch'd in a pit hard by Herne's oak, with obscur'd lights; which at the very instant of Falstaff's and our meeting, they will at once display to the night."*

Mistress Ford: *"That cannot choose but amaze him... The hour draws on! To the oak, to the oak!"* (V.iii)

[Enter Sir Hugh Evans disguised (the quarto indicates that Sir Hugh enters *"like a Satyre,"* possibly to explain the reference to *"Welsh devil."* Pistol is dressed as Hobgoblin and the others as Fayries. They have circlets of candles around their heads; hold tapers [little torches] in their hands; probably they have rattles too] *"Trib,*

trib, fayries, come; and remember your parts: be pold, I pray you, follow me into the pit and when I give the watch-'ords, do as I pid you: come, come, trib, trib." (V.iv)

So, at the final, long-anticipated climax to *The Merry Wives of Windsor*, that old horny-dog Falstaff is duped by Mistresses Page and Ford into showing up at Herne's Oak in Windsor Forest at the hour of midnight. Thinking he is going to get it on with both of them, Falstaff is merrily sporting a pair of buck's horns atop his head, in ritual evocation of Herne the Sex Stag-God of the English Celts. This extremely colorful and lively speech, famous in the canon, replaces six kind of dry lines in the quarto, and considerably heightens the expectation of the meeting:

Falstaff: *"The Windsor bell hath struck twelve* [It is twelve o'clock]; *the minute draws on!* [The appointed time is near] *Now the hot-blooded* [horny] *gods assist me! Remember, Jove, thou wast a bull for thy Europa, love set on thy horns.* [This is a reference to metamorphic Greek mythology, whereby Zeus turned into a bull to carry away Europa. This is a dirty joke, if you consider that 'horn' is slang for 'penis.'] *O powerful love, that in some respects makes a beast a man; in some other, a man a beast. You were also, Jupiter, a swan for the love of Leda.* [Another Greek reference, regarding Leda of Aetolia, taken by Zeus in the form of a goose. If you've ever seen an impassioned goose, you'd know this is kind of a disturbing image.] *O omnipotent Love, how near the god drew to the complexion of a goose!* [The irony of love, says Falstaff, is that it causes the gods to demean themselves to the level of geese.] *A fault* [slang for 'intercourse'] *done first in the form of a beast—O Jove, a beastly fault! And then another fault in the semblance of a fowl—think on't, Jove, a foul fault!* [Falstaff is punning, here.] *When gods have hot backs* [sweat during intercourse], *what shall poor men do? For me, I am here a Windsor stag* [he says that he is a stag, because he is wearing Herne's horns], *and the fattest, I think, i'the forest. Send me a cool rut-time* [mating season], *Jove, or who can blame me to piss my tallow?* [Deer grow lean during mating season and urinate frequently. The saying is that they piss their tallow (fat) away.] *Who comes here? My doe?"* [Enter Mistresses Page and Ford]

Mistress Ford: *"Sir John! Art thou there, my deer? My male deer?"*

Falstaff: *"My doe, with black scut?* ['Scut' is a frank Elizabethan word, meaning exactly what you think it means.] *Let the sky rain potatoes; let it thunder to the tune of Green Sleeves, hail kissing-comfits and snow eringoes; let there come a tempest of provocation, I will shelter me here."* [All of this is very provocative. "Potatoes" refers to the Spanish, i.e. sweet potato, as opposed to the Irish variety. Kissing-comfits are sweetmeats, meant to make your breath sweet enough to kiss your sweetie. "Eringoes" are the candied roots of sea-holly. All of these are thought of as aphrodisiacs. With "I will shelter me here," Falstaff probably throws his arms open wide, as if, "let us seek shelter from the storm together, my darling."]

Mistress Ford: *"Mistress Page is come with me, sweetheart."*

[This next jaunty interlude replaces a few dry lines in the quarto, punching up the comedy considerably.]

Falstaff: *"Divide me like a brib'd buck, each a haunch: I will keep my sides to myself, my shoulders for the fellow of this walk; and my horns I bequeath your husbands. Am I a woodman, ha? Speak I like Herne the Hunter? Why now is Cupid a child of conscience, he makes restitution. As I am a true spirit, welcome!"* [All this sequence, Falstaff is speaking in terms associated with deer-hunting, or (as in this case) deer-poaching. A "brib'd buck" is a poached deer, who has to be cut up quickly before the sheriff or keeper of the woods finds you. Getting busted with a "brib'd buck" was serious business. "Haunch" means the upper leg, such as the thigh; Falstaff wants the Wives to separate his thighs. Sides straining in passion is a common Shakespeare metaphor; "shoulders for the fellow of this walk" refers to the custom of leaving the shoulders of the deer behind as gratuity for the "fellow of the walk" or the guy who "kept" the forest—the forest steward. "Horns" is a cuckold reference, to a man whose wife steps out on him, causing him to grow cuckold's horns in shameful consequence; more on this below. "Woodman" means both a "person of the woods" and is a pun on the fact that "wood" is slang for "penis." All of this makes Falstaff like Herne the Hunter. "As I am a true spirit": that is, the true spirit of Herne.]

[Noise within]
Mistress Page: *"Alas! What noise?"*
Mistress Ford: *"Heaven forgive our sins!"*
Falstaff: *"What should this be?"*
Mistress Page: *"Away!"*
Mistress Ford: *"Away!"* [They run off]

The Horned God of Wytches 87

Falstaff: *"I think the Devil will not have me damn'd, lest the oil that's in me should set hell on fire; he would never else cross me thus."* [Enter others, disguised as fayries, with tapers. All this next section, poetry replaces the less effective prose found in the quarto]:

Mistress Quickly: *"Fayries, black, grey, green and white, you moonshine revellers and shades of night, you orphan heirs of fixéd destiny, attend your office and your quality. Crier Hobgoblin, make the fayrie oyes* [noise calling the fays to order]."

Pistol [as Hobgoblin, in the place occupied by "Puck" in the quarto]: *"Elves, list your names; silence, you airy toys. Cricket* [a feyrey named 'Cricket'], *to Windsor chimneys shalt thou leap; where fires thou find'st unrak'd and hearths unswept* [in places that have not been tidied before the maids went to bed], *there pinch the maids as blue as bilberry; our radiant queen hates sluts and sluttery."* [This is a reference to Elizabeth as the Moon-Goddess ('radiant queen'); also interesting in light of the wandering Night-Ladies traditions, whereby goddesses visited homes at night and were offended by messiness.]

Falstaff: *"They are fayries; he that speaks to them shall die: I'll wink and couch* [lie on the ground and cover my head]: *no man their works must eye."* [Lies down upon his face]

Evans: *"Where's Bede? Go you and where you find a maid that ere she sleep has thrice her prayers said, raise up the organs of her fantasy* [dirty joke, saying that good maids are rewarded with erotic dreams], *sleep she as sound as careless infancy, but those as sleep and think not on their sins, pinch them, arms, legs, back, shoulders, sides and shins."*

Mistress Quickly: *"About, about; search Windsor Castle, elves, within and out: strew good luck, ouphes, on every sacred room: that it may stand till the perpetual doom in state as wholesome as in state 'tis fit, worthy the owner and the owner it. The several chairs of order look you scour with juice of balm and every precious flower: each fair instalment, coat, and several crest, with loyal blazon, evermore be blest! And, nightly, meadow-fairies, look you sing, like to the Garter's compass, in a ring: th' expressure that it bears, green let it be, more fertile-fresh than all the field to see; and* Hony soit qui mal y pense *write in emerald tufts, flowers purple, blue, and white; like sapphire, pearl, and rich embroidery, buckled beneath fair knighthood's bending knee: fairies use flowers for their charactery. Away; disperse: but till 'tis one o'clock, our dance of custom round about the oak of Herne the hunter, let us not forget."*

Evans: *"Pray you lock hand-in-hand; yourselves in order set; and twenty glow-worms shall our lanterns be, to guide our measure* [dance] *round about the tree. But, stay, I smell a man of middle-earth!"* [Ah, so that's where Tolkein got that from.]

Falstaff: *"Heavens defend me from that Welsh fayrie, lest he transform me to a piece of cheese!"*

Pistol: *"Vile worm! Thou wast o'erlooked even in thy birth!"*

Mistress Quickly: *"With trial-fire touch me his finger-end* [she's going to hold fire to Falstaff's fingers]: *if he be chaste, the flame will back descend and turn him to no pain; but if he start, it is the flesh of a corrupted heart!"* [This is a reference to the old 'trial by endurance' tests. If Falstaff can withstand being burned, he is pure. As he cannot, of course, this means he gets punished more.]

Pistol: *"A trial, come!"*

Evans: *"Come, will this wood take?"* [They burn Falstaff with their tapers]

Falstaff: *"O, o, oh!"*

Mistress Quickly: *"Corrupt, corrupt and tainted in desire! About him, fayries, sing a scornful rhyme, and as you trip, still pinch him to your time!"*

SONG: *"Fie on sinful fantasy!*
Fie on lust and luxury!
Lust is but a bloody fire,
Kindled with unchaste desire,
Fed in heart, whose flames aspire,
As thoughts do blow them higher and higher!
Pinch him, fayries, mutually;
Pinch him for his villainy;
Pinch him and burn him and turn him about,
Till candles and starlight and moonshine be out!"

[They all pinch Falstaff. A "noise of hunting" is heard (probably a hunting bugle is blown). All the fayries run away. This final verse appears only in the Folio; in the quarto, the last assault of the feyries upon Falstaff is unscripted. One imagines that this was too sloppy for Shakespeare to let stand.]

[Falstaff pulls off his buck's head and rises. Enter Mistress Ford, Mistress Page, Master Ford, and Master Page.]

Master Page: *"Nay, do not fly, I think we have watch'd you now: will none but Herne the Hunter serve your turn?"*

Mistress Page: *"I pray you, come, hold up the jest no higher. Now, good Sir John, how like you Windsor wives?"*

Quarto differences

In the 1602 quarto *Merry Wives,* Sir Hugh Evans costumes himself as a *"Satyre."* Then, since it is he who responds to the line: *"give them their charge* Puck, *ere they part away,"* we assume it is Sir Hugh (disguised like a satyr) who is indicated by *"Puck."* Since this character is replaced by "Hobgoblin" in the Folio, we assume that satyrs, pucks, and hobgoblins are all sort of interchangeable for Elizabethans.

In his notes, Craik identifies "satyre" as a "goat-footed wood-god (the usual sense in Elizabethan literature)." Improvisation of modest means being the Elizabethan theatrical norm, Craik allows that: "If he [Sir Hugh] disguises himself in a cloak of shaggy material he may pass, for the purposes of the stage direction, as a 'satyr.' " [199] In other words, if Sir Hugh drapes some fabric of shaggy cloth over him—perhaps even an actual shaggy animal-skin, a bearskin perhaps, acquired from the bear-baiting pit next door to the theater, perhaps—Craik feels that this would strike them as sufficient to imitate a satyr.

The quarto *Merry Wives* plays up the connection between Herne and stags even more than the Folio. Instead of the Herne Speech (Folio, IV.iv.), Mistress Page has the brief lines in Scene 15: *"Oft have you heard since* Herne [printed 'Horne'] *the hunter died, that women to affright their little children, says that he walks in shape of a great stagge."* They anticipate meeting Falstaff *"disguised like* Horne, *with huge horns on his head... Then would I have you present there at hand, with little boys disguised and dressed like Fayries, for to affright fat* Falstaff *in the woods."*

The quarto introduction to Scene 18 informs us, *"Enter Sir John with a Bucks head upon him,"* implying that in the original production, Falstaff was outfitted with a genuine stag's head, horns and all.

Falstaff: *"Well, I stand here for* Horne *the hunter* [disguised as Horne (Herne) the hunter], *waiting my Does coming."*

Sir Hugh: *"I smell a man of middle earth... See I have spied one by good luck, his bodie man, his head a buck."* [The half-man/half-beast state attributed to Falstaff here is reminiscent of Bottom in *A Midsummer Night's Dream*]

Falstaff: *"*Horne *the hunter quoth you: am I a ghost? S'blood the Fayries hath made a ghost of me: what hunting at this time at night?... How now, who*

---

199 T.W. Craik, ed. *The Merry Wives of Windsor* (Oxford: Oxford University Press, 1994), p. 207n

have we here, what is all Windsor *stirring? Are you there?"* Later, Sir Hugh tells him: *"I was also a Fayrie that did helpe to pinch you."* Falstaff: *"I, 'tis well I am your May-pole"*—referring to the fact that they have been running around him in a circle as if Falstaff were a Maypole.

The joke on Falstaff (which he deserves, being a liar and a con) is that he thought he was going to be Herne the Horned in Windsor Woods; he thought he was going to get it on in major manner with two merry wives. Ah, but they turn the tables on him. Instead of being Herne the Stag in rutting glory, poor Falstaff becomes instead the deer hunted upon by sudden preying humans.

Cuckold

Elizabethans have two ways in which to use horns metaphorically. One is as a sign of *potent virility*, of rampant masculinity—not a far-fetched association for a people who worshipped the stag and his mighty rack. This is the meaning behind the blessing of a precinct with the horn-sign of the god, and behind the triumphant celebration after the hunt. The other instance of the horn metaphor is the famous *cuckold joke*. It was believed (or at least people pretended to believe) that a man whose wife cheated on him grew horns as consequence; hence Othello's famous speech about feeling horns budding on his forehead because he thinks that Desdemona has been unfaithful. For some reason the Elizabethans found this situation to be a bottomless font of mirth, ripe humor indeed—one cannot find an Elizabethan comedy that is not chock-full of cuckold jokes. Who knows when horns acquired this other meaning, but it proved popular with the Elizabethans, who were very concerned about the idea of cuckoldry. Unfaithful wives challenged their sense of orderliness. Briggs points out the association with horns probably originally belonged to the adulterer (where they make more sense, and where, as Briggs says, the name cuckold belonged "first and naturally.") "When the odium shifted to the injured man the horns may have gone with the name."[200] Perhaps this shift in symbology was recent to Shakespeare's time; a tension in attitudes seems to be suggested by the line in the Horn Dance scene (IV.ii) from *As You Like It*: *"Take thou no scorn to wear the horn; It was a crest ere thou wast born: thy father's father wore it, and thy father bore it: the horn, the horn, the lusty horn is not a thing to laugh*

---

200 Briggs, *Pale Hecate's Team*, p. 182

to scorn." Since "horn" was a slang-word for a penis (preferably an erect one), the cult of horn-worship seems at times to have been a cult of penis-worship (thereby going a long ways towards explaining why men would preserve it as a custom).

The problem is that the degree to which horns are taken to refer to cuckoldry in Elizabethan drama is overstated. The Elizabethans used horns as cuckoldry jokes a lot, yes, but they used horns for other metaphoric purposes too. Inevitably, however, editors will interpret every reference to horns as a cuckoldry reference, and this is at times plainly incorrect. For instance, in *A Midsummer Night's Dream* (V.i), Moonshine, Demetrius, and Theseus have three horn references, one after the other. Both Demetrius and Theseus's references may refer to cuckoldry. Inevitably, however, all three references are described as cuckold references; this is not true in Moonshine's case. According to Moonshine, his lantern represents the *"hornéd moon."* This phrase refers to the crescent moon, making a comparison with the horns of the crescent moon and the horns of an animal (a primitive idea, by the way). Marlowe's *Tamburlaine* uses the phrase, and Jeffrey Burton Russell comments on the connection (claiming that the phrase refers to the "lunar pull" upon animals, meaning, presumably, their sex drive).[201] The point is, Moonshine's reference is not, as so many editors will claim in footnotes, a cuckoldry reference.

More ritual impersonations of the God

As the God is impersonated (on two different levels) in *The Merry Wives of Windsor,* so is He impersonated in the many Puck/Robin Goodfellow Plays. Puck/Robin Goodfellow clearly being a favorite character, *A Midsummer Night's Dream* is but the most well-known of a notable sub-genre of the Elizabethan/Jacobean stage, i.e. a play that features Puck/Robin. Continuation upon the path of the Robin Goodfellow Plays leads to divergent trails, not all of them nice.

The early Christian Church had a tendency towards authoritarian conformity; this may be seen in the suppression of the esoteric and mystical Gnostic Gospels in the early centuries of the Christian Era and in the continuing punishment of "heretical" developments in Christian thought throughout the Middle Ages (the

---

201 Russell, *Witchcraft in the Middle Ages,* p. 47

ultimate heresy being Protestantism, which drove the Catholics nearly crazy). The early church tended as well to "stamp out" the pagan religions of Europe, in part by attributing pagan religion to Satan and by black-washing pagan deities as Satanic counterfeits.

It is obvious that this holy smear campaign was employed against the Goodfellow (which initially must have puzzled the pagans, who apparently felt so fondly towards Robin that they called him a Good Fellow). Folkloric mores plainly adopted the convention of Robin as a "devil" and as "devilish"; the church's enforcement of orthodoxy is too ruthless to have permitted dissension. William Baldwin submits to the dictates of the Christian "Establishment," by associating Robin with demons, "goblines," and succubae: *"the ayry spirits which we call Demons, of which kind are incubus and succubus, Robingoodfellow the Fairy, and goblines."*[202] Rowland's *More Knaves Yet* achieves an assimilatory compromise between Robin as a sprite and as a devil:

> *Amongst the rest, was a good fellow devill,*
> *So called in kindness, cause he did no evill,*
> *Knowne by the name of* Robin *(as we heare)...*
> *Who came a nights, and would make Kitchins cleane*
> *And in the bed bepinch a lazie queane...*
> *Amongst the creame bowles and milke pans would be,*
> *And with the country wenches, who but hee.*[203]

To be "with" country wenches, and to be Robin Goodfellow for being "with" country wenches, is a naughty thing, in this context.

It is equally clear that this convention is no more than lip-service paid to an idea; for all that the early seventeenth century makes the concession of Robin as a "devil," he is never less than a completely pagan figure. (The Elizabethan/Jacobean Ages are masters at this sort of "double-speak," whereby they say one thing and hold a completely different idea.)

Two anonymous plays—*Wily Beguilde* and *Grim, the Collier of Croydon*—both adopt the convention of Robin-as-a-devil and subvert the concept—implying that their audience is able to shift associations of Robin, as context warrants.

---

202 Purkiss, *At the Bottom of the Garden*, p. 162
203 Briggs, *Anatomy of Puck*, p. 72

Wily Beguilde
>Peter Plod-All: *"Pray ye, sir, is your name Robin Goodfellow?"*
>Robin: *"My name is Robin Goodfellow."*

A rollicking, jocular little comedy is *Wily Beguilde* (printed in 1606, with no division into acts or scenes). Robin in *Wily* is technically one of the "up-to-no-good" characters. A really basic play structure is "good" characters, beset upon by "up-to-no-good" characters (this is *Hamlet, Othello, Lear, Richard III*, etc). A frequent use of this device is young lovers, in danger of being separated by unsuitable suitors—*Romeo and Juliet* is a tragic version of this storyline. In much milder fashion than *Othello* or *Lear, Wily Beguilde* finds Robin supporting his friend Churms in Churms's wooing of the young lady, who wants instead to be free to marry the handsome stud Sophos; Robin is therefore one of the forces acting in opposition to the union of true love (which did ne'er run smooth).

It should be noted that Robin acts in loyalty to his pal Churms (who probably never has any luck with ladies), directing his mischief against others in support of Churms. At one point, Robin sets off generously to treat Churms to a quart of wine, suggesting a character who enjoys sharing largesse. Robin in the play is a carouser; Churms looks for him *"in every alehouse in the town"* and Robin is called a *"good cup-companion."* It is noteworthy that *Wily Beguilde* expects that Robin would be a fine bloke with whom to swig a few; to the English, anyone who makes an admirable tavern-buddy cannot be bad at all.

Nonetheless, Robin is called "the devil" throughout, as in Fortunatus's *"And, for the devil, I will conjure him"*—meaning Robin Goodfellow. Robin tries to frighten Sophos by pretending to be the Devil: *"Now I am clothed in this hellish shape* [meaning that he has put on a suit of leather], *if I could meet with Sophos in these woods, O he would take me for the devil himself!"* Fortunatus condemns Robin as an *"audacious villain"* and Sophos agrees: *"Sure, he's no man, but an incarnate devil, whose ugly shape bewrays* [betrays; reveals] *his monstrous mind."*

While the play concedes Robin as a devil, though, it also denies the convention. Robin does not consider himself a devil; when he is beaten by Fortunatus, he protests: *"O good sir, I beseech you... O hold your hands; I am not a devil, by my troth!"* All the other characters reference Robin and his doings: Mother Midnight makes her entrance addressing Will Cricket. *"Why, William, we are talking of Robin Goodfellow. What think you of him?"* (Apart from the Dickensianly-named *Churms the Lawyer*, characters such as Mother Midnight, Will Cricket, and Robin Goodfellow lend an inevitable faerey-tale air to *Wily Beguilde*, as Fortunatus and Sophos impart a classical one.) Peter Plod-All respectfully calls Robin *"a very cunning man"* and asks *"reverence of your worship."*

Robin Goodfellow [seeking his friend Churms]: *"Nay, prythee, stay. Who wilt thou tell him would speak with him?"*

Will Cricket: *"Marry, you, sir."*

Robin Goodfellow: *"I? Who am I?"*

Will Cricket: *"Faith, sir, I know not."*

Robin Goodfellow: *"If thou seest him, tell him Robin Goodfellow would speak with him."*

Robin Goodfellow [chuckling after Will Cricket has left]: *"Mass, the fellow was afraid. I play the bugbear* [a troublesome pagan spirit] *wheresoe'er I come and make them all afraid."*

⁓

Robin's basic storyline in *Wily Beguilde* is that he promises his mate Churms that he will get rid of the hot dude Sophos (Churms's rival for the lady's love, against whom Churms does not stand a chance) by scaring Sophos in the woods. Robin does this by disguising himself as a devil: *"I'll put me on my great carnation-nose, and wrap me in a rowsing calf-skin suit, and come like some hobgoblin, or some devil ascended from the grisly pit of hell, and like a scarbabe* [I have no idea what this is] *make him take his legs: I'll play the devil, I warrant ye."* Robin cannot logically be a devil if he is going to disguise himself as a devil ("play the devil"); it is notable that in his disguise, he will be both *"like some hobgoblin, or some devil,"* which implies a cultural assimilation of the pagan hob to the Christian Devil. It is also notable that Robin's disguise (that will make him into a "devil") is a *"rowsing calf-skin suit."*

For all that he is going to be a "devil," the Hell that Robin describes is a very pagan one, unaffiliated at all with Lucifer's Inferno. Popping out to terrify Sophos, Robin informs him that: *"The high commander of the damned souls, great* Dis, *the duke of devils and prince of Limbo Lake, high regent of* Acheron, Styx, and Phlegeton, *by strict command from* Pluto, *hell's great monarch, and fair* Proserpina, *the queen of hell, by full consent of all the damnéd hags, and all the fiends that keep the Stygian plains, hath sent me here from depth of underground to summon thee to appear at* Pluto's *court!"* We may see here a cornucopia of Classical reference, but nothing of satanism. The pagan woods haunted by Robin are the same ones into which the forest-god Sylvanus sends *"a lovely train of satyrs, dryades, and water nymphs... to tune their silver strings."*

Fortunatus thwarts Robin by leaping out and beating him up—this is a favorite theme in medieval folk-story, whereby a supernatural being is bested (frequently violently) by a stout-hearted mortal. Robin begs him to stop, insisting that he is not a devil. As humiliation, Fortunatus forces Robin to stand on a stool and discuss his parentage *("make a preachment of thy pedigree")*. Robin hops atop the furniture and explains that he was begot by a boat-wright and a *"refuséd hag"*: and *"in a whirlwind forth of hell she came: o'er hills she hurls, and scours along the plains; the trees flew up by th'roots, the earth did quake for fear... and by her means I learn'd that devilish trade."* (This description sounds very much like the Wild Ride of Holda or the Faery Rade of the Gyre Carling of Scotland.) When his hag-mother died, *"her fellow-fiends"* complained to *"grim Pluto and his lady queen"* about Robin and got him kicked out of hell.

Notice that in this tale, hags (witches) are assimilated to damnation and hell just as is the pagan Hobgoblin. There are references to Robin as a witch, such as his first entrance, whereupon Will Cricket exclaims: *"Zounds, I think he be a witch!"* Robin is called a *"water-witch"* and offers Plod-All a love-powder and a potion. He says to Peter Plod-All, *"experience hath taught me so much craft that I excell in cunning"* [hitting two words—'craft' and 'cunning'—that are often used as shorthand for 'witchery'].

Robin's intention in scaring Sophos is more mischievous than malevolent: I'll *"make fine sport with him,"* he says. The play ends with Robin commiserating with his old pal Churms and planning (like Laurel and Hardy or like Bogie and Claude Rains at the end of *Casablanca*) to relocate to a new vicinity *"where we are not known and there set up the art of knavery with the second edition"*—leaving open the teasing possibility of a sequel.

Collier of Croydon

By appearing as a character in a play, Robin is impersonated in a cultural context as surely as Superman is impersonated in movies and on television. *Grim, the Collier* [Coal-miner] *of Croydon,* another play whose author is unknown, plays upon the "dual-identity" of Robin as both a devil and as the pagan Goodfellow as creatively as *Wily Beguilde,* in another instance in which the pagan God is acted out upon the stage.

Grim was adapted (with many adjustments) from Machiavelli's novel *The Marriage of Belphegor* (Belphegor being an Old Testament fertility-god later recast as a demon); although *Grim* was printed in 1662, it is clearly much older (among other things, it references the "new world" of America). It is thought that *Grim* means to draw upon traditions of the seasonal Mummers' Plays; Katharine Briggs feels that the "whole" of *Grim the Collier* "resounds with echoes of the mumming plays."[204] A number of the play's characters—the Sooty Collier (or someone with a blackened face, justified as being either a coal-miner [collier] or a chimney-sweep), the Miller, and the Friar—are much used in the folk-songs, games, and plays that typify the Mummers' celebrations. The nature of the speech also suggests to Mother Briggs that the author was reminded of a mummers' play and introduced such whole-heartedly into the central theme.

The Prologue to *Grim* is clearly in the manner of Mumming, with a spirited rhyming opening that finishes with an introduction of the archetypal character St. Dunstan. *Grim* apparently means to be a comedy, along the spooky Satanic lines of *Rosemary's Baby,* to judge from the Prologue's initial words.

Prologue: Our *"plot I dare not tell for fear I fright a lady with great belly* [he fears their play is so frightening, it may induce miscarriage]: *or should a scold* [an assertive, aggressive woman] *be 'mong you, I dare say she'd make more work than the devil in the play* [this is the first promise of mischief-working devils to come]. *Heard you not never how an actor's wife, whom he (fond fool) lov'd dearly as his life, coming in's way did chance to get a jape, as he was 'tired in his devil's shape* [the actor gave his wife a terrible shock, as she came across him while he was still attired in his devil's costume]; *and how equivocal a generation was then begot* [a *Rosemary's Baby*-like joke on the inhuman quality of children born of devilish parents] ... *this I dare to say, here is no lecherous devil in our play* [the Prologue promises that the devil in their play will behave himself and not make

---

204 Briggs, *Anatomy of Puck,* p. 77

advances on the ladies]. *He will not rumple Peg, nor Joan, nor Nan, but has enough at home to do with Marian* [Marian is another character inherited from the Mummers' Plays; this may also be a joke on the identification of Robin Hood with Maid Marian, in which case the audience would have to associate Robin Hood with Robin Goodfellow, and Robin Goodfellow with the play's devil—all at once—for the joke to work] *... but if your children cry when Robin comes* [here again, the Prologue means Robin Goodfellow, who is thought of as both kindly and scary in their kind-of contradictory folklore], *you may to still them buy here pears or plums* [this is an endorsement of the food vendors peddling their wares in the theater]. *Then sit you quiet all who are come in, St. Dunstan will soon enter and begin.*"

Grim is an enjoyable, though uneven work, made complicated by a number of disguised identities. Its main theme (distressing to our modern minds) is the difficulty posed to harmonious marriages by *scolds* or *shrews*—uppity women who rail and talk back to men and who will not accept an appropriately docile and submissive servitude in their matrimonial relationships. Shakespeare's *Taming of the Shrew* is the most infamous of this genre.

Grim starts first with the Prologue, before introducing St. Dunstan, famous as an Abbot of Glastonbury. Dunstan alludes to himself as a national hero associated with several notable Anglo-Saxon kings, making mention of his birth in West Saxony and entry in "*that sacred register of holy saints,*" the *Golden Legend*. A drowsiness then steals over Dunstan, and he falls asleep, to dream the third beginning of the show.

Dunstan's dream takes place in Hell, but not a Hell overseen by Satan. Rather (in the pagan manner favored by English dramatists of the period), Hell is governed by Pluto, attended by "*princes of darkness, Pluto's ministers,*" the lords of Cocytus, Styx, and Phlegethon, as well as the Cretan King Minos and the Furies (I.i). They are sitting in judgment of Malbecco, whose flighty wife has inconsiderately taken to spending her time "*amongst a crew of satyrs wild.*" Puzzled that "*marriage* [is] *now become so great a curse*" and that women "*have lost their native shame,*" Pluto's council *("our awful synod")* resolves to send Belphegor to dwell among mortals for "*a twelvemonth and a day,*" to take a wife and see how goes the state of matrimony. Belphegor asks that his servant-devil Akercock accompany him and Pluto agrees. "*Mark well the process of the devil's disguise, who happily may learn you to be wise. Women, beware! and make your bargains well; the devil, to choose a wife, is come from hell."* (I.i)

The next we see Belphegor (I.iii), he has dressed himself as a Spanish physician, intending to cure the daughter of an earl who has been struck with a strange malady of speechlessness. Belphegor figures that if he can rescue the maid from her silent condition, the girl's father will allow Belphegor to marry her. His man Akercock is dressed *"in a tawny coat,"* which might well be a reference to a costume of animal-skins. Anticipating Belphegor's marriage, Akercock wonders if he [Akercock] *"shall now and then have, as it were, a course at base with her* [Belphegor's projected wife]?" Belphegor nixes this idea, explaining that monogamy is one the plagues of wedlock.

Like *Wily Beguilde*, *Grim the Collier* plays upon the various aspects or personae of Robin Goodfellow, including jokes about his devilish association. In a kind of abrupt shift in dramatic logic, the stage directions inform that Akercock enters the next scene (II.i) *"as Robin Goodfellow,"* so Akercock the demon-from-hell apparently stops being a demon-from-hell and starts being the familiar folkloric hero of English folk-story. It is evidence of the play's clumsiness that this change is not explained; it does indicate the close parallel observed between (pagan) devils and the Goodfellow. Essentially, Robin stops being a demon-minion to Belphegor and continues the play as the independent-minded sprite beloved by all (he also begins to refer to himself as "Robin," such as at the end of the Second Act: *"They all shall want ere Robin shall have none"*).

Dunstan is already praying earnestly over the mute lass, plotting fasting and masses and the turning of beads with aves and creeds. Posing as a doctor, Belphegor boasts of the *"love I bear to secret arts"* (magic), by which he has *"increas'd my wealth";* restrains Dunstan's harp from playing by means of sorcery and *"spells";* and cures the maid's silence by straining the juice of an exotic herb taken *"from the plains of new America,"* that can *"bind and unbind nature's strongest powers."* (II.i)

Robin's jesting nature is frequently seen as he stands apart from the action, tossing off barbed one-liners into the audience (in much the manner of a stand-up comic today): *"Call you this making of a woman speak? I think they all wish she were dumb again"* and *"This is the bravest country in the world, where men get wives whether they will or no"* and *"who keeps a shrew against her will had better let her go."* (II.i)

Through a deception, Belphegor is tricked into marrying the shrewish Marian. Robin therefore becomes her servant as well as Belphegor's and engages in a bawdy exchange with his new mistress: *"As it falls, quoth ye? Marry, a foul fall it is."* ["Fall" is a euphemism for "sex"; "foul" one for "nasty" or "gross."]

Marian: *"Base rascal, dost thou say that I am foul?"*

Robin: *"No, it was foul play* ["play" is also a euphemism for sex] *for him to fall upon you."* Whereupon Marian *"giveth Robin a box on the ear."*

Mortals quite often were on the uncomfortable end of Robin Goodfellow's abuse and misrule. Stories do however turn the table and occasionally allow humans to get some of their own back (which must have been very satisfying, in a sturdy, earthy peasant kind-of-way); as in *Wily Beguilde,* Robin Goodfellow gets beaten up by a wrathful denizen of Middle Earth. The harsh Marian is too much of a milady for Robin to bear; he enters at the top of the Third Act *"with his head broken"* [bandaged], complaining of his mistress's short-tempered and demanding nature. *"Zounds! I had rather be in hell than here... Robin means not to stay to be us'd thus. The very first day... her nimble hand began to greet my ears with such unkind salutes as I ne'er felt... but I'll no longer serve so curs'd a dame; I'll run as far first as my legs will bear me... here to stay with Mistress Marian— better to be so long in purgatory! Now, farewell, master! But shrewd dame, fare-ill! I'll leave you, though the devil is with you still!"* (III.i)

Robin disappears until the top of the Fourth Act, when he enters after having adopted a disguise. He is dressed *"in a suit of leather, close to his body; his face and hands coloured russet-colour, with a flail."* Robin: *"The doctor's self would scarce know Robin now... thus therefore will I live betwixt two shapes; when as I list, in this transform'd disguise, I'll fright the country-people as they pass; and sometimes turn me to some other form and so delude them with fantastic shows. But woe betide the silly dairymaids, for I shall fleet their cream-bowls night by night, and slice the bacon-flitches as they hang. Well, here in Croydon will I first begin to frolic it among the country lobs."* Robin ceases to be the devil Akercock in any form and becomes the folkloric Robin one-hundred percent (which transformation is explained as his hiding from angry Marian and is signaled by his dressing in a skin-tight suit of animal-skins). He intends to set about his traditional pastimes of playing tricks on mortals and muggles, by changing shape and skimming the cream and swiping bacon and what-not.

In the course of adjusting himself to his new neighborhood, Robin discovers Grim the love-sick Collier (coal-miner) of Croydon. Grim is hoping to marry the country-maid after whom he pines and a parson promises to wed them: *"Tomorrow is Holy-rood day, when all a-nutting take their way; within the wood a close* [an open glen or glade] *doth stand, encompass'd round on either hand with trees and bushes; there will I despatch your marriage presently."* (II.i) Holy-rood Day sounds very like an autumnal festival (associated with gathering nuts and—with *"take their way"*—I think we can assume a little sexual license as well; Holyrood is also a royal residence in Edinburgh, built at the turn of the sixteenth century near the ruins of a twelfth-century abbey). Since *Grim* is thought structured deliberately so as to suggest seasonal Mummers' Plays, it may be that the Cult of Robin Goodfellow was remembered in a mumming rite associated with Holy-rood Day—sort of the way that *The Merry Wives of Windsor* may have been inspired by a mumming ritual that associated Herne the Hunter with Windsor Forest; likewise, the way that Santa Claus is associated with Christmas may be the way that Robin was associated with the nutting festival of Holy-rood. The "close" in the woods where the parson means to marry Grim and his girl seems very similar to the *Nemeton,* the sacred Celtic temple-grove in the forest.

Alas! There is a very interesting sub-plot about the parson (named Shorthose), who it seems is a lecherous individual who means violently to take Grim's girlfriend for himself. This strikes us as an unusual take on medieval clergy; Katharine Briggs reminds us, however, that (as so many Robin Hood ballads attest) the common people could hold extremely ambivalent feelings about churchmen and of course we today have our own cultural experience with sexually rapacious men of the cloth. Finding his sense of justice offended by the corrupt churchman, Robin pledges to support Grim and his lovey-dovey. *"I like this country-girl's condition well; she's faithful and a lover but to one. Robin stands here to right both Grim and her."* (IV.i)

Robin's means of righting a wrong are simple. In a scene that must have played as riotously funny, Robin *"beateth the priest with his flail"* and then goes after the crooked priest's accomplice, a miller: *"Now, miller, miller dustypoll, I'll clapper-claw your lobbernoll!"* [This nonsensical doggerel is very much in the nature of a Mumming Play rhyme.] Robin *"beateth the miller with a flail, and felleth him." "I'll thrash you for your knavery! If any ask who beat thee so—tell them 'twas Robin Goodfellow!"* (IV.i)

Robin follows Grim and his sweetie back to Grim's house (where apparently Robin is invisible) and amuses himself with his fond diversion of flipping out one-liners, until Grim's girlfriend produces a mess of cream. Then Robin decides to reveal himself and *"falleth to eat"*: *"Ho, ho, ho, my masters! No good fellowship! Is Robin Goodfellow a bugbear grown, that he is not worthy to be bid sit down?"*

Grim reacts with alarm: *"O Lord, save us! Sure, he is some country-devil; he hath got a russet coat upon his face!"*

Robin: *"Some men call me Robin Goodfellow."*

Grim: *"O Lord! Sir, Master Robert Goodfellow, you are very welcome, sir!"*

Robin: *"This half year have I liv'd about this town, helping poor servants to despatch their work, to brew and bake, and other husbandry... Well, now the night is almost spent; since your affections all are bent to marriage and to constant love, Grim, Robin doth thy choice approve; and there's the priest shall marry you."*

Grim: *"Master Robert, you were ever one of the honestest merry devils that ever I saw!"*

Robin: *"Now joy betide this merry morn and keep Grim's forehead from the horn* [this is an example of the famous Elizabethan cuckold-joke]: *for Robin bids his last adieu to Grim and all the rest of you."* (V.i)

This jaunty and flamboyant sign-off ends Robin's participation in the show as the Goodfellow. At the conclusion of the play, however, he re-appears as Akercock, with Belphegor, as they report on their adventures to the Synod of Hell. In an odd sort of denouement, Belphegor displays the horns of cuckoldry given him by his wife and Pluto commands that no other devil ever make fun of anyone's wearing horns on their heads. *"It thundereth and lighteneth. Exeunt omnes."* *Grim*'s ending reminds me in some ways of the "origin of" type of comic book that explains how Superman got his red cape or Green Lantern got his power battery. In the play's charmingly haphazard fashion, the conclusion seems to postulate a solution to the dilemma, How did devils get their horns?

Commenting upon the relationship between Robin and devils, Katharine Briggs reminds us that the devils in *Grim* are "innocent even in intention; their errand is one of pure justice."[205] For all that he is a devil in the play, Robin remains the easily recognizable sprite of folklore; his character "is thoroughly English" and "like the true Robin Goodfellow he is on the side of justice."[206]

As further commentary upon devils and folkloric wights—the English version of the Danish folk-story *Friar Rush* (well known to the sixteenth-century English in chap-book form) follows the same pattern of storyline as *Grim the Collier*. Initially, Satan sends a devil in the guise of a monk to lead other monks at an abbey astray. At the abbey, the disguised devil tempts the monks to quarreling, lasciviousness, and gluttony (Mother Briggs observes that the satirizing of friars was popular in England and elsewhere from the fourteenth century onwards). As the "wandering tale trickles on" during the "unsystematic" and episodic English chap-book treatment, the devil becomes less of a devil and (as in *Grim*) begins pronouncedly to act like a hobgoblin. Uncovered by the slacker monks, the devil changes into a hob-like horse and is banished to haunt a ruined castle. Displaying an "innocent good-fellowship," he takes pleasure in seeking out taverns and the company of rustics.

Tiring of being a castle-ghost, he embarks upon a hobgoblin's career, serving one master with dutiful speed and "prodigious labours." He plays tricks upon a wanton priest who courts his mistress (again with the wanton priests); he even advises one master how devils may be cast out, a highly inappropriate thing for a devil to do. Far from returning him to his devil's hell, various versions of the legend transform Friar Rush into a paganistic will-o'-the-wisp. Like the *Coal-miner of Croydon*, the folk-story *Friar Rush* suggests that the English (at any rate) tended to interpret devils as hobgoblins.[207] Similar might be the case of the minor devil *Pug* in Jonson's *The Divill is an Ass* (c. 1616). Given permission to make iniquitous sport among mortals for a day, he proves to be an incompetent devil, as he is misled and deceived by knavish human trickery before being carted off to Newgate Prison at the end. Briggs decides that he is "no fallen angel," but a poor, sad, discomfited little sprite, much like a boggart, dobie, bwbach, or some other such as are

---

205 Briggs, *Anatomy of Puck*, p. 75
206 Briggs, *Anatomy of Puck*, p. 76
207 Briggs, *Encyclopedia of Fairies*, p. 181

outwitted by mortals in faerey story. The name *Pug* derives from the same root as *Puck* or *Pixie*.[208]

Robin officially becomes Robin in *Grim the Croydon Collier* at the top of the Fourth Act (Act IV.i); this shift appears to be signaled by a dramatic change of costume. As I see it, Robin has three costume changes in *Grim;* the first is whatever devil's costume he wears as Akercock at the start (and close) of the show. Stage notes indicate that (between the first and third scenes) he changes from his devil's costume and assumes a "tawny coat" (possibly a coat made of animal-skins). A third costume change comes prior to the Fourth Act, when: *"Enter Robin Goodfellow, in a suit of leather close to his body; his face and hands coloured russet-colour, with a flail."* This appearance—in close-fitting leather, with his hands and face painted red (russet-color)—apparently identifies once and for all the undeniable Goodfellow.

In *Wily Beguilde* as well, there is a body of wealth identifying Robin with the tanned skins of beasts. At the start of the show, a comic juggler interrupts the actor speaking the Prologue, who threatens the saucy fool: *"I'll make him do penance upon a stage in a calf's skin... his calf-skin jests from hence are clean exil'd."* It is very interesting the apparent association of calf's skin with the performance of penance; this foreshadows Robin's humiliation ritual when the butch Fortunatus forces him to stand on a stool—Robin (the actor who interrupted the Prologue) therefore does penance upon the stage in a calf's skin. It is also noteworthy that the calf's skin is associated with jesting, hence with that archetypal figure of jest—the Fool. (The Fool is distinguished by his drooping horned head-caps; the concept of the horned clown brings us back around to horned *Harlequinn*). That the same actor who plays Robin is the jester who steals focus from the Prologue is revealed in a line of Will Cricket's, when he says of Robin: *"Why, Robin Goodfellow is this same... calf-skin companion!"*

Throughout the show, Robin keeps commenting ahead to the point when he will terrify Sophos in the woods, after he has dressed in a suit of leather. He says to Peter Plod-All: *"I'll rather put on my flashing red nose and my flaming face and come wrapped in a calf's skin and cry: Bo bo!"* Perhaps in the dialect this works out to "Boo Boo." He essentially says that he will adopt the same disguise

---

208 Briggs, *Anatomy of Puck*, p. 73

that Robin adopts in *Grim the Collier*—he will paint his face red (a "flaming face") and wear a calf's skin (the flashing red nose, I am not sure about—it sounds a little like Rudolph the Red-Nosed Raindeer.

Later, Robin plans his costume change: *"Well, let's go drinke together; and then Ile go put on my divelish roabes—I meane my Christmas Calves skin sute, and then walke to the woodes, O Ile terrifie him I warrant ye!"* Here Robin registers some confusion over the implications of his costume—at one point his leather vestments are *"divelish roabes"*—and then he corrects himself and calls them *"my Christmas Calves skin sute* [suit]." The fact that Robin first identifies his calf's skin clothes with Christmas (or the winter solstice, a super mystical time in the pagan calendar) and then calls them "devilish robes" says pretty much everything there is to say about original European paganism and the antagonism of the devil-obsessed medieval Church.

The fact that (by the time of *Wily Beguilde*) wearing animal-skins was supposed to be recognized as satanic is put plain by the fact that Sophos is supposed to think that Robin (finally making his much-anticipated appearance in his calf's skin-suit, his face painted fiery-red) is the Devil (but a pagan devil, come at the order of Pluto and Dis, not a Christian devil). Upon seeing him, Sophos exclaims: *"But stay; what man or devil, or hellish fiend comes here transformed in this ugly, uncouth shape?"* The fact that the play has so been leading up to Robin's turn in his leather suit implies that it is meant to be one of the highlights of the show, suggesting that an audience will be happy to sit three-quarters of the way through a show, if they know that Robin dressed in leather is going to come along. This seems to me like the awaited moment when Spider-Man first puts on his Spidey-Suit or Batman his Bat-Suit—or Santa Claus his red suit; the moment when a folkloric character and his characteristic apparel become one. All of this suggests a vital folk-identification of *Robin the Goodfellow* with *leather clothes*.

To Wear the Skins of Beasts

The custom of wearing skins seems to have originated in tests of valor. German youths were said to kill an aurochs (a now-extinct bovine creature of Europe's dim past, similar to a bull) in a pit single-handedly, as a coming-of-age thing; Norwegian tales equally describe young men killing bears in tests of manhood. Certain sagas imply shamanic traditions for training warriors, utilizing the ritualistic use of skins; Sigmund and his son, on a revenge quest, isolate themselves in the woods, dressed in wolf-skins and speaking like wolves. (This suggests groups of men living in the woods, as the Irish Fianna did, learning warrior-skills by strict discipline and stern teachers.) Scandinavian tradition otherwise held that shape-changers wore a wolf-skin belt when they left the house at night, to prowl about as wolves; Ulf Bjalfason, in *Egil's Saga*, is thought to be a shape-changer, called "Evening-Wolf." [209]

Northern warriors seem to have made shamanic associations with wild beasts: the berserks fought like wolves, howling and baying and fighting in a band, heedless of threat, resembling the solitary bear in terms of mass, horrifying aspect, and in the ruthless application of killing power. The berserks and the wolf-coats are part of a wider Scandinavian tradition connecting people with animal-metamorphosis; the swan-maidens are of this tradition. Bears and wolves are shown beside warriors on helmet plates from Swedish or Alamannic graves; some are animal figures, others are men with animal heads.[210]

Mystical powers were attributed to the skillful use of skins: a Gaelic ritual called *taghairn* (a complicated form of divination) involves wrapping someone in the warm skin of an animal freshly killed, then laying him beside a waterfall, where he is left alone. The roar of the falls will reveal the future to him; a similar custom, of sitting at a cross-roads on a bull's hide or a bear-skin, is one that "indicates heathen sacrifice," according to Grimm.[211]

According to legends of the history of Britain, collected by *Geoffrey of Monmouth*, Brutus emigrated to England in obedience to a vision sent by Diana. *The vision was received as Brutus slept outdoors on a doe's hide*. The custom was not roundly popular, however, as the penitential called the *Corrector et Medicus* (included in Bishop Burchardt of Worms's *Decretum*) condemned the heathenish New Year's Day custom of sitting on a bull's hide at a crossroads to learn the future. *Otherwise, the custom of wrapping someone in an animal-*

---

209 Davidson, *Myths and Symbols in Pagan Europe*, p. 79
210 *Myths and Symbols in Pagan Europe*, p. 79
211 Grimm, *Teutonic Mythology*, vol. III, p. 1115

skin was understood as a healing or as a protective rite—according to William of Malmesbury's twelfth-century story about the *Witch of Berkeley*, she was laid to rest *wrapped in the skin of a stag*, in order to protect her soul from the Devil. Some idea of how pagan customs were demonized may be had in the 1222 chronicle which reports of a Jewish necromancer, who *purchases a boy and wraps him in the skin of a dead man* in order to learn the future.[212]

Further evidence of the purifying powers ascribed to animal-hide is the Germanic custom of Holzberndorf, in Upper Franconia, wherein a boy acts the *Eisen-berta*. Clad in a cow's skin, *he goes about ringing a bell, giving nuts and apples to good children*.[213] In Highlands Scotland, a similar ceremony occurs, whereby the *Hogmanay* lad makes Midwinter visits wearing a *cow-skin* (Hogmanay being the last night of the year); *the boy runs around each house three times before he and his companions receive refreshment*. As a charm against "*witch-craft and infection*," everyone must smell a burning piece of sheep-skin.[214] The Hebrides keeps a similar Halloween custom, whereby a youth dressed in cows hide goes around the village, bringing *blessings to the houses with the fumes of a burning hide*.[215]

Various fayrey-stories attach significance to the wearing of furs or skins. In the well-known fable of *Thousandfurs*, or its French version *Donkeyskins*, the heroine *wraps herself in a coat of furs, and blackens her face*, in order to escape her incestuous father. *Thousandfurs* sounds suspiciously like *Cinderella* at times; the three dresses that Donkeyskins has—*one as gold as the sun, another as silver as the moon, the third as glittering as stars*—sound suspiciously like the dresses which fell to Cinderella from a magical tree.[216] Ginzburg speculates that Cinderella's magic dress may originally have been a shaman's costume; this is undoubtedly the explanation for Thousandfurs' attire as well.[217]

The wearing of animal-hide is associated with heroism in many ways, as a sort of shamanic badge of honor. The *Ragnars-*

---

212 Kittredge, *Witchcraft in Old and New England*, p. 47
213 Grimm, *Teutonic Mythology*, vol. IV, p. 1370
214 Alford, *The Hobby Horse*, p. 67
215 Briggs, *Anatomy of Puck*, p. 77
216 Maria Tatar, *The Annotated Classic Fairy Tales* (New York: W.W. Norton and Co., 2002), p. 117
217 Ginzburg, *Ecstasies*, p. 248

drapa is a ninth-century poem attributed to the poet Braggi, otherwise called *The Lay of Ragnar Shaggy-Breeks*. It tells the story of the heathen Dane *Ragnar Lodbrok*, against whom *Edmund*, king of East Anglia, had to defend his kingdom. *Lod-brok* means "Hairy-breeks" or "Shaggy-pants"; Ragnar was called "lodbrok" after the manner in which he won his wife. *She was guarded by a snake, which prevented anyone from approaching her. Ragnar had an inspiration, however, and made himself a set of breeches and a cloak out of hide, which he wore with the hairy side out. He boiled these in pitch and allowed them to harden; they thus made excellent armor against the snake.*[218] The Gaelic *Tam Linn* is likewise associated with furry pants:

> *Tam o' the Linn had nae breeks to wear*
> *So he cut him a sheepskin to make him a pair*
> *He wore them skinny side out and wooly side in*
> *Now ain't I fine, said Tam o' the Linn*

Otherwise, in the Irish tale of *Tom o' the Goat-skin*, the hero comes to the court of the king of Dublin, clad in skins and armed with a club.[219] *In a bit of a supernatural association*—the fondness of the English *hob* for animal-skin clothing or for suits of leather is reminiscent of the *witch's familiar* and its customary animal form.[220]

There were certain specific occasions upon which it was traditional to dress in animal-hide. A horn dance is performed in *As You Like It* which suggests a long-ago ritualistic custom of adorning the hunt's victor in the skin of the kill. *Late summertime was the time for fairs,* another opportunity for men to perform plays with elements of deer-song in them. Fairs were a chance to see burlesques and mimes (reflections of fertility rites), involving actors clad in animal-skins and horns, or in foliage and greenery. Through such avenues, the masquerades performed in the Christmas and Easter Mummers' Plays were transported to the professional stage—to shows such as *Wily Beguilde* and *Grim the Collier of Croydon*.[221] And there were deeply heartfelt customs across Europe that identified

---

218 Marshall, *Everyman's Book of English Folktales*, p. 182
219 Nutt, *Studies on the Legend of the Holy Grail*, p. 134
220 Purkiss, *At the Bottom of the Garden*, p. 153–5
221 Laroque, *Shakespeare's Festive World*, p. 188

certain significant "turns" in the year's progress with the magical appearance of skin-clad *ritual-animals.*

Ooser

The *Dorset Ooser* (pronounced oo-sir) was carefully photographed in 1891, the picture reproduced in Murray's *The God of the Witches.* The Ooser was a bull's mask, used as a ritual-animal in Midwinter festivities, and a wonderful example of folk-art—a human face, with lively expression. The effect is of some stereotypical jungle-savage, both ferocious and comic all at once. One wearing the Ooser must have looked like a proverbial wild man from Borneo let loose in some quaint nineteenth-century English village. It had two great bulging eyes and a rounded boss in the center of his forehead (the place of the third eye in Eastern traditions). The jaw was moveable; he had a fine head of curly bull's hair and a beard; he was adorned with an impressive set of bull's horns. It is easy to imagine children shrieking with delight at the terrifying, capering Ooser, and one has only to look at the mask to be sure that the Ooser would indeed caper. Doreen Valiente offers the suggestion that "ooser" derives from the Old English *Os,* meaning "god."[222] Similar would be the Padstow *Obby Oss. Osmond,* as in "Melbury Osmond" (or I guess, as in "the Osmonds," like Donnie and Marie), means "god-protection"; it should be noted that *Os* is similar to the odd American word *Oz.*

The Dorset Ooser came to someone's attention, who recorded it in an 1891 book on Somerset and Dorset. They found it in a village called Melbury Osmond, in the possession of a family who, when they moved, took the Ooser with them. Shortly thereafter, the Ooser disappeared, never to be seen again. Perhaps someone feared the Ooser's leaving his ancestral home, or maybe they just wanted the mask for themselves, or maybe there was some act of spite involved. Or perhaps some Purityrannical individual (Purityrannical: "tyranny of the Puritan") freaked out over the blatant heathenism of the Ooser. Whatever the reason, the Ooser vanished.

The Ooser is an example of the "masking" rites, or *ritual-animal masquerades,* continued seasonally throughout Europe. In this instance, the Ooser, or Bull's Mask, was associated with the Yule-tide

---

222 Doreen Valiente, *An ABC of Witchcraft: Past and Present* (Custer, Washington: Phoenix Publishing, 1973), p. 95

and the Twelves of the year. It was during this period that spirits were like to be about, the dead roamed into people's homes in search of refreshment, and Holda and Perchta made great processional tours, *accompanied by ghosts and faeryes*. Animal-masquerades are often noted at these times.

Doreen Valiente further informs that a collection of Dorset folk-lore, published in 1951, refers to the Christmas appearance of the Ooser, or Wooser, worn by a man dressed in animal-skins. According to the book, the custom continued until the turn of the last century. In 1911 a Dorsetshire paper recounted a man's scaring girls *"dressed in a bullock's skin, and wearing an ooser"*—innocent times, when such things were news. Dorset is, by the way, near the Cerne Giant, whose name attests to his connection with horns and whose legend attests to his powers of fertility. Kingscote, Gloucestershire, had a similar custom—a *Wooser,* also called the *Broad,* accompanies the Christmas wassailers. A *Wooset* of Wiltshire was a similar Bull, an annual figure at Yule-tide in Stourton, made of a *real bull's head*, bottle eyes, and a sacking body with a rope tail (and a man inside). The Wooset went about, knocked on doors with his horns, and, once inside a house, chased people around and made as to terrify them. In 1908, he had been in the same family for over a hundred years.[223] Violet Alford locates cultural connotations in the Wooset that lead to *Wurse,* the Archfiend in Layamon's *Brut,* the *Wood-woose,* and, eventually, to *Herne* and *Cernunnos*. The presence on the European timeline of (1) horned divinities in pagan Europe and (2) masquerades of horned animals in medieval Europe implies a connection. While the medieval customs of the bull-horned Midwinter wassailer are not an overt expression of heathenism, they imply what the original religious customs may have been.

The Minehead *Sailors' Horse,* of Somerset, wears a large, cone-shaped tent which hangs from a frame about his shoulders. This is sometimes painted with large circles, or (should anyone not recognize him) with "Sailors' Horse" in large letters; the upper part of the costume is adorned with bits of ribbon and cloth. Before his spring tour, the Sailors' Horse observes Warning Night, according to an account written in the nineteenth century. On the night of April 30, accompanied by a drummer, the Horse and his gang

---

223 Alford, *The Hobby Horse,* p. 59

repair to a crossroads, where the gang dances about him.[224] (This is something—*dancing at a crossroads on May Eve*—which *witches* were said to do, and is an example of European folk-custom imitating folklore.) Otherwise, the Horse dances again the next day at Whitecross Roads, where a pretty girl is selected *May Queen*.

In much the same manner, the *Land's End Horse* had a head, a neck, and a body covered with either a hide or blanket; he went out with Cornish guisers dressed in bullocks' hides with the horns left on; sometimes a version of the *St. George Resurrection Play* was performed.[225]

The *Boeuf de Meze*, the Meze Ox, is of the French province Languedoc. He has a head with great horns, and a tent-body so large seven or eight men must move him. He appears at the local fete in August, accompanied by trumpets and drums; has a song of his own; and tries (when he can) to rush into the crowd and overturn people.[226] At Amelie-les-Bains in Vallespir, a bull-mask, the *bou-rouch*, appears with his bride (a man in drag) and makes a riot running in and out of shops and cafes. Being near the Spanish border, two toreros excite him; when folklorist Violet Alford observed this rite, she was astonished to discover that the Bull was also joined by someone dressed as Charlie Chaplin, complete with bowler, jacket, and trousers.

In Austria, the *Schiache Perchten* (supposedly the goddess *Perchta* Herself) dress in long sheepskin coats, devil-like masks, wooly wigs, and goats' horns; they sometimes carry brooms or shovels.[227] At Mittendorf, the *Oat-Goat* appears, to ensure a good oats-crop; he is accompanied by guisers wearing fur coats, horns (sometimes as many as eight), and huge cow-bells about their waists. They jabber nonsensically and make great leaps into the air. As the Alpine slopes carry us into Slavic Europe, we come across the *Koranti*, clad in skins and horned, who welcome spring by running from precinct to precinct. Like the runners of the Swiss and Austrian Alps, the Koranti create a din with their cow-bells and drums. Slovenia observes the plow procession, in which gaily decorated trees fastened onto plows are taken about, a whiffler cracking a long whip,

---

224 *The Hobby Horse*, p. 45
225 *The Hobby Horse*, p. 35
226 *The Hobby Horse*, p. 93
227 *The Hobby Horse*, p. 129–133

and the plow being guided by one of the horned and hide-covered Koranti, who sings a wassail song. In Iceland, a certain "monster" used to appear at feasts, with a wooden mask outfitted with glass eyes, ram's horns, and lighted candles in his nostrils. He wore a sheepskin, or (if need be) a quilt, and frightened people at the assembly, while two "shield-maidens" (guys in drag) made as if to restrain him.[228]

Alford reports that in Lincolnshire it was an Old Sow which appeared at harvest suppers, running about on all fours under the feet of the females. She notes that this illustrates, in Britain as elsewhere, the interchangeability of animal-masks. The point was not so much this animal or that animal, but the appearance of a ritual-animal at the appropriate period. On the whole, the people of Europe seemed to think it better to keep these rites going, or at least seemed to feel that they would miss them if they didn't.

The animal-disguises which occurred in Europe are probably related to more general mythology concerning the *spirits of the dead*. In many of the seasonal "dressing up" rituals, effort is made to turn people into representations of the *spirits of the dead* and to imitate the behavior of the wild dead as much as possible. We thus find customs whereby people invade the homes of others, or demand some sort of edible or monetary offering as propitiation, or are permitted to indulge in light theft or prankster hijinks. These will be noted as on-going Halloween customs.

Folklorists note that associations are sometimes made between Otherworldly figures and animals. The Highlands faery-women, the *baobhan sith*, had cloven feet; the Greek *kallikantzaroi* were hybrid goat—or ass—creatures, who emerged from the underworld during the Twelve Days—the same period in which the *benandanti* fought ecstasy battles, and the dead roamed about, led by *maternal goddesses*. In *Ecstasies,* Ginzburg includes a map outlining the areas of Europe in which nocturnal journeys, fertility-battles, and apparitions of the dead took place alongside semi-animal apparitions and animal-masquerades.[229] The same regions in which trooping processions took place centered around ritual-beasts are the regions that credited the Wild Hunt—and the Wild Hunt was joined by the ranks of the dead. Lawson recognizes in the "simple coun-

---
228 *The Hobby Horse*, p. 125
229 Ginzburg, *Ecstasies*, p. 98

try people" of the Aegean and the Greek mainland, and in the legend of the kallikantzaroi, a firm belief in the "chthonic spirits inhabiting the deep places of the earth." He concludes that "persons dressing themselves as animals, and behaving like animals during the Twelve Days of the Kalends represent demons [spirits, I would say], who, during that time are permitted to emerge from the underworld."[230]

In other words, the European seasonal customs of dressing like animals may have started as a rite of placation, a means of amusing and gratifying the spirits who were about at these times; this makes an association between *spirits* and *animals*. The animal-masker is often accompanied by other guisers, persons (mostly men): dressed in drag; dressed as merrymakers; dressed as faeries or other spirits. The animal-masquerades take the form of some beast of mythical stature, like the horse, or else of some horned beast, such as the ram, goat, deer, or bull. Otherwise, they take the form of a sacrificial animal, which, often, is the same thing as being horned.

Condemnations

The heathen origins of such customs were so apparent, and the people's devotion to their traditional ways so strong, the church was obliged to engage in strenuous opposition. One of the first condemnations was that of Pacianus, bishop of Barcelona in 370 CE, who feared that, by criticizing the *"stag play,"* he in fact prolonged its pagan life.[231] Augustine (387–430 CE) demands: *"If you ever hear of anyone carrying out that most filthy practice of dressing up like a horse or a stag, punish him most severely."*[232] Caesarius of Arles (470–542 CE) despised dressing up in the heads of beasts (as Falstaff seems to do in *The Merry Wives of Windsor*, over one thousand years later).[233] St. Isidor (636 CE) wrote with annoyance of pagans who, on the Kalends of January, dressed in the shapes of beasts, and ran *"about hither and thither";* in 923 CE they were still doing the same thing.[234] It is significant that it is midwinter (the

---

230 Alford, *The Hobby Horse*, p. xv
231 *The Hobby Horse*, p. 19
232 *The Hobby Horse*, p. 20
233 *The Hobby Horse*, p. 20
234 *The Hobby Horse*, p. 21

same seasonal period frequently associated with the good ladies) and the Kalends of the New Year, that was often the date for the animal-guisers.

Also in the seventh century, St. Aldhelm of Wiltshire was disgusted to think that *"the impious"* had once worshipped stags and horses *"in crude stupidity,"* and inside temples (Alford points out that the Anglo-Saxons of his own time were still doing so).[235] Regino of Prum, in 915 CE, told the Germans of his congregation (who lived in a still isolated stretch of country, where paganism probably lingered) that they had done as heathens had, when they went about on the first of the year *"in the guise of a stag or a calf. May you repent..."*[236]

Lest we should think that any of this prohibition impressed the stubborn common-folk of Europe, let us consider the fact that in the tenth century, Pseudo-Theodore of Canterbury felt compelled to thunder a ferocious condemnation: *"If anyone on January 1st goes about dressed as a stag or a calf, identifying himself with the nature of beasts, dressing in the hides of animals, those who in such ways change themselves into animal forms... such things are devilish."*[237] This lets us know that—at roughly the same time that the *Canon Episcopi* tells us that women fly at night with a pagan goddess—men spend the first of the year "going about" in the hides of animals, "identifying with the nature of beasts" and "changing themselves into animal-forms." Burchardt of Worms threatened his diocesans with penance for putting on the guise of a calf or a stag and St. Eligius of Rouen spoke against both dressing as a stag, and *"the preparation of tables overnight."*[238] The latter refers to the custom of leaving the table set (while one sleeps) as a sign of hospitality towards the visiting Good Women who travel at night, again linking a Wandering Woman custom with the male custom of dressing like a stag. Masquerades involving stags or calves were specifically condemned by the Pseudo-Cummean Excarpsus; the Burgundian penitential; the Scarapsus of St. Permin in Alamannia (c. 724 CE); and the Merseburg penitential.

So little effect did any of this have that *Le Roman d'Alexandre*, a

---

235 *The Hobby Horse*, p. 21
236 *The Hobby Horse*, p. 21
237 *The Hobby Horse*, p. 22
238 *The Hobby Horse* p. 22

fourteenth-century Flemish manuscript given as a wedding present to Elizabeth Woodville, ill-fated queen to Edward IV, has an illustration showing men and women linked in a line; the men are masked, as a stag, a hare, and something like a horse. Another page shows a *cervulus*, a stag-impersonation, enacted by a boy under a sheet.[239]

Rituals of death and rebirth

Of similar note to the Dorset Ooser, but of different season, is the *Obby Oss,* or *Old Hoss,* ceremony observed on May Day in Padstow, Cornwall. The Old Horse is another example of a ritual animal—significant, *as the horse was a major symbolic figure to the Celts.* The Padstow event has become an exceedingly famous affair, attracting so much attention now that locals complain about the crush of tourists and news reporters who appear each year to commemorate the Hoss's appearance. If you type "Obby Oss" or "Old Oss, Padstow" into YouTube, you will find several good video postings of the celebration.

The earliest known records of the Oss date from 1803.[240] The Oss is a man in a fantastic costume made of a long black tarp, tented over a large circular hoop at the shoulders; all told, the Oss resembles a giant, walking witch's hat—*there, I've said it.* The ritual-beast dances through the streets while everyone comes to watch and sing and to make merry. Observers of the ceremony speak of the strange "old-world atmosphere" created by the Oss's procession.

The Obby Oss proceedings begin the night before, when a group strolls about the town, singing the Night Song. At midday the next day (May Day), the door to the Golden Lion tavern is flung open, and out comes the Hoss and all his retinue.[241] The Old Hoss is sometimes accompanied by figures such as Lively Mac, who keep the fun going. Until the mid-nineteenth century, the Oss was kept company by men-women dressed in scarlet cloaks, in imitation of the nationalistic legend whereby *the French were driven off by the Oss and a band of Cornish women in their red coats.* At other times the Oss has been accompanied by a rough-looking man dressed

---

239 *The Hobby Horse,* p. 24
240 Valiente, *Natural Magic,* p. 156
241 Alford, *The Hobby Horse,* p. 39

incongruously in a dainty dress with a bonnet and his face painted red. This man was identified as "All Sorts" to Violet Alford, who reports that he no longer seems to walk with the Hoss. *This is also a type of drag known today as "gender-fuck," pardon the expression, which aims to be aggressively masculine and feminine at once.*

The Padstow streets are traditionally decorated with greenery, for there is a secret to the Obby Oss ceremony. The Teaser goes ahead of the Hoss by a few paces, guiding the huge creature (who likely can not see very well out of his giant, tent-like disguise). The Teaser waves a ceremonial club before the Hoss, performing a dance which involves defined steps and hypnotic waves of his instrument. (The dance is traditional; when Alford saw the ceremony, she observed the club handed to an elderly lady and some children, all of whom could imitate perfectly the Teaser's steps and use the club exactly as he did.) The Oss follows the Teaser's graceful, drooping dance. As he dips and sways, and as the crowd sings about him, the Oss periodically sinks down to the ground, lying in a great, black, inert, heap. His companion rubs and strokes him, as do children brought up to the Horse; he then rises back to his feet, and resumes his dance. *This same process will be repeated again and again throughout the day, as the Obby Oss dies, and is reborn, dies and is reborn. This is the secret to the Obby Oss ceremony and to any number of ritual-pantomimes.*

Seasonal rites of blackening fertililty

An ox sometimes replaces the German *Schimmel*, the White Horse, at festive occasions, his head usually made from a bucket. Whether Ox or Horse, he falls dead when struck, only to leap up again a moment later.[242] The *Wild Horse* of Antrobus, in Chesire, is a horse-skull on a pole. He appears after the performance of the Mummers' Play on All Soul's Day, and is so old that he is said to fall to pieces as he expires in his mock death: *"Poor old horse, poor old horse,"* everyone croons.[243] In the Hobby-Horse Play of La Soule (Pays Basque), the horse is gelded (a symbolic death), then leaps in the air at the play's conclusion (in a symbolic resurrection).[244] The streets of Krakow are enlivened by the *Laikonik* on Corpus

---

242 *The Hobby Horse*, p. 117
243 *The Hobby Horse*, p. 7
244 *The Hobby Horse*, p. xx

Christi day. The horse (ridden by a man dressed as a Tartar) rushes through the crowds to the cathedral, when he dies on the steps and has to be removed. Alford comments that this is a "rudimentary death," but is comparable to "a hundred other animal guisers."[245] A clumsy cow, known as the *Limodje,* appears on feast days at Presles and other villages in the Basse-Sambre, in Belgium. A vet accompanies the cow, who periodically falls sick and has to be revived. This pantomime echoes "scores" of other folk-drama deaths, and may be accepted as "just one more degraded seasonal rite."[246]

A strong dose of fertility-magic is often heavily mixed in with the ritual animal-masquerades. The Oss traditionally makes a point to chase girls about, sometimes smearing them with blackened hands, or perhaps catching them under his coat for a moment. It is understood that this promotes fertility in the girls, often in the form of an imminent pregnancy. This theme is spread across Europe in the animal-guises; it is universally understood that, when the ritual-beast nudges or rubs against a woman, or backs her against a wall, he is magically impregnating her. The superstition is that the woman will then find herself with child within the year's time.

French bears in Roussillon blackened Carnival participants with fertility-magic, before being captured by cross-dressed brides, who disappeared with the bears down the street in a wild gallop.[247] Chimney-sweeps often accompany wedding parties in England, Hungary, and elsewhere, blackening being so thoroughly understood as a fertility-ritual.[248] In Germany, the White Horse makes his appearance on St. Nicholas's Day accompanied by the Feen (fayryes), which are men dressed as old women with blackened faces.[249] In the Swiss Alps, guiser bridal couples are accompanied by *Schnabelgeissen* (goats' heads carried on sticks) and an accordionist who has blackened his face. Otherwise, a guiser group was made up of a pretend-bride and groom, accompanied by a *blackface devil.*[250]

---

245 *The Hobby Horse,* p. 8
246 *The Hobby Horse,* p. 8
247 *The Hobby Horse,* p. 95
248 *The Hobby Horse,* p. 141
249 *The Hobby Horse,* p. 116
250 *The Hobby Horse,* p. 128

The Oxfordshire St. George Play

[The mummers enter singing and walk around in a circle, before standing off to one side.]

King Alfred: "*I am King Alfred and this here is my bride* [which bride is without a doubt a man in a dress]. *I've a crown on my pate* [head] *and a sword by my side.*" [He stands aside.]

King Cole: "*I am King Cole and I carry my stump. Hurrah for King Charles! Down with Old Noll's Rump!*" [This may be an allusion to Cromwell and the Rump Parliament.]

Giant Blunderbore: "*I am Giant Blunderbore, fee fi fum*! [This should sound very familiar.] *Ready to fight all—so I says, 'Come!'* [Enter Little Jack—a boy] *And this here is my little man Jack—a thump on his rump and a whack on his back! I'll fight King Alfred, I'll fight King Cole, I'm ready to fight any soul! So here I, Blunderbore, takes me stand, with this little devil Jack at my right hand, ready to fight for mortal life! Fee fi fum!*"

[Enter St. George, the "leader of the dance."]

St. George: "*I am St. George of Merry England—bring in the morresmen, bring in our band!*" [The morris-men dance to a fife and drum. When the dance is concluded, St. George continues—] "*These are our tricks—ho! men, ho! These are our sticks—whack men so!*"

[The Dragon roars and comes forward.]

The Dragon: "*Stand on head, stand on feet! Meat, meat, meat for to eat! I am the Dragon—here are my jaws! I am the Dragon—here are my claws! Meat, meat, meat for to eat! Stand on my head, stand on my feet!*"

All sing [several times]: "*Ho! Ho! Ho! Whack men so!*" [The drum and fife sound; all fight and ("after general disorder") fall to the floor]

[Enter Old Doctor Ball;]

The Doctor: "*I am the Doctor; I cure all ills—only gullup my potions and swallow my pills; I cure the itch, the stitch . . . and the gout, all pains within and all pains without. Up from the floor, Giant Blunderbore!* [The Doctor gives Blunderbore a pill and Blunderbore rises] *Get up, King! Get up, Bride! Get up, Fool, and stand aside!* [He gives them all pills] *Get up, King Cole, and tell the gentlefolks all—there never was a Doctor like Mr. Doctor Ball! Get up, St. George, old England's knight—you have wounded the dragon and finished the fight! Now kill the Dragon and poison Old Nick—at Yule-tyde, both o'ye cut your stick!*" [The Doctor forces a pill down the Dragon's throat, who dies in roaring convulsions. Enters Father Christmas.]

Father Christmas: *"I am Father Christmas! Hold, men, hold! Be there loaf in your locker and sheep in your fold; a fire on the hearth and good luck for your lot; money in your pocket and a pudding in the pot! Hold, men, hold! Put up your sticks; end your tricks; hold, men, hold!"*

[All sing, while one goes around with a hat for gifts.]

All: *"Hold, men, hold! We are very cold! Inside and outside, we are very cold. If you don't give us silver, then give us gold from the money in your pockets—hold, men, hold!"*

A Chorus: *"God A'mighty bless your hearth and fold, shut out the wolf and keep out the cold! You gev' us silver, keep you the gold, for 'tis money in your pocket—hold, men, hold! God A'mighty bless &c."* [Exeunt omnes]

The Oxfordshire St. George Play was printed in 1874; its preserver informed that it had been transcribed verbatim in 1853 from an actor of the play. The writer remembered the play from 1839; it had been the custom "from time immemorial," to perform the show at the "houses of the gentle-people" (and then later the vicarage) during the Christmas season, from December 21 to Old Christmas Eve (January 5). The performers of the play believed themselves to be true inheritors of the tradition; the man from whom this account was taken had first performed the piece in 1807, as he said his father had done in the previous century.[251]

Gassner feels certain that the pagan Celts and Teutons had developed some super-primitive proto-type of theater, well before the conversion of the Roman Empire to Christianity.[252] It is impossible to judge the earliest point on the European timeline upon which might be located pagan drama, but Gassner assures us that we are safe in assuming that some early form of theater ("intimately related to seasonal rites dealing chiefly with winter and spring") was "well established" by the time that Christianity was introduced into Europe.

---

251 Joseph Quincy Adams, ed. *Chief Pre-Shakespearean Dramas* (Houghton-Mifflin, 1924), p. 353

252 John Gassner, ed. *Medieval and Tudor Drama* (New York: Applause Books, 1987), p. 28

The Horned God of Wytches

Such theater—pagan dramatic pieces—come down to us as re-enactments of death and resurrection rites, concerned with the death of vegetation (sometimes symbolized as the death of animals) during the cold winter and the blossoming rebirth of spring. The medieval Christian world assimilated the magical pagan mysteries into folk-performances that re-enacted death and resurrection; the dramas betray their pagan origins by being traditionally performed at Christmas and Easter (the winter and spring festivals of Christianity). Folklorist Bob Pegg feels that the recurring theme of death and revival demonstrates that the plays may be viewed as "debased fertility rites of non-Christian or pre-Christian origin."[253] He cites another authority (who wrote prior to the First World War) as agreeing: "The Mummers' Play, degenerate and undeveloped though it may be, bears distinct traces of a ritual origin..."

Mummers' Plays—known generically as "death and resurrection" plays—began to be printed around the mid-1740s, implying interest at that time; the plots are simple: someone dies and is brought back to life (the comparison with the Obby Oss tradition is clear). A popular form is the *hero-combat play*, which appears widespread over northern, central, and southern England, southern Scotland, and northern Ireland. Characters tend to be exotic and reflect British adventures in the world (such as the Crusades)— Alexander, St. George, King George, the King of Egypt, the Black Moroccan Prince, the Turkish Knight, Bold Slasher, and the Indian King have all been found as participants. Typically a fight ensues and some heroic soul is killed and reborn, resurrected by the Doctor.

A really, really recurrent motif is the appearance of the Doctor, who performs a miraculously magical cure. I have this obstinate theory that the individual designated the Doctor may at one time have been identified as the Witch or as the Healer. I have no proof of this, but I find it significant that a member of the modern medical profession has been otherwise introduced into ancient rituals of rebirth; some of the doctors' speeches, such as that in the Leicestershire St. George Play, sound very like witches boasting of their healing powers in Burning Times drama.

---

253 Bob Pegg, *Rites and Riots: Folk Customs of Britain and Europe*. (Poole, Dorset: Blandford Press, 1981), p. 102

The *Plough Plays* depict an animal killed and reborn, or depict the ritual death of the Old Father; the *Sword Dances* tend to be of the *Hero-Combat* or *Champion* variety, which show the death of the company's captain or some other individual. The Sword Dances perhaps reflect a dim memory of animal (or even human) sacrifice to the spirit of vegetable life; they were possibly introduced into England by the Danes and Saxons (*Beowulf* refers to a sword-dance [*"sweorda-gelac"*] as a metaphor for combat). In the Revesby Sword Play (the first folk-play recorded) a madman fights first a Hobby Horse, then a giant worm; the madman's sons kill him, then revive him by stamping on the ground. The Sword Dance and the Morris are performed; the Sword Dance trick of interlocking all the blades, so that they are lifted by a single hilt, is accomplished.[254]

> *A ring, a ring, we enter in*
> *To see this merry act begin.*
> *We'll act it right, we'll act it left,*
> *We'll act it on the public scale,*
> *And if you don't believe these words I say,*
> *Step in St. George and clear my way.*
> —The Pace-Egg Play of the Yorkshire Pennines[255]

St. George of Merrie England

An immensely popular version of the "death and resurrection" play is the *St. George Play,* featuring England's patron saint, famous for dispatching a dragon; Thomas Hardy presents a St. George Play (based upon those recalled from his youth) in *The Return of the Native.* For all that the saint is a beloved figure in English folklore, he may well be a late assimilation; his dramatic custom of being killed in order to be reborn seems to have less to do with Christianity and more to do with the ancient renewal rites of the Near Eastern vegetation-gods Attis and Thammuz.

The "George" of St. George irresistibly links up with the "George" of *George a Green* or *George o' the Green* or *Green George,* the famous Pinner (woods-keeper) of Wakefield and the subject (like Robin Hood) of a popular cycle of ballad romances. Elizabethan literature teems with references to George: *The Merry Wives of*

---

254 Laroque, *Shakespeare's Festive World*, p. 53
255 Pegg, *Rites and Riots: Folk Customs of Britain and Europe* p. 104

Windsor (I.i); *Henry IV, Part II* (V.iii); and Drayton, in the twenty-sixth song in *Polyolbion*. The Pindar of Wakefield was popular as a sign for public-houses and "as good as George a Green" was a proverbial saying for many generations.

Green Man

The rebirth theme and the association with greenery suggest that St. George, the patron saint of England, may serve as an aspect of the *Green Man,* the artistic motif which may be found in both pagan and medieval architecture, and which represents the spirit of nature as a mysterious leafy mask, or as a man's face peeping through a veil of vegetation, or sometimes as a leafy man disgorging vegetation. It may be too that the legend of St. George is intertwined with that of the old British light-god *Bel/Belenos,* counterpart to *Lugh/Lugos.*[256] As "Bel" is the same root whence the spring holiday *Beltain,* hence St. George's connection to the May games.

Harmony and union with the world of nature are best demonstrated through the *Green Man,* who is kind of hard to talk about, because he is more of a visual kind of thing. In his definitive book *Green Man: the Archetype of our Oneness with the Earth,* William Anderson first detects the Green Man both in the pagan nature-worship of the Celts (seen as a version of Cernunn the Horned One in the St. Goar pillar [possibly fifth century BCE] and in the Gundestrup Cauldron) and as a version of the Mediterranean and Near Eastern gods of the death/rebirth cycle—*Dionysos, Tammuz, Osiris, Adonis, Attis*—through whom the renewing properties of the vegetative world are celebrated in the many cults of mystery-religions popular throughout the Roman Empire. Anderson believes that the leafy mask of the Green Man derives from the foliate-mask worn by initiating priests of the Dionysiac rites.

Virtually all medieval summer festivities had a strong Green Man theme attached. A corbel carving (c. 1350) in the cathedral nave at Exeter may represent the May King, with the suggestion of a marvelous leafy head-dress.[257] At Thann (Haut-Rhin) a misericord carving shows the garlanded head of the May Queen, next to the head of a young man wearing a cap (probably the Summer King);

---

256 Anderson, *Green Man,* p. 28
257 *Green Man,* p. 28

above both is the head of a Green Man. The Green Man theme appears universal; during the May season, the Romans celebrated the fertility festival of the *Floralia* and the imported festival of the *Magna Mater* (Great Mother).[258] In this, the tree designated as the sacred *Attis-pine* (symbolizing the god Attis) was ceremonially carried to the Palatine temple in Rome—as the Maypole was later carried to the festival-field.

Otherwise, Green Man customs abound in medieval Europe—decorating *people and things* with flowers and greenery; *disguising* people, often with greenery and flowers; decorating *animals* with flowers and greenery; *leading people and things* decorated with greenery around to *various places,* also decorated with greenery, in order to accomplish various symbolic *tasks;* designating *ceremonial roles,* etc.[259] In England, the young people spent the night before May Day in the woods, taking horns and other instruments and not being chaste. They interrupted their non-chastity long enough to cut boughs off the trees, which they decorated with wreaths of posies, setting them in the doors and windows of houses by sunrise.

The true vibrancy of the Green Man theme is seen in medieval cathedrals, as demonstrated by various instances cited above. The powerful feeling held for the Spirit of Nature Itself was clearly so strong—one can conduct tours of Europe, specializing in Green Man churches. An example of the incorporation of the Green Man into actual Christian worship would be the figure called the *Compagnons du Loup Vert,* who partook in the Epiphany services at the church of St. Firmin in Picardy (we note the connection with the *Ember time* of midwinter). Wearing a *wolfskin* painted *green* and covered with *vegetation,* he would arrive at the church bearing a candle garlanded with flowers and station himself at the altar during the Mass. This kind-of pagan custom was discontinued in 1727.[260]

Ever-renewing cycle of life

Mummers' Plays, with their almost idiotic sing-song rhymes, offer the same comforting repetitiveness as do children's games; in depicting the death and resurrection, death and resurrection,

---

258 Russell, *Witchcraft in the Middle Ages,* p. 51
259 Grimm, *Teutonic Mythology,* vol. II, p. 785–7
260 Anderson, *Green Man,* p. 27

of St. George, they provide almost Hindu-like assurance of rebirth. Their customary performance during the renewal seasons of midwinter and spring indicate a willingness on the part of the actors to align their energies with the mighty energies of the turning earth. Laroque feels that (in like manner) the seasonal enactment of animals was meant to serve as a "magical means of triggering the reawakening of natural human and animal forces. Originally, the dances, masquerades and music were designed to revive the sleeping forces of fertility, at the end of the winter." [261]

In other words, the ritual mumming of animals (like the proto-theatrical Resurrection Plays) is inherited from pagan rites of regeneration which both proclaimed faith in—and sought to implement and make effective—the magical process of the rebirth of nature. As Doreen Valiente says of the Obby Oss: "He is the representative of the old god of the life-force, the power of fertility for humans, animals, and all nature, ever dying and being resurrected from death. He is the ever-renewing cycle of life." [262] *Perhaps in recognition of this, another custom is said to be observed regarding the Obby Oss. The Obby Oss's cloak, worn over the circular frame, forms a sort of canopy beneath him. It is said that the man impersonating the Obby Oss traditionally goes naked under the canopy.*

Clad in the hide of animals

Which brings us back to Puck/Robin Goodfellow: A complicated figure is positioned at the crux of all this—an actor playing an animal and a priest guiding a ritual occasion. We return to the interesting fact that both *Wily Beguilde* and *Grim the Collier of Croydon* take pains to place Robin in a suit of leathern animal-skins. Act IV of *Grim* opens with a description: *"Enter Robin Goodfellow, in a suit of leather close to his body; his face and hands coloured russet-colour, with a flail."* Since *Grim* mimics the elements of Mummers' Plays, Katharine Briggs finds it "probable that Robin Goodfellow had at this time some part in the mummers' play." [263] The mention of Robin's calf-skin disguise in *Wily Beguilde* strengthens this belief: "It is possible that Robin Goodfellow in a calf-skin suit may have taken the part of the man sweeping the floor with a broom, who is still one of the characters in many of the traditional mummers'

---

261 Laroque, *Shakespeare's Festive World*, p. 48
262 Valiente, *Natural Magic*, p. 156
263 Briggs, *Anatomy of Puck*, p. 76

plays."[264] (This would also explain Puck's appearance at the end of *A Midsummer Night's Dream*, when he appears to sweep up with a broom in the play's final scene.) There are other references to calf-skins among the mummers, suggesting that other characters may have worn skins as well.

The detail about sweeping the ritual-space with a broom is very interesting, as the early English Traditionalists were (still are, for all I know) very into sweeping bad energies away from the consecrated area prior to ritual; it sometimes seems as if every witch-book from the 1960s and early '70s shows a photo of Maxine Sanders or Janet Farrar sweeping with their ritual brooms somewhere.

More interesting still is finding Puck/Robin presiding over the death/rebirth ritual of the Mummers' Plays, *clad in the hide of animals*.

Fires

Jacob Grimm directs our attention to the "numerous ceremonies" associated with fires in early nineteenth-century Germany (the Easter fire, the Midsummer fire, etc) that give evidence of old pagan customs—such as rubbing the flame, leaping the fire, throwing flowers into the flame, baking and distributing loaves and cakes, performing the "circular dance."[265] In like manner, Grimm brings up old sacrificial plays, "still performed in parts of Gothland," wherein young fellows disguise themselves, blackening their faces. *"One, wrapt in fur, sits in a chair as the victim."* He holds in his mouth straw-stalks, which reach to his ears and which resemble sow-bristles—reminiscent of the sacrificial boar, such as that offered by the English at Yule.

> *"He's made an altar for me, faced with stone... he's reddened the new altar with ox blood."*
> —The Verse *Edda* [*Song of Hyndla* (10)][266]

The Norse equated making something red with making it enchanted or holy; this came about through cultural memory of *sacrificial blood* and the process whereby a sacrificial candidate becomes

---

264 Briggs, *Anatomy of Puck*, p. 77
265 Grimm, *Teutonic Mythology*, vol. I, p. 43
266 Larrington, *The Poetic Edda*, p. 254

The Horned God of Wytches 125

(for being a sacrifice) something sacred. Any sacrificial ritual will possess a certain duality of character. There is a quality of the somber, as a living creature is dispatched from the world. There is also a large element of the celebratory and the ecstatic, for the bloodied animal propitiates the gods and (hopefully) brings prosperity to the tribe. The sacrificial beast also, in more primitive times, simply meant dinner for the hungry ritualists, who did not have the convenience of a nearby A&P or Piggly Wiggly. Any sacrifice would then naturally tend to turn into a feast, with the spirit of the sacrificial animal imagined to enjoy the feasting immensely.

Is this the secret to the legends of Puck and Robin Goodfellow—Robin who was identified with the deer and Puck whose name means "goat"? Were they at one time imagined as the spirits of the sacrificial animals upon whom the hunting-tribes of Europe depended?

And were they imagined as well as the skin-clad priests who performed the sacred sacrifice—the magical animal-men who interfaced with the universe and with animal-herds on behalf of the tribe's well-being?

Is this the significance to Robin Goodfellow's wearing leather in *Wily Beguilde* and *Grim the Collier of Croydon*?

Was Robin Goodfellow originally the skin-clad Trois Freres Sorcerer, the first animal-shaman of Europe?

> *"The records of the Middle Ages show that the ancient god was known in many parts of the country, but to the Christian recorder he was the enemy of the New Religion..."*[267]
>
> —Margaret Murray, *The God of the Witches*

A kind of ironic thing is that Margaret Murray postulated that the pagan fertility-god worshipped by the witch-cult of Europe was impersonated by priests *dressed in suits of leather*. "In many religions the disguising of the principal personage—whether god or priest—as an animal is well known"[268]; the "ritual disguise was

---

[267] Murray, *The God of the Witches*, p. 19
[268] Murray, *The Witch-Cult in Western Europe*, p. 60

not merely a mask over the face, but included a covering, possibly of leather or some other hard and cold substance, over the whole body and even the hands."[269]

The basis to *Margaret Murray's* theories is the assumption that the documents and confessions of witch trials are accurate to the extent that they describe an outline of pagan traditions—it being a tactic of authorities to describe pagan activity, but with a bias. Thus statues of pagan gods are of "demons," pagans leave offerings to "demons," etc. Murray becomes suspicious that when the god of the witches appears, he is described as a demon. *"It is impossible to understand the witch-cult without first understanding the position of the chief personage of that cult. He was known to the contemporary Christian judges and recorders as the Devil, and was called by them Satan, Lucifer, Beelzebub, the Foul Fiend, the Enemy of Salvation, and similar names appropriate to the Principle of Evil, the Devil of the Scriptures, with whom they identified him."*[270] *"The consequence,"* as Murray reminds us, *"is that the pagan people are now regarded as having worshipped the Principle of Evil, though in reality they were merely following the cult of a non-Christian Deity."*[271]

The importance of distinguishing between Principles of Evil and non-Christian Deities is astoundingly pertinent today, as the emerging modern Neo-Pagan movement (fueled by the initiating fire of Wicca) meets the fundamentalist Purityranny ("tyranny of the Puritan") of triumphantalist Christian Evangelism. It was an innovation on Murray's part to see that—if the conquering Church *demonized* pagan religion—they undoubtedly *demonized* the pagan God as well. The possibility that our own modern conception of the Devil might reflect a *demonized* portrait of the original pagan God of witches is a new wrinkle in the study of Christian theology.

It has long since been an established convention that Murray was a crackpot whose notions of an organized pagan Resistance Movement, finally exterminated (in the manner of the Cathars) by the Church during the Burning Times of Witches—constitutes fanciful nonsense at best and an appalling lack of historical probity at worst—despite the fact that, as Ginzburg noted (in *The Night Battles*, p. xiii), there was an essential "kernel of truth" to Murray's thesis.

---

269 *The Witch-Cult in Western Europe*, p. 63
270 *The Witch-Cult in Western Europe*, p. 28
271 Murray, *The God of the Witches*, p. 33

Murray refers to a "continuity of belief and ritual which can be traced from the Palaeolithic period down to modern times"; following a line "of anthropological inquiry," one may discern the "survival of an indigenous European cult and the interaction between it and the exotic religion [Christianity] which finally overwhelmed it."[272]

Based upon the evidence of the Trois Freres Sorcerer and other such matter, Murray intuits an aboriginal Horned God amongst the Paleolithic, Neolithic, and Bronze Age peoples, associated with hunting-animals and the life-renewing properties of the universe. "After the general introduction of agriculture, the Horned God remained as a great deity, and was not dethroned even by the coming of the Iron Age. It was not until the rise of Christianity, with its fundamental doctrine that a non-Christian deity was a devil, that the cult of the Horned God fell into disrepute."[273]

Murray based her primary hypothesis—that the Hero-God of one religion will become the Devil of an usurping religion—upon her study of her chosen field of expertise, Egyptology. "In ancient Egypt the fall from the position of a high god to that of a 'devil' is well exemplified in the god Setekh, who in early times was as much a giver of all good as Osiris, but later was so execrated that, except in the city of his special cult, his name and image were rigorously destroyed. In the study of the Horned God this fact of the fall from godship to devildom must be borne in mind."[274]

As the Egyptians did with Setekh (reasons Murray), so would the Christians with Cernunnos and Puck. "In the thirteenth century the Church opened its long drawn-out conflict with Paganism in Europe by declaring 'witchcraft' to be a 'sect' and heretical."[275] "The fifteenth century marks the first great victories of the Church.... The Pagans fought a gallant, though losing, fight against a remorseless and unscrupulous enemy [so Murray characterized the medieval church]...they [pagans] clung to their old faith [paganism], and died in agony unspeakable [in the witch-persecutions of the Burning Times] rather than deny their God.... I have traced the worship of the Horned God onwards

---

272 *The God of the Witches*, p. 13
273 *The God of the Witches*, p. 14
274 *The God of the Witches*, p. 15
275 *The God of the Witches*, p. 21

through the centuries from the Palaeolithic prototypes, and I have shown that the survival of the cult was due to... a stratum of the population... strong enough to keep it alive." [276]

Murray felt that the priests of the Witch-Cult assumed the ritual role of the God: "The deity of this cult was incarnate in a man, a woman, an animal... though as God that place was infinitely higher in the eyes of the congregation than any held by a mere human being." Therefore, when witches (tortured into confessions) described adoring the Devil in their Sabbats, they meant (figured Murray) that they worshipped their pagan God in the human form of His priests: in these confessions, "the god was often spoken of as wearing the skin or attributes of an animal." [277]

Murray's assertion that pagans of Europe were organized into uniform covens, venerating a Fertility-God embodied in the form of a High Priest is a little outlandish. But in a subtle sense...

The Horned God was clearly impersonated, in a ritualistic manner of sorts, not by pagan priests celebrating Samhain or Beltain—but by actors performing the ritual of drama.

Select individuals, in a public forum, kept alive cultural memories of the pagan God during the Elizabethan and Jacobean Ages—by acting him out upon a stage.

Murray's belief that, since the Devil is so often described in terms of leathery skin, the priests of the witch-cult must have worn skins to impersonate Him, kind of predicts the appearance of Robin Goodfellow in *Grim the Collier* and *Wily Beguilde* dressed in suits of leather.

"The suggestion that the Devil was a man, wearing either an animal's skin or a mask in the form of an animal's head as a ritual disguise, accounts as nothing else can for the witches' evidence as to his appearance and his changes of form.... The witches never admitted in so many words that the Devil was a man disguised, but their evidence points strongly to the fact. In some cases the whole body was disguised, in others a mask was worn, usually over the face." [278] It would be interesting to know where else Murray thinks a mask would be worn.

---

276 *The God of the Witches*, p. 14
277 *The God of the Witches*, p. 12–13
278 Murray, *The Witch-Cult in Western Europe*, p. 61

Devil

"Devil" derives from the Latin *diabolus*, Greek *diabolos*, from *diaballein*, "to slander."[279] Professor Russell specifically denies a connection with the Indo-European root *div-*, often cited in this context. *Div*—yields "deus," divine, diva, as well as the Indian Vedic *devos*, which are supernatural beings of light who fight for good. Also related are such names as *Djevs* and *Deivos*, from which are derived the original Indo-European names for the Sky God: Zeus, Jovis, etc.

Christian demonology finds its roots in Jewish concepts of evil, derived from the traditions of the ancient Near East. The first outlines of the Devil began when the Israelites commenced discrediting the religion of the agricultural Great Mother of their pagan neighbors; thus, things associated with the Mother's cult—such as pigs, snakes, and spirits—came to be perceived as *evil*. This holy prejudice is seen in a number of ways—in Old Testamant references to the "whores" (meaning the goddess-priestesses) of Babylon and Egypt, for instance, and in stern prohibitions away from the ways of heathens, despised by the One God. The subsequent name *Beelzebub,* the "prince of demons," is a corruption of the name of the Canaanite fertility-god *Baal* ("Lord"), as the patron-god of the city of *Zebul; Baal* may also be seen as the root-name of the pagan god *Baalphegor* worshipped in the Old Testament by the Moabites on a mountaintop. German heretics in the 1150s were said to make offerings to a demon named *Belphegor,*[280] which is otherwise one of the demons in *Grim the Collier of Croydon*. Baal's consort, the life-giving mother-goddess *Asharoth* or *Astarte* became the arch-demon *Astaroth*.[281]

---

279 Russell, *Witchcraft in the Middle Ages*, p. 103

280 *Witchcraft in the Middle Ages*, p. 129

281 Gareth J. Medway, *Lure of the Sinister: The Unnatural History of Satanism* (New York University Press, 2001), p. 54

The Exile into Babylon (586–538 BCE) introduced the Jews to Persian *Zoroastrian dualism*. This helped the Jews conceive an adversary to God; Satan begins to appear in texts for the first time.

All cultures believe in evil (or at least chaotic) spirits. As far as is known, evil *as fundamental principle* started with the Persian *magos* Zoroaster, whose dates are unclear. Preaching what were then novel innovations, Zoroaster taught that: there was only one god; there would be a final judgment; there were two principles at work in the world—good and evil. Humans, having capacity for choice, must pick one or the other.

Under the influence of the Persian Empire, the Jews incorporated these ideas— *Satan*, in the Old Testament, is not a personal name, but means "an adversary." In the books of Samuel, David is a *satan* to the Philistines, and (used as a verb) God sent an angel to *satan* (or oppose) Balaam in Numbers 22:22. In the Talmud, *satan* is the ordinary word for an evil spirit; in the New Testament, Satan is transliterated into Greek letters and translated as *diabolos*, "one who throws against" or an adversary (*dia-*, "against" and *bolos*, "throw"). The *b* changing into a *v*, this eventually became *diavolos*, hence the medieval *divel* or devil.[282] In the Dead Sea scrolls, *angel* (Hebrew: *malaakh*) more often than not meant a "devil" rather than an "angel"; since the Christians called good spirits *angels* (meaning "messengers"), they tended to call evil spirits *demons*, from the Greek *daemon*. (On the other hand, pagans tended to equate demons or daemons with benevolent spirits and even deities.)[283] *Lucifer* or *Phosphoros*, the "Shining One," nearly became a name for Jesus (*"I am the Phosphoros,"* Revelation 22:16).

---

282 *Lure of the Sinister*, p. 52
283 *Lure of the Sinister*, p. 53

It is significant that, by the first century of Christianity, Jewish writing has become increasingly apocalyptic and therefore more inclined to dwell darkly upon Satan. Early Christianity follows the lead of both contemporary Jews and Gnostics in detailing a demonology and in equating pagan gods with *demons*. (It should be noted that both the Jews and early Christians treated the Greek, Philistine, and Canaanite pantheons the same, turning the foreign gods into evil spirits.) With the addition of Catharist dualism in the twelfth century, the Devil begins to approach his status as an eternal, cosmic principle.[284]

Distinctions were noted in the Ancient World concerning supernatural beings—distinctions ignored by the early Christians. The Greeks differentiated the *daimonion* (an evil spirit), from the useful spirit, the *daimon;* to the Aegean mind, the universe was full of spirits and sorcerers worked magic in cooperation with the daimones.[285] Homer uses *daimon* almost as a synonym for *theos*, "god," and Socrates shamanically claimed a personal *daimon*, who spoke advice into his ear. Medieval scholars dismissed the difference between good and bad spirits altogether, classifying all spirits as *demons;* church missionaries, influenced by Jewish and Gnostic thought, considered their work cut out when they got to Europe and found a bunch of pagan magic-users, whom they considered ipso facto demonolaters.

Otherwise, it may have been that a perception of hostile spirits of the dead—or the spirits of animals or humans outside the community—contributed to the concept of the evil demon. Equally, demons may represent personalizations of the hostile forces of nature and fate, or (Freud-like) they may be the projections of violent and uncontrollable forces that we feel within ourselves. As Russell notes, there is a curious relationship between our will and the demon that we have projected from our darkest desire.

What specifically interests here is the fact that the Devil was an import into Europe from somewhere else, another foreign belief (like Christianity) which had to be planted in the European soil. The Devil's path in Europe is uneven; neither the Celts nor the Teutons had any concept like the Devil. He barely makes an impression in either England or in Italy, and he never made it to Russia.

---

284 Russell, *Witchcraft in the Middle Ages*, p. 101–108
285 *Witchcraft in the Middle Ages*, p. 103

Heresy and dualism

The first execution for heresy took place in 1022 under Robert of France—the details of this initial "discovery" of heretical practice will become standard. Heretics (the convention will go) meet in *secret places,* caves or underground buildings, lit by torches. Heretics *chant names* until some *demon* appears—the lights are *extinguished* and frenzied *orgies* ensue. The children born subsequently are *burned up* after eight days (in a perversion of the baptismal practice). The substance thus gotten is used in *blasphemous parody* of communion. Genuinely pagan ingredients are to be found in this stew; when filled with the Unholy Spirit of their twisted sacrament, the heretics had angelic (shamanic) *visions;* they were *transported* from place to place without loss of time (the benadenti legend); they adored the Devil, who appeared as a *beast* (shamanic animal-worship), an angel of *light* (Celto-Teutonic solar-divinities), or as a *black man* (another pagan shamanic motif, denoting one of another world). Such dualist doctrines had not been seen since the Gnostics and comprised the blueprint for "devilish" witch assemblies, characterized by orgies, cannibalism, and human sacrifice (especially that of children). Demonstrating that these slanders were no innovative inspiration is the fact that the same non-human, monstrous crimes of depravity had been self-servingly alleged against the Jews by the Syrians; against the early Christians (hyper-ironically) by the Romans; against the Gnostics by the established Christians; and now against heretics, and then—eventually—witches.[286] A long succession of heresy trials follows, playing upon the same themes, throughout the fourteenth and fifteenth centuries, with the transistion from "heretic" to "witch" accomplished in the fifteenth century without much difficulty.

The addition (or invention) of the Devil to the Christian mythos was not necessarily a healthy circumstance. Katharine Briggs says that the Devil loomed so large in the minds of Puritans that they were in danger of falling into *Zoroasterian dualism,* meaning the conception of dualing gods: one beneficent, the other cruel and wicked.[287] The Devil was so ever-present in the minds of mortals during the seventeenth century that Protestants conceived of

---

286 Russell, *A History of Witchcraft,* p. 59
287 Briggs, *Pale Hecate's Team,* p. 151

even ghosts as demonic (the consequence of having done away with Purgatory).

First pact

The first European story of a pact with the Devil is that of *Theophilus*, a precursor to Faustus. According to Kittredge, Theophilus enjoyed a "triumphant career throughout the Occident for a millennium," his story translated from Greek to Latin in the ninth century and then into English about the year 1000. He was popular fare in the pulpit, his legend read in church at matins, and he became a "stock item in medieval collections of miracles and exempla."[288] He became also a French poem in the thirteenth century and the subject of a popular troubadour drama. Sculptures of him can be recognized in Beverley Minister and in the Lady Chapel at Ely.

Theophilus was the bursar of a church at Adana in Northern Cilicia c. 538 CE. Demoted by a jealous superior and seeking revenge (in an un-Christian sort of way), Theophilus consulted a Jew (who was of course, being a Jew, also a sorcerer). This Jew summoned the Devil: *Theophilus signed a contract with his own blood and got his office restored.*

An important part of the story is that nothing ultimately happens to Theophilus—the Blessed Virgin kindly intercedes on his behalf at the fateful hour, tearing up the document of damnation. It is super-significant that in such early stories as that of Theophilus, the Blessed Virgin (or somebody) would save the misguided person at the last minute, to be forgiven; in contrast with later medieval fable, initially there is not necessarily terrible consequence for covenanting with the Arch-Fiend—in fact, it is possible to have a happy ending. Also—it must be noted that, in early "sell the soul" stories, persons who make pacts with the Devil tend to hold equal, if not superior, power, as the Devil is seen as one who could be controlled by humans.[289] Magical manuscripts have a great deal to say about retaining control over demons and magical spirits; the excessively aggressive tone of many directions is, to a great extent, meant to force demonic forces into submission. All these ideas will change wholly by the sixteenth century.

---

288 Kittredge, *Witchcraft in Old and New England*, p. 239
289 Jeffrey Burton Russell, *A History of Witchcraft: Sorcerers, Heretics, and Pagans* (New York: Thames and Hudson, 1980), p. 78

The story of Theophilus was included in the *Golden Legend*, a thirteenth-century best-seller, and "caught on" to such an extent that Pope Silvester II (who, being of a mechanical mind, made clocks and other such wizard-like gadgets) was assumed to have sold his soul, as was Oliver Cromwell—hence his victory at Worcester.

Originally, attitudes towards the Ultimate Evil seem to have been relaxed and reasonable. Reginald Scot cites one John Davie, who consoles his wife after she sells her soul to the Devil in an impulsive moment: *"Be content, (quoth he) by the Grace of God, Jesus Christ can unwitch us: for none evill can happen to them that feare God."*[290] Likewise, a woman was brought before a synod in Darmstadt in 1582. The conclusion of the proceedings was for *"the people to be taught that all that happens to them is not to be ascribed to sorcery, for much is sent by God or happens naturally, and no one can be injured by sorcery further than God permits; repentance, prayer and other Christian means are to be employed, and the defamation of innocent persons to be wholly avoided."*[291] Presumably the church did not find these comforting attitudes helpful in cementing its authority and so we find increasingly hysterical accounts of the Devil and devil-worship.

A couple of funny stories about Faustus give some idea of the paranoia that came to surround the Devil. The wizard Faustus conjures onstage in Marlowe's show, a device which seems to have fascinated the Elizabethans, but horrified the Puritans. A bit of sixteenth-century urban mythology has it that—during some production of *Faustus* somewhere—while *"Faustus was busie in his magicall invocations, on a sudden they were all dasht, for... there was one devell too many amongst them."* Another story cautions that the actor's magic-working resulted in the *"visible apparition of the Devill on the stage... (the truth of which I have heard from many now alive, who well remember it) there being some distracted with that fearfull sight."*[292] (A suspicious number of incredible Elizabethan things are attested to on the authority of Someone Who Said So.) The stories are funny, *but the Devil is quickly attaining the majesty of his satanic self and it is becoming more and more accepted that there is no*

---

290 Briggs, *Pale Hecate's Team*, p. 14
291 *Pale Hecate's Team*, p. 14
292 *Pale Hecate's Team*, p. 127

way to win with the Fiend of Hell. In the play *The Devil's Charter*, Pope Alexander conjures with the Devil; the Devil (as the Devil will) betrays him by appearing seated in Alexander's throne, wearing the Pope's ceremonial robes. Mephistopheles tempts Faustus out of his soul. A Renaissance prince muses upon a supernatural encounter: *"The spirit that I have seen may be the Devil; and the Devil hath power to assume a pleasing shape; yea, and perhaps out of my weakness and my melancholy, as he is very potent with such spirits, abuses me to damn me."* (*Hamlet*, II.ii.610–15) And damned many were.

Un-demonizing the Devil

Jacob Grimm said, of the addition of the Devil to European pagan folklore: *"Christianity could not but receive, just as heathen Polytheism was expiring, a visible bent towards Dualism, which afterwards philosophy tried to resolve into a general principle of good and another of evil. When we compare the cheerful tone of Greek myths with the harshness and grimness imparted to the legends of our Middle Ages by the intrusion of an all-too positive Devil, we see that the contrast comes out not so much in the original texture of the popular beliefs, which is everywhere the same or similar, as in the colour laid upon it; and therefore our inquiry is entitled to resolve a whole mass of devil-phenomena back into the milder forms of ancient spirits and gods."*[293]

Folklorist Katharine Briggs agrees with Grimm; she sees the differences between the puckish Puck of *A Midsummer Night's Dream* and the half-human Robin of *Wily Beguilde* as "truly" representing "varying strains of folk tradition."[294] While the hobgoblins, brownies, and pucks of folklore might be characterized variously as ghosts, minor devils, kindly domestic elves, or mischievous but ultimately well-intentioned spirits—"It seems likely that the kindly feeling had survived from pre-Christian times, and the ghost belief may have been a survival of primitive ancestor worship, reinforced by psychic phenomena. The devil theory was that taught by the church."[295]

In other words, examining the folklore, it becomes apparent that the Devil was an alien and late insertion into the European mythos. Since the European pagan God was painted over by Chris-

---

[293] Grimm, *Teutonic Mythology*, vol. III, p. 986

[294] Briggs, *Anatomy of Puck*, p. 71

[295] *Anatomy of Puck*, p. 71

tians so ardently, in a perverse way, we can gain an understanding of the pagan God by looking back from the figure of the Devil. If we "un-demonize" the European Devil, we often can see the pagan God.

It is a pretty sure thing that one may judge how important or vital a concept was to the Celts and the Teutons by how vehemently it was slandered by the church. Take for instance the bizarre medieval fixation upon the pagan theory of the *supernatural lover*— rendered in Christian orthodoxy as the soul-stealing demonic seducers the *incubi* and *succubi*.

European pagans enthusiastically accepted the notion that children could be born through the union of a mortal and a supernatural or divine being. "The belief in spirits which fathered children on human women was a pagan Celtic superstition before it became a Christian one."[296] In the *Tain*, the Irish hero Cu-chulaidh was conceived upon his mother by the sun-god *Lugh* as she slept near the Brugh na Boyne (a significant *sidh*), at the fateful time of Halloween (Samhain). Irish kings supposedly received the passionate favors of the territorial-goddess *Maeb* on the night of their inauguration; Andro Man apparently told his examiners that he had *"carnal dealings"* with the faerey Queen. It was asserted of popular figures as a commonplace that they came of half-otherworldly parentage; inevitably the Devil squirrels his unpleasant self into this otherwise fortuitous equation. It is revealing then that legend will pass down to us the information that *Merlyn* (the supreme wizard of the British people and of all time) *was fathered by the Devil*.

An example that early traffic with the Devil was regarded far more complacently than it would be several centuries later is the Arthurian ensemble of writings called the *Vulgate Cycle* (c. 1215–30), one of the first times that the master magician makes an appearance. Geoffrey of Monmouth's 1135 *History* begins this theme, with Merlyn's mother claiming to have been impregnated by an otherworldly spirit: *"I know only one thing: when I was... resting in my chamber, there often appeared to me a most handsome young man. He would take me in his arms and kiss me on the mouth. After a few moments he would disappear."*[297]

---

296 Cavendish, *King Arthur and the Grail*, p. 108
297 Markale, *Merlin*, p. 9

It is noteworthy that, by the time of the *Vulgate Cycle*, this incubus has become the Devil himself. According to the *Lancelot in Prose* (c. 1230): *"The devil...assumed his human form and, while* [Merlyn's mom] *slept, he came to her and had carnal knowledge of her."*[298] Merlyn's mom, upon realizing what has happened, visits her confessor. What happens next is significant. She is absolved, on condition that she *"eat only once on Friday and abstain from all lust except for that which comes in sleep and which no one can guard against. She promised him. The devil understood that he had lost and was very angry."*[299] The general leniency and tolerance of the situation is in marked contrast to later demonic stories, as is the character of the eldritch Casanova, which changes from an amorous lover, to a grotesque demonic molester, to being the Scourge of Hell himself. Cavendish finds another interpretation for Merlyn's otherworldly begetting, reading it as a stand-in for "something which was probably common...the state of being half Christian and half pagan, of adopting the new religion without surrendering the old."[300]

Conjuring and commanding

The Middle Ages observed the same magical conventions as did the Greeks, the Babylonians, and the Assyrians—not surprising, as Middle Ages magic was based upon Greek, Babylonian, and Assyrian manuscripts. These considered that the universe was filled with magical spirits who could intervene (if approached properly) on behalf of humanity. Medieval sorcerers maintained a distinction between good demons that could be relied upon for help, and bad demons, which were to be avoided. A medieval manuscript on sorcery calls for the use of pentacles (inscribed with Kabbalistic names) *"to influence good spirits favorably."*[301]

Often early devils and demons were associated with these magical spirits, who could be raised and commanded. This implies that—when the Devil was first introduced—he was confused with the older concept of magical spirits. Thus, Bale (in 1547, attacking the Catholic mass) claimed that, *"It serveth all wytches in*

---

298 *Merlin*, p. 13

299 *Merlin*, p. 13

300 Cavendish, *King Arthur and the Grail*, p. 108

301 Emile Grillot de Givry, *Illustrated Anthology of Sorcery, Magic and Alchemy* (Zachary Kwinter Books, Ltd., 1973), p. 109

their wytcherye, all sorcerers, charmers, inchaunters, dreamers, sothsayers, necromansers, conjures, crosse dyggers, devyll raysers, myracle doers," etc.[302] The point is that Bale apparently considers *"devyll raysing"* to be something akin to "raising spirits," an adequate medieval way to express conjuring and magic-use.

In this context, the conjuring in Shakespeare's *Henry VI, Part II* (I.iv), becomes significant. Bolingbroke and Mother Jourdain call forth a spirit, who *"riseth"* out of the stage's trapdoor. He is imprisoned within the magic circle which they have made and consecrated, and so must answer their questions. *Of interest is the name which the spirit bears*: Asnath, *sometimes* Asmath. *It is not hard to see that this is an anagram for* "Satan," *or, in medieval pronunciation,* "Satham." *Needless to say, this gives a good idea how the spirit may have been costumed for the scene.* One can imagine the stir which this would cause at the box office, when it is learned that the price of admission includes an unparalleled opportunity to witness *the raising of the Devil himself* on stage!

But the point is that the spirit is under the power of Bolingbroke and Jourdain (as he is held fast inside their charmed circle) and must answer the questions which they put to him. When they have heard enough, they dismiss him: *"Descend to darkness and the burning lake! False fiend, avoid!"* This is the ideal medieval magical situation: the conjurers confident and forceful with the spirit (and therefore in charge of the situation), armed with the power which their magical preparations have given them. This is the situation which Faustus hopes to exploit. *But Faustus's Devil is the crafty kind, who outwits and dooms all those foolish enough to traffic with him.* And here we therefore see the difference in the early Devil (associated with magical spirits and thought malleable) and the later Devil (the architect of evil and screwer of humanity).

In the romance tales of *Charlemagne and his Peers*, magicians continue to control demons. The wizard-hermit who comforts Angelica reads from a magical book, whereby a goblin appears to serve them; *Malagigi the enchanter* casts spells out of magical books; these cause people to fall asleep, or cause *demons to appear out of the air*, to be mounted as transports by Malagigi; Malagigi summons the demon Ashtaroth to bring Rinaldo to him.[303] It is

---

302 Kittredge, *Witchcraft in Old and New England*, p. 466
303 Bulfinch, *Bulfinch's Mythology* p. 532

surely out of these traditions that Prospero the Mage is attended by his servant-spirit Ariel in *The Tempest;* also related are the animal-familiars that cohabited with witches, magically performing the beldames' bidding. Fantasies of secret supernatural minions attached themselves to impressive historical figures as well; Grenville, Raleigh, and Drake were all said to possess personal devils.[304]

There is an important burlesque tradition concerning devils in the Middle Ages, casting devils in the buffoon-roles otherwise filled by Robin Goodfellow or by Falstaff-masked-as-Herne. The Mystery and Morality Plays, as well as the Mummers' Plays (such as the Lutterworth Christmas Play), use devils as comic characters, played by clowns for laughs. Laroque explains this "conjunction of laughter and devilry" as a "distant association of the burlesque with agricultural fertility rites" which underlies "beliefs in fairies and witches."[305] The use (or misuse) of devils as comic foils explains their presentation in plays such as Greene's *Friar Bacon and Friar Bungay* (c. 1590).

Friar Bacon displays an exceptional irreverence towards the very idea of devils. Friar Bacon spends the entire play summoning, ordering, controlling, and commanding devils and there is never a question but that Bacon is the superior entity. As an instance, he conjures a devil to carry off Friar Bungay (*"I'll fetch this Bungay straightway from Fressingfield..."* [II.iii.164]), leading to the amusing sight of a costumed devil hoisting the pudgy monk over his shoulder and trotting off the stage with him. Christian and pagan theology unite in the assertion (III.ii.61) that Lucifer and his devils are *"subject under Luna's continent,"* implicitly connecting the magic-using friars with mystical moon-energies and elevating the moon-goddess Luna to the position of Deity Supreme to devils (it is not the Father and the Son to whom devils are subject, according to *Friar Bacon*—it is Luna the Moon-Mother). And at the end of the play, in a deliberate slap to any sort of Puritan morality, Bacon's servant Miles actually decides to accompany the devil on a kind of holiday in hell. Since all *"tapsters"* (bartenders) are in hell, Miles figures there must be *"good tippling-houses* [bars] *there,"* where he can find *"a lusty fire there, a pot of good ale, a pair of cards."*

---

304 Briggs, *Pale Hecate's Team,* p. 160
305 Laroque, *Shakespeare's Festive World,* p. 26

In another comic exit, Miles leaps onto the devil's back: *"O Lord, here's even a goodly marvel, when a man rides to hell on the devil's back!"* "Exeunt, roaring." (V.ii.)

Merry Devil

At times, devils are so thoroughly assimilated to the side of beneficent magic, they are regarded as "good." Such an instance is the anonymous play *The Merry Devil of Edmonton*. The show was probably first performed around 1604, often revived (*"sundry times Acted by his Majesties Servants, at the Globe, on the banke-side"*), and printed around 1608. It was included in the Shakespeare Apocrypha (unknown works attributed to Shakespeare at one point or another) and alluded to in 1616 by Jonson in the Prologue to *The Divell is an Ass*.

Without doubt inspired by *Faustus*, *The Merry Devil* opens at the moment where *Faustus* ends, introducing Peter Fabell (the eponymous Merry Devil) as he awaits the fateful coming of his attendant-demon—*for the time has come when Fabell's contract is up and he must away to an eternity of damnation in hell*. However, Fabell's attendant-demon doesn't seem like the brightest bulb in the neighborhood, as Fabell is able to trick him (fairly easily) into sitting in an enchanted chair (perhaps one which has had a magic circle drawn about it). The demon is unable to move from his magical prison and Fabell blackmails him into an extension of his contract. (Briggs notes that a popular folkloric theme is someone's outwitting the Devil, reinforcing the superiority of English native intelligence when compared to the dullard laggards of the Infernal Depths.)[306] This (the first scene in the show) completely ends the demonic sub-plot of *The Merry Devil;* the show goes on to demonstrate how Fabell (a popular magic-user and wizard) leads a gang in springing a girl from the harsh prison of a convent, so that she might marry the handsome hottie boyfriend that she desires and that her father opposes. In going to great lengths to unite young lovers, Fabell "acts as the rather puckish good genius" of the play: *"And let our toyle to future ages prove, the devill of Edmonton did good in Love."*[307]

Fabell is esteemed as a magician; he has *"long at Cambridge read*

---

306 Briggs, *Pale Hecate's Team*, p.122
307 *Pale Hecate's Team*, p. 125

the liberal arts, the metaphysics, magic, and those parts of the most secret deep philosophy" (I.iii.14–16); demonstrates a masterful command of spirits more hobgoblin than devil by promising his friend that, "*Ile make my spirits to dance such nightly Jigs along the way twixt this and Totnam crosse* [a crossroads] ... [Those that come] *shall lose their way; and scrambling in the ditches, all night shall whoop and hollow, cry and call, yet none to other finde the way at all*" (I.iii.135–144); and puckishly plays magic tricks upon the nuns, compelling them to engage in sexy games (II.ii).

Despite the ostensible Christian setting, there is a pronounced pagan quality to much of the play—such as Smug's pledge that he will, "*when it shall please the goddesses and the destinies, be drunk in your company!*" (II.i.20) As well, a gentle pagan invocation ("*I cast my holy water pure on this wall and on this doore, that from evill shall defend and keepe you from the ugly fiend: evill spirit, by night nor day, shall approach or come this way; Elfe nor Fary, by this grace, day nor night shall haunt this place*" [III.ii.26–35]) seems to contrast deliberately the harshness of medieval Christian piety: "*Rise at midnight to your matins, read your Psalter, sing your Latins. And when your blood shall kindle pleasure, scourge yourself in plenteous measure.*" (III.i.43–46) Note: in an enjoyably spooky scene, a sexton fears that he is being haunted in the churchyard by many spirits, including the ghost of Master Theophilus. (IV.ii) Fabell wins admiration all round when (in the manner of the pagan marriage-god Hymen at the close of *As You Like It*) he calls down blessings upon the newly-wed couple (V.ii.122–140)—an act that also has the effect of reinforcing his devotion to goodness, in the manner of Puck in *Midsummer*.

For all that Fabell traffics with spirits relentlessly, his appellation "the Merry Devil" suggests an irrepressible joie de vivre. "Devil" refers to his status as a magic-worker, but bears a positive connotation, born out by the trust and esteem that his fellow characters demonstrate towards him. In the case of Peter Fabell, "Devil" is as upbeat and affirmative an adjective as one could find.

Variable role

Of the number of "Devil Plays" of the Elizabethan/Jacobean Ages, only *Faustus* takes the Devil at all seriously; everyone else treats devils as stooges. The popular press produced an exceptional number of tracts, broadsides, and pamphlets, against which popular tradition can be gauged. Two periods were especially prolific, 1580–1628 and 1643–1700, the second even more so than the first. The literary treatment of witches at the beginning of this period was often humorous or sympathetic—as, curiously, frequently was that of the Devil. As the witch-scare increased, treatment of witches grew far more serious. Plays, however, such as *The Merry Devil of Edmonton, The Pranks of Puck, Friar Rush, Friar Bacon and Friar Bungay* are all evidence of a light-hearted treatment of devils—and even at the height of the witch-craze, the 1655 *Witch of the Woodlands* details jocular and non-Puritanical pranks played upon a cobbler by witches.[308] This provides an example of how unimpressed the (Protestant) English were over the Devil, and offers a startlingly vivid contrast with the Catholic Continent, who freaked out over demonism so thoroughly they began hysterically to set people on fire over the matter.

In the arena of British folk-legend as well, the Devil's role (so observes wise Mother Briggs) is "rather variable," implying that he was somewhat misunderstood by a native populace that really had no cultural context for a being irrationally dedicated to evilness.[309] Like *giants* in some stories, the Devil is susceptible to trickery and may be gulled into impossible tasks; distracted by fool's errands; and in general may successfully be "mocked and deluded" by humans. Like giants (and like the *aboriginal gods* of the British Isles), the Devil has the habit of lifting and hurling stones, sometimes burying whole towns with shovel-fulls of dirt; the Brits goddess *Caillech Berra*, for instance, likewise was supposed to have created whole sections of rocky coast by dropping the stones she was carrying when her overburdened apron gave way. Like Odinn "and other pagan gods" (King Herla, for instance), the Devil heads the spectral ride that hunts for lost souls, galloping forth with the *Dandy Dogs* or with *Dando* the damned priest (damned because he wouldn't stop hunting long enough to observe his priestly duties). Many legends feature the Devil in the pagan role of the *huntsman of souls*—in Scandinavian legend, the Devil carries away wood-wives; in English tradition, witches.

In folklore, as in the dramatic traditions, the Devil is frequent-

---

308 Briggs, *Pale Hecate's Team*, p. 27
309 Katharine Briggs, *British Folk-Tales and Legends: A Sampler* (London: Routledge Classics, 2002), p. 151

ly impotent against the skillful wielding of the magical arts; numerous instances relate the compulsion or coercion of the Hellish Lord by the superior power of magic—Sir John Schorn assumed control of the Devil by conjuring him into his boot.[310] Mother Briggs reminds us that (in stout British legend, at least) a "dauntless heart" and a cunning wit are often all that is required to best the Great Fiend (who frequently exits British story seeming distinctly not-so-Great).

Ways in which the Devil in folklore is essentially like pagan deities

The belief that a magic-worker utilized spirits in order to perform magic led to the belief in *familiars* or *imps* (spirits associated with specific magicians, who helped facilitate their sorceries). These familiar-spirits were often identified with *small animal-characteristics* (a trend noted even late in the Hunt-Times, after the familiar had become generally identified with demonism). Likewise forest-spirits and the domestic sprites of folklore were associated with animal characteristics—generally furriness and possession of animal parts—a small stature, *diminutiveness*, is also a feature here. Significantly, demons are sometimes portrayed with just these same characteristics, implying an attempt (on somebody's part) to demonize these helpful, native creatures and creating a confusion gap, in which *demons* and *sprites* appear to be one and the same.

Instances where the Devil falls into this confusion gap are noteworthy, as they suggest a generalized confusion of the Devil with familiar-spirits and domestic sprites. It is significant that, for instance, during the *Dauphine trials* of 1421–1440 (in which it is mostly peasants and shepherds that are accused), the Devil is overwhelmingly described as one of the Little People of folk legend. He is usually a *little black man* or a little man dressed in black clothes. The names given to demons in these trials are decidedly non-demonic: *Brunet, Corp-diable, Griffart, Guillaume* or *Guillemet, Pierre, Borrel, Jean, Tartas, Revel, Guli, Juson,* and *Ginifert.* As Russell observes, "Mischievous, but hardly awful names."[311]

Sara Williams had notable names for her devils, such as *Hoberdidaunce* (named after the subject of a *"merry tale"* told by her Mis-

---

310 *British Folk-Tales and Legends*, p. 152
311 Russell, *Witchcraft in the Middle Ages*, p. 217

tress *"as they were at worke,"* concerning a creature *"that used his cunning to make a Lady laugh"*), which hardly sounds hellish. Other names by which she called her imps were: *Killico, Frateretto, Tocobatto, Lustie Jolly Jenkin, Delicat, Puffe and Purre, Lustie Dickie, Molkin, Wilkin, Kellicocam, Maho, Modu,* and *Hob*. These are incongruous names for demons and devils; "Hob" is plainly a hobgoblin name and "Fraterreto" seemingly derives from the Latin *Frater* ("brother," hence "fraternity"), which would give a friendly sort of impression, one would imagine. Numerous others look like nothing so much as seventeenth-century names for pets ("Kellicocam" and "Killico" remind too much of "calico" not to imagine they were not associated with cats, as does certainly "Puff and Purr"). It is fascinating that Sara said she knew these *"very strange names"* because they were *"written upon the walls of Sir George Peckhams house, under the hangings, which they said were names of spirits."*[312] "Hangings" are wall-hangings, a customary means of period home-decoration, which (according to Sara) mask the inscribed names of these "spirits"; this sounds like the kind of secret occult detail that might be imagined by an accused witch, after the Stockholm Syndrome has set in and she has acquiesced to the supernatural horror-show her examiners insist upon.

Grimm observes that "witches' devils have proper names so strikingly similar to...those of elves and kobolds," at times it seems as if "all devils' names of that class are descended from older folk-names for those sprites."[313] A survey of these names provides a glimpse into the "old elvish domestic economy" of the Middle Ages. For instance, many names for the Devil can be discerned as deriving from healing-flowers and herbs: *Wolgemut* (origanum), *Schone* (daisy), *Luzei* (aristolochia), *Grunlaub* (leaf), *Lindenzweig* (twig), *Eichenlaub* (oak), *Holderlin* (elder), *Kranzlein* (garland)— Grimm offers two entire pages of examples as proof. *Flederwisch*, a name used by witches, is also the folkloric name of a kobold.

Murray notes that many of the Devil's names given by Alsatian witches from 1585–1630 are diminutive: *Hammerlin, Peterlin* (this not only means "Little Peter," it means "parsley"), and *Kochloffel*.[314] Suzanne Gaudry, in her confession, gives *Petit-Grignon* as the

---

312 Briggs, *Pale Hecate's Team*, p. 157
313 Grimm, *Teutonic Mythology*, vol. III, p. 1062–3
314 Murray, *The God of the Witches*, p. 38

name of her demon-lover.[315] James Stewart, apprehended at Irvine in 1618, said that the Devil appeared *"in the similitude and likeness of a black little whelp."*[316] English witches were calling the Devil, as well as numerous imps, spirits, and familiars, by the cozy name of "Tom" until well into the 1660s (see *The Witch of Edmonton);* this intrigues Judy Grahn, as English lesbians of today are called Toms.[317]

The faerey-story of *The King of Ireland's Son and the Well of the Western World* reads like a veritable catalog of Celtic mythic motifs.[318] The King of Ireland's son (1) goes *hunting* in the snow where he (2) kills a *raven*. He therefore falls under (3) the *taboo* that he can never sleep two nights under one roof until he finds [this should sound really familiar] a woman whose (4) *skin is white as snow, whose hair is black as raven's wings, whose lips are red as blood* [this litany pops up a lot in Celtic stories]. The youth must go to the Eastern World to do this, an (5) exotic *Otherworld*. He passes (6) a funeral. Creditors are holding the body for payment of a debt. The youth is (7) generous, and pays the debt. A (8) *small, green man* mysteriously appears to accompany the youth. The man has with him five champions with (9) *superhuman powers*—one can see far, one can run fast, one can blow super-breath. The short green man can (10) swell in size. They get to the castle where a *raven-haired woman* lives; (11) spikes are set all around, with (12) the heads of hapless suitors stuck upon them. The woman is (13) capricious, and gives the youth gifts, only to steal them back from him. The *small green man* steals them back yet again, and returns them to the youth. (14) Pins of slumber in pillows cause people to fall asleep inopportunely; one fellow goes to sleep with his head on a (15) *horse's skull* [in which, natch, there is a pin of slumber]. One of the champions has to go to the (16) *Well of the Western World* [this sounds a lot like the World-Tree Yggdrasill of Norse myth] and fetch back (17) *three* (18) bottles of *healing*. To do this, he has (19) to *race* against (20) an old *hag* [reminiscent of the story of Macha].

---

315 Alan C. Kors and Edward Peters, *Witchcraft in Europe: 1100–1700: A Documentary History* (Philadelphia: University of Pennsylvania Press, 1984), p. 267
316 Murray, *The God of the Witches*, p. 133
317 Grahn, *Another Mother Tongue*, p. 299n
318 Briggs, *Anatomy of Puck*, p. 207

The thing that cracks me up about this story is that the heroine, the beautiful woman with the "skin as... etc.," works to the hero's detriment; she is a very subversive faery-tale princess. The Celts are a famously tempestuous people; this seems to extend to their fayrie-tale figures. Otherwise, what intrigues is the *small, green man*, who appears out of nowhere, to assist the hero.

He is like small, mysterious men in general who appear in folklore. In the Fenian story of Diarmid and the *Daughter of King under the Waves*,[319] Diarmid is helped by a small russet man, reminiscent of Robin in *Grim the Collier*, with his face painted russet (red). Otherwise, small gray or black men turn up in folklore and faerey-tales in a number of ways: *Rumplestiltskin* and *Tim Tom Tot* are two of this variety; *Faerey Patch* and *Belly Blind* are helpful goblins not unlike *Puck*. The fact that these beings are often colored recalls various dwarf/feyrie-stories wherein the spirits are colored; John Walsh (a cunning-man and a healer, who was examined in 1566) said that faeries were colored white, green, and black.

In 1588, Alesoun Peirsoun, of Byrehill, Fifeshire, claimed that *"thair come ane man to hir, cled in grene clothis* [green clothes, a frequent detail in Celtic stories of supernatural folk], *quha* [who] *said to hir, Gif scho* [if she] *wald be faithfull, he wald do hir guid* [good]."[320] Previously, she had discussed the Good Neighbors in her testimony; it seems clear enough that she is describing one thing and her judges are hearing something else. The man who comes to visit her is perceptibly pagan in origin, one of the "good society" tradition which is stretched from Central/Eastern Europe to the Scottish Highlands, as his *green clothes* make clear (green clothes being one of the signals in Celtic folklore as to this sort of origin). Alesoun's examiners (however) seem happy enough to accept all this as evidence of devil-worship.

Folklore recognizes an amiable spirit called *Blue Breeches;* the witch-tortured children of Mohra, Sweden, said that the Devil was an old man with a red beard, long garters, and *blue stockings*. In German stories, the Devil appears as *Green-coat,* or as a *hunter in green*.[321] The so-titled Faerey-Tale of the Brothers Grimm (#101) tells of a soldier who makes a bet with the Devil; the Devil is a man

---

319 Nutt, *Studies on the Legend of the Holy Grail*, p. 195
320 Murray, *The Witch-Cult in Western Europe*, p. 241
321 Grimm, *Teutonic Mythology*, vol. IV, p. 1607

in a *green coat* with *cloven hoofs*. To win the bet, the soldier must wear both the *green coat* and a *bear-skin* (sleeping in it too) for *seven years*.

This faerey-tale may be seen as an example of a Celtic *initiation story*. In a very shamanic circumstance, the supernatural *Man in Green* challenges the soldier, just as the medieval epic *Sir Gawain and the Green Knight* begins when the Green Knight dares Sir Gawain to face him again. The soldier is challenged to wear the Man's (supernatural) green coat (symbolic of affinity with the renewing *vegetation of the earth*) and a bear-skin, wearing *animal-skins* being an ancient pagan custom, prohibited continually (and ineffectually) by the church. The soldier then reverts to being a *Wild-Man* (one who lives in the wilds like an animal, also a pagan motif). The point is, the soldier is hard-core, *sees the difficult task through to its fullest conclusion, wins the bet, and gets a beautiful bride* as consequence. *Some revisionist individual* along the way, though, is presumably uncomfortable about the soldier "winning" his contest with the devilish *Man in Green* and so tacked on a *gratuitous ending* about the soldier *losing his soul* after all. This ending (the one used by the Grimms) makes *no sense* and seems to exist simply to reinforce the church's didactic point about *not making bets* or having anything to do with *cloven-hoofed green men*.

Interestingly, the devils described in French Switzerland are colored— some are red, others are blue, black, or brown. Most, however, are green, which implies that they have grown out of forest spirits.[322] The Egyptians similarly used to paint the face of Osiris green to demonstrate his vocation as god of vegetation and resurrection. *This may explain the enduring conviction that witches' faces are green.* Generally speaking, however, the color most often associated with the Devil in the Middle Ages is *black*. This identification is a very old one in Christendom, probably growing out of a Jungian fear of the darkness of death and the night. There is probably also attached a superstitious fear of the Arabs encountered in the Crusades and of the Africans encountered by Portuguese, Spanish, and Italian traders, thereby encouraging the wretched Western prejudice against dark-skinned people.[323] The idea that the Devil is *red* is a

---

[322] E. William Monter, *Witchcraft in France and Switzerland: The Borderlands During the Reformation* (Ithaca: Cornell University Press, 1976), p. 112

[323] Russell, *Witchcraft in the Middle Ages*, p. 217

fairly modern one and may have grown out of the New World fear of the Native Americans. In an association rife with irony, African natives used to imagine devils as white.[324]

The situation becomes somewhat less charming when one reflects that—in many instances—congress with *small, colored people* constituted traffic in demonism. Suzanne Gaudry's 1652 examination at Rieux is typical: She consistently applies diminutives to her demonic lover. He *"called himself Petit-Grignon, that he would wear black breeches…"*[325] Also, *"that the devil appeared to her, being in her lodgings in the form of a man dresed in a little cow-hide and black breeches."*[326] This testimony, by the way, is taken as Suzanne Gaudry is tortured on the rack. It is interesting that—in her desperation to describe some sort of supernatural lover to her torturers, astutely realizing that only this will end her torture—she hits upon the idea of (1) a small man (2) dressed in a little cow-hide (3) and black breeches.

In addition to being conceptualized in the friendly, diminutive form of imps and familiar-spirits, and being associated with significant pagan colors—the Devil may have inherited other attributes from the old heathen gods. The Devil's pitchfork may be either two—or three—pronged. When three-pronged, it becomes a trident, and as such, possibly associated with the threefold power over earth, sea, and air (or over the underworld, earth, and air) ascribed to *Hekate;* in like manner, the tenth-century idea that *Herodias* ruled over one-third of the world may be derived from the three-fold powers of Hekate. During the fifteenth century (the first that the Devil's presence at the Sabbat is consistently assumed),[327] this three-fold association is demonstrated by the Devil's presiding over the revels by sitting on a tripod.[328] Similarly, the three-faced Devil of Dante seems without precedent, save for Hekate.[329] (Or perhaps save for the triple-formed Celtic gods.) Russell notes that the Devil is furnished at times with a thunderbolt or a hammer, suggesting the influence of the Norse gods; Dr. Murray notices

---

324 Grimm, *Teutonic Mythology*, vol. IV, p. 1603
325 Kors and Peters, *Witchcraft in Europe*, p. 267
326 *Witchcraft in Europe*, p. 274
327 Russell, *Witchcraft in the Middle Ages*, p. 218
328 *Witchcraft in the Middle Ages*, p. 247
329 *Witchcraft in the Middle Ages*, p. 115

such when she comments that—at the Alsatian trials—one of the names given for the Devil was *Hammerlin,* possibly a diminutive for Thor.[330]

Other ways in which the Devil is like pagan gods

A localized English name for the Devil came to be "Old Harry."[331] This may derive from the Saxon *hearh,* a name for a hilltop sanctuary: Mount Harry, of the Sussex Downs, and the Old Harry Rocks, on the South Coast (supposed to have been placed by the Devil) are examples. As Doreen Valiente imagines, before he became the Devil, " 'Old Harry' [was] the Old One who was worshipped on the hills." Other dialect terms for the Devil include "Old Hornie" (for obvious reasons) or "Old Poker," from the Old English *pucca* or Welsh *pwca,* two species of poltergeist-like spirits; likewise, "Old Scratch," from the Germanic forest-spirit, the *skratte* or *schrat.* "Old Nick," another nickname for the Devil, is taken from *Nik,* an Old English name for *Wod,* forcing the suspicion that English places now associated with the saint Nicholas were once associated with either the Anglo-Saxon *Wodan* or *Nik.* The very old Staffordshire church where the Abbots Bromley Horn Dance is performed is dedicated to St. Nicholas, and the oldest parish church in Brighton, Sussex, is that of St. Nicholas, built on a hill where local tradition claims a pagan stone circle once stood. "It is not difficult to see how Nik and his Waelcyrges contributed to the idea of Old Nick and his witches," concludes Mother Valiente.

A story wherein pagan gods are specifically conflated with the Devil

A biography of *St. Collen* (a truculent seventh-century Welsh saint) identifies the faerey-king with demons. The story is so evocative of native heathenism, and describes so well the almost comic clashes between clerics and native faith, it deserves repeating. *Of a "pugnacious and restless disposition,"*[332] Collen made his way to Glastonbury Tor, building a hermitage at its base.

Glastonbury Tor is—with the exception of Stonehenge—the most amazing heathen spiritual site in England. It is essentially a

---

330 Murray, *The God of the Witches,* p. 38
331 Valiente, *An ABC of Witchcraft,* p. 258
332 Briggs, *Encyclopedia of Fairies,* p. 345

prehistoric, man-made, terraced hill in Somerset, around which much mythology and historical speculation have grown. A stone circle once stood atop the Tor, later replaced by the Christian church which now lies in poetic ruins (so the site's eminence as a place of pagan power is clear, as the Christians sought to coopt it). The area is believed to have been visited since Neolithic times, and inhabited since the Mesolithic; flints are found dating from 10,000–2000 BCE. There is much evidence of Bronze Age settlements, with the ruins of nearby villages dating to the third or fourth centuries BCE. The area must have been a very important religious site; in Arthurian legend, the Tor is heavily associated with *Avillion* or *Avalon*. Festivals were held there from the twelfth century to the early nineteenth.

At Glastonbury, Collen devoted himself to a career of meditation and contemplation. One day, however, he overheard two locals speaking of a local superstition. According to them, the king of the fayres—*Gwin ap Nudd* (pronounced "Neeth")—kept his revels atop the Tor at night. Collen rebuked the men for speaking of demons from hell and they warned him against giving grievance to the Otherworld Lord. That evening, an invitation was delivered for the churchman to visit Gwin in his home. Accordingly, armed with his indomitable faith, Collen climbed the famous twisting spiral-pathways of the Tor.

Gwynn ap Nudd ("Gwynn, son of Nudd") rules the Phantom World in the Mabinogion *legend of* Culhwch and Olwen, *also one of the first Arthur stories.* Otherwise in Welsh folklore, Gwynn fights a yearly contest for the beautiful spring-maiden Creiddylad (a variation on the Persephone myth); in time Gwynn became king of the *Plant Annwvyn,* the Welsh version of the *Tuatha de Danaan,* the faerie-people who live under the ground and near springs and wells. Plainly Gwynn managed the transition from Celtic mythology to Christian era folk-tradition. As Gwynn is Welsh, as is Collen—and Glastonbury is not—it seems as if Gwynn must have migrated to England along with the Welsh saint.

When Collen arrived at the top of the Tor, he saw what to all eyes seemed to be the glittering banquet of the ferey-court. The Savior's power was strong within him, though, and Collen perceived the court for what it truly was—a pack of snarling demons, gobbling dirt and animal dung. Collen splashed about him the flask of holy water which he had brought and the demon-horde vanished, howling back to hell. *Collen was left alone atop the Tor in the moonlight.*

We note anew the process, whereby a purely pagan figure, on the basis of some characteristic which doesn't really jibe with Christianity, is made out be the Devil.

Discredited gods

The Devil's progress in Europe seems an assimilative one. At first, it is necessary to get across to the pagans the idea that what they do, their methods of worship, their deities, etc., were "devilish" things—demons are stressed more in early theology than the Devil is. The Devil seems to turn up more steadily as the Christian era advances; Europe having no native concept of the Devil, he is confused with paganism, with magical spirits, with familiars. His appearance is not constant; he is often described as human or in a variety of monstrous animal-shapes. The association with hoofs and horns begins in the twelfth and thirteenth centuries, as does an association with animal skins. *These will eventually replace all others as the premiere characteristics of the Devil.*

The Devil's association with witches is one of integration: it is not until the fifteenth century that the Devil begins to make consistent appearances at the witches' Sabbat, and it is not until thereafter that witchcraft is automatically seen as devil-worship. In some places (such as England), the witches' connection with the Devil will remain perfunctory at best.

The eminent Anne Llewellyn Barstow notes something worthwhile, concerning religious differences between the East and the West. Like the other First-Peoples of Europe (and indeed all over the world) primitive Russians worshipped nature. Other people in Europe (however) eventually personalized aspects of nature into deities—hence the *pantheons of gods* of the Greeks, the Romans, the Celts, and the Teutons. Unlike other peoples in Europe, the Russians never split nature into humanistic counterpoints; they always worshipped nature as a great, pantheistic whole. Simply put, the Russians venerated no pantheon, but nature herself.[333] The difference becomes crucial as one factor becomes clear: the Russians—who had no pagan pantheon—never developed a demonological system either.

---

333 Anne Llewellyn Barstow, *Witchcraze: A New History of the European Witch Hunts* (San Francisco: Pandora, 1994), p. 82

In fact, Russian witches, observing neither the Devil nor the Devil's Sabbat, sometimes appear very different from witches described in traditional medieval Western sources. *This suggests anew (to Professor Barstow) that the demons of Middle Ages Europe were actually* discredited gods.

The extreme medieval emphasis on the Devil suggests, as Professor Barstow points out, that he had been in fact a powerful pagan god, outlawed by the church as the Devil. "Satan is the Westerners' lost God," Barstow concludes finally.

Barstow comes to the realization that her perception approaches "the oft-disputed theory of Margaret Murray that Western witchcraft was a continuation of the ancient European pagan religion." An understanding of the process whereby a pagan Deity was *demonized* by the medieval church into Satan—reinforced by the fact that no comparable process took place in Russia, which (having no native deities) had nothing to demonize—all of this "illuminates that part of her [Mother Murray's] argument" which Barstow cannot dismiss: "evidence for ancient 'folk religious' practices [found] throughout the Western witchcraft material."

Murray (the Grandmother of Witchcraft) "erred by forcing her evidence too far." "Still, her attention to what people were doing, to folk ritual and belief, was on the right track."[334]

Briggs apparently agrees with Barstow that the figure we call "Satan" represents a demonized form of the Lost Pagan God of Europe. If the accusation of Devil-worship was based partly upon the determined identification of pagan gods with demons—then the association of witches with devils is therefore "virtually an accusation of an older heathenism."[335]

Monstrosity

To the medieval mind, *monstrosity* was the result of things not following a natural order. When they wanted to represent something as unnatural, medieval people depicted it as being a misshapen composite of human/animal parts. This, to their mind, represented something out of the natural loop; in the contortions of a grossly fantastic body, people were meant to understand the distortions which sin worked upon the soul. *Monstrosity* was under-

---

334 *Witchcraze*, p. 83
335 Briggs, *Pale Hecate's Team*, p. 218

stood as a graphic and didactic symbol of the *power of sin* to warp and to dislocate; Bosch is the best known example of this school of the grotesque.[336]

The Devil is presented in a variety of ways throughout the Middle Ages. One such category is what I call the Scary Composite. *Boaistuau's 1597 picture of the Devil enthroned shows him as possessing a cat's face and (Lilith-like) bird feet.* Likewise, a woodcarving from Lycosthenus's 1577 *Chronicle,* depicting the *Witch of Berkeley* story, shows the woman being carried off by *a horned figure with bird feet;* in Molitor's 1489 portrait of a woman's seduction, the Devil is distinguished by *a clawed foot.* Why is the cloven hoof now associated with the Devil, and not the clawed bird's foot?

At other times the Devil is depicted as a lizard-like figure with wings. This is his representation in *Newes from Scotland* and in Guazzo's illustrations. *Why is the goat-man the image of the Devil now, and not the reptilian lizard-man?*

In confessions of the Devil's pact and whatnot, the Devil is either described as a Man in Black (the predominant image) or (usually in early cases of the Sabbat) as a great lord, sometimes enthroned and wearing a crown. At other times, the Devil is perceived as a young rake, who, likely as not, seduces a young woman. *At other times,* the Devil is presented as a goat-like man. The image of the Devil as a goat-like man, then, is not the predominant image in the Middle Ages. Other representations of the Devil are as well-known or as influential. Each of these other images was, at some point, as authoritative a depiction of the Devil as any other. Each had, at some point, the same potential to dominate the Western imagination.

The first question is, *why does this goat-image stick?* Always, this is our image of the Devil now, what we inevitably conjure in our Western minds—the horned guy with cloven hoofs and a pitchfork. Why is this our image of the Devil, not the lizard-man, not the monstrous composites? *Why does this picture of the goat-like man cling to Western culture with such tenacity? How did he get to be the Devil?*

Perhaps because he was originally the God to the pagans of Europe—and in libeling him and terrifying people away from his worship, the medieval church *demonized* the pagan God—

---

336 Russell, *Witchcraft in the Middle Ages,* p. 112

a magical beast-man born of the woodlands—into the Devil. Consider—

Olaus Magnus's *History of the Northern Folk* (1555) includes an illustration variously translated as "The Elves' Dance" or the "Dance of the Faeries"; Murray includes it in her book *The God of the Witches*. The creatures depicted, though, resemble neither elves nor fays to our mind, looking as they do like *satyrs*. The creatures all have goats' legs, cloven hoofs, tails, and horns. Stylistically they resemble devils, which fact offers a clue as to where Western culture's satyr-like concept of the Devil comes from.

Another illustration from the book depicts the Devil carrying off the Witch of Berkeley. The Devil looks oddly like the fayries of the other picture—he has horns and animalistic feet. The pictures together suggest a bad-tempered version of the gamboling elves stealing a woman away on horseback. Together, the two pictures suggest the process whereby, as Murray averred, the old gods of Europe were demonized into the Devil of the Christians.

The fays of Magnus's book somewhat resemble the Greek *kallikantzaroi*, the half-men, half-animal creatures who dwelled under the world. Ginzburg infers a primitive connection with the *spirits of the dead* from the connection between the kallikantzaroi, *animals,* the *underworld,* and *dates upon which the dead were thought to roam.* The resemblance between the kallikantzaroi and the elves of Magnus's book suggest that just such a connection accounts for other European ideas about faeries—*supernatural beings* are mixed up with *animal-characteristics,* ultimately revolving around a perception of the *departed.* It also suggests a connection between fayries and animalistic creatures, best exemplified by the *goat-like* Puck. This identification extends to other folkloric creatures, such as the *shaggy lobs* of England.

The witch Anne Bodenham is depicted in *The Kingdom of Darkness* conjuring with her spirits in a circle; the imps are shown as little *goat-like men*. Robert Kirk, in *The Secret Commonwealth of Elves, Fauns and Fairies,* connects elvish creatures with *goat-like men,* as does Thomas Nashe, in *Terrors of the Night.* Ben Jonson's *Oberon, the Faery Prince* (presented at court on New Year's Day, 1611) presents satyrs acting as faeries. The satyrs associate themselves with the ecstatic rites of Dionysos/Bacchos, which is interesting, as their rites in the masque have *elements in common with the witches' Sabbats.* They sing a song to the *"cunning lady Moon"* and *"Midwife Juno,"* following with an *"antic dance full of gesture and swift motion."* Prince Henry appears, in a chariot pulled by *"two white bears"* (probably two men wearing bearskins). Sylvans are also present in the drama (editors' notes to the Norton edition of Jonson give *"denizens of the forest"* as definitive for *"sylvans"*); they are guards before the prince's palace, *"armed with their clubs and dressed in leaves."* "Akin to satyrs, fauns, and sileni, sylvans were natives of Italy (they had no Greek existence). They were shy little wild creatures." [337]

The Devil was not the first mythic being in Europe to have hoofs

The Devil is frequently identified in folk-story by his cloven feet; as an instance, Sarah Bowre said of the Devil, that he *"had strange sort of Feet, like a Cows,"*[338] a particularly zoomorphic impression of the Arch-Fiend, in the manner of Celto-Teutonic animal-cults. Otherwise, the image of Satan as a hoofed man has become stereotypical. A really representative Shropshire legend relates how an improvident group of men once held a card game (upon which they even, horrors compounded upon horrors, placed wagers) on a Saturday night, rashly continuing their wickedness past the hour of midnight, when the Holy Day of the week began. A stranger entered at that moment. One of the players noticed the stranger's cloven feet—that man instantly was blasted to bits, leaving a mucky stain that could not be washed clean. At the nightly stroke of midnight thereafter, a ghostly troop of horse-riders marched the length of the house, making such a racket as to wake the dead. (A similar story is told to explain part of the haunting of Glamis Castle).[339]

The hoofed feet of the Devil are the tell-tale sign that lead us from the Enemy of Christians back to the original European Divinity that the imported legend of the devil was meant to obscure. For in European forest-legend—*and has European folk-culture any other type of legend?*—hoofed beings abound, clomping all the way back at least to the Celtic deer-gods Cernunn and Herne. (Grimm

---

337 Robert M. Adams, *Ben Jonson's Plays and Masques* (New York: W.W. Norton & Co, 1979), p. 350n

338 Briggs, *Pale Hecate's Team*, p. 155

339 Briggs, *British Folk-Tales and Legends* p. 156

observes a connection of "goat's feet" between "wights and elves" and satyrs; dwarfs, too, are said to "dart through the wood on pointed hoof.")[340]

John Walsh, a cunning-man and a healer, was examined in 1566. Walsh described his visits with the faeries at *"great heaps of earth,"* or prehistoric barrows, the prototypical feerye-sidh. Otherwise, Walsh explained that he had a familiar, or spirit-helper, who appeared *"sometime like a man in all proportions, saving that he had cloven feet."*[341] This is in keeping with old Celtic tradition, *whereby gods and spirits are given animal-parts from time to time,* and in opposition to Christian custom, which *demonized* any human/animal composite.

A like instance may be seen in the Highlands legend of the *Baobhan Sith,* the "Faery Women."[342] Like all other Celt goddesses, these were beautiful women in green dresses with long flowing hair, who could appear as crows or ravens. More importantly, they sometimes had deer's hoofs. Later ages turned these supernatural ladies into fearsome creatures. *Mackenzie relays a story of hunters who sought shelter from a storm. Imagine their delight when they were joined by three mysterious women, who began to dance with the men. One of the hunters, however, noticed a* hoofed foot *peeking from beneath the dress of one of the ladies—a hoofed foot, with blood dripping from it. That man ran outside and hid with the horses. The next morning he found that the* baobhan sith *had sucked his friends dry of their blood.* This vampiric story may be compared with that of the Italian witch, the *striga,* whom folklore likewise transformed into a bloodsucking demon. Germanic swan-maidens too sometimes have cloven-feet, a sign of their otherworldly status; kobolds (house-spirits) have horses' hoofs, as do the Greek *kallikantzaroi*—as does the Devil, significantly.[343]

Too much goat-worship

As evidence of the forced link between the Devil and animal/agricultural pagan gods, Russell says of the Devil: "he is often

---

340 Grimm, *Teutonic Mythology,* vol. IV, p. 1411
341 *"The examination of John Walsh,"* printed in Barbara Rosen, ed. *Witchcraft* (New York: Taplinger Publishing, 1972), p. 69
342 Briggs, *Encyclopedia of Fairies,* p. 16
343 Grimm, *Teutonic Mythology,* vol. III, p. 994

dressed in shaggy animal skins, suggesting a [close] connection with chthonic ['from beneath the earth'] deities."[344]

We come to understand how sacrificial animals came to be deified as gods. Pope Gregory the Great (d. 604), speaking of the Langobards, said that the head of a goat was held aloft, and that *"the people bowed before it."*[345] Likewise, the "hallowing" of a he-goat is a well-attested tradition of the antique Prussians; the Slavonian god Triglav is represented by three goats' heads. Since, in faery tales, the Devil appears as a bleating goat, Grimm asks, "May it not be that the figure of the he-goat sacrificed by the heathen was afterwards by the christians transferred to the false god?"[346]

The Christians plainly had conflicted feelings about the horned ritual-animal, the goat, as evidenced by numerous stories apparently meant to discourage people away from too much goat-worship. In a very pagan circumstance, when William Rufus was slain in the first year of the twelfth century, the Earl of Cornwall had a vision of a huge *black goat* carrying the mortally wounded king on its back. Kittredge feels that subsequent versions of the story, which claim that the goat bore the heathen king away *to his Judgment,* have the sound of monkish interference.[347] As do stories of the pious Bartholomew, who chose Farne for his hermitage in the twelfth century. It was an unfortunate choice, as *goat-riding devils* soon appeared to haunt a little nearby island—hideous devils who resembled *dwarfs* with long beards and cowls. (St. Dunstan was likewise plagued by the Devil, in the curiously pagan forms of a bear, a dog, and a fox.) St. Godric, another twelfth-century hermit, was equally tormented by demons who appeared in his cell as *black dwarfs.* These dwarfs could shamanically change into bears, eagles, or crows, and bellowed like oxen.

A similar story tells of a girl who danced with the *Julbuk,* a ritual animal-disguise of northern Europe, featuring a goat's head carried on a stick by a man dressed in hides or blankets. Imagine the girl's surprise when she discovered that the ritual goat she had been dancing with was none other than—*the Devil!*[348] Since the

---

344 Russell, *Witchcraft in the Middle Ages*, p. 114
345 Grimm, *Teutonic Mythology*, vol. I, p. 52
346 *Teutonic Mythology*, vol. III, p. 995
347 Kittredge, *Witchcraft in Old and New England*, p. 175
348 Alford, *The Hobby Horse*, p. 123

goat was once the center of ritual pagan celebrations, it may not come as a surprise to find that, later, a black goat was said to supervise the witches' assembly. In Puy de Dome in 1594, Jane Bosdeau's lover took her to a witches' meeting, where *"there appeared a great Black Goat with a Candle between his Horns."*[349]

Such instances begin the tradition of a *satanic goat* presiding over the witches' Sabbats—culminating in the infamous artwork by the nineteenth-century occultist *Eliphas Levi* of the sinister Goat-God *Baphomet*, whence the *goat-face etched onto the inverted pentagram*—today the recognized cultural sign for *Satanism* and an immense annoyance to modern Wiccans, as it demonizes both our Deity and our religious symbol. *What a distressing journey*—from a primal connection with the *spirit of the goat*—to a conceptualization of *Puck* as an expression of the *natural world*— to the *satanic Goat-God* keeping implacable watch over the *damnation of witches*.

An ultimately alienating journey as well: as the *deified goat* expresses a *oneness with nature*, while the *demonized goat* erects barriers of suspicion between worshipful mortals and the *marvelous world of nature*.

Traditional depiction of devils

The traditional depiction of devils begins to be seen. An illustration from Nathaniel Crouch's *Kingdom of Darkness* (1688) shows women dancing back-to-back in a *circle* with demons. The demons are drawn as *goat-men*, with horns and goat's legs; a man in a tree plays a pipe (a popular image for the Sabbat).

The Trooping Portrait depicting the *Sabbat on the Brocken* shows women floating in the air in ecstasies and flying aloft magical rams. Many pipers play and people throng about the mountaintop, directed and encouraged by *goat-legged horned men* with flaming hands.

Very similar is the *Sabbat at Eichstatt*, included in the 1693 German translation of Remy's *Demonolatreiae*, which features a woman boiling a cauldron within a *magic circle*, whilst people line up to kiss a goat on its butt and in the distance people dance around a hilltop. Women fly through the air atop goats; pipers play. Leading the routs of the damned is the same smiling *goat-man*, his fiery hands held aloft.

---

349 Murray, *The Witch-Cult in Western Europe*, p. 68

The Horned God of Wytches

These are typical delineations of demons—*horned, with goat's legs and cloven hoofs.*

Yet they also resemble *perverted portraits* of pagan creatures—the goat-men laughingly leading humans to heedless damnation look like psychotic satyrs or corrupt versions of the Horned Gods like Cernunnos and Hernunn.

One can imagine some priest standing before such illustrations, explaining to a dumb and illiterate group of peasants—these things (dancing around a hill or mountaintop; piping music; unrestrained celebration and joy—a notable feature of all these illustrations is the suggestion of abandonment and ecstatic pleasure) are *evil*, whereby souls are lost. These beings—*goat-like men with horns and hoofs*—these are *evil* beings, who will lead one into the *damnation of hell*.

> *Graunt that no Hobgoblns fright me,*
> *No hungrie devils rise up and bite me;*
> *No Urchins, Elves or drunkards Ghoasts*
> *Shove me against walles or posts.*
> *O graunt I may no black thing touch,*
> *Though many men love to meete such.*[350]
>
> —Day's *Law Tricks:*

Birth of Merlin

Awestruck though Christians might have been by the Devil, plain-folk English plainly felt that he would be no match (no way) against their own native magic-working wonder *Merlin*, the Pride of the British Shores—as the climatic scene of the anonymous play *The Birth of Merlin* makes evident.

Merlin doesn't actually make his appearance until half-way through the play; the first half concerns itself with the war between Christian Britain and the invading pagan Saxons. In a peace-making move, the British King Aurelius marries the Saxon Queen Artesia—causing considerable consternation among the pious British over the infiltration of the Christian court by pagan "infidels" (the play's term). A magical demonstration ensues, as a Saxon sorcerer boasts that he can make appear anything he desires, *"beneath the moon, the centre of the earth, the sea, the air, the region of the fire..."* (II.iii) The sorcerer summons the Champions of the Trojan

---

350 Briggs, *Anatomy of Puck*, p. 72

War (never mind how a fifth-century Teutonic enchanter is going to be familiar with the Trojan War); the Champions *"charge"* at one another until a Christian hermit shows up, instantly robbing them of their powers. A really common motif is the Christian hermit who shows up and robs the enchanter of his magical powers.

The second half of the play finds a rustic girl made pregnant by a man later revealed to be—the Devil! As in *Rosemary's Baby,* the Devil requires a mortal woman to carry his infernal seed. For all that he is sired of the Devil, the play makes clear that Merlin is destined for greatness: *"Whilst men do breathe and Britain's name be known, the fatal fruit thou bear'st within thy womb shall here be famous till the day of doom."* (III.i)

The Light-Goddess Lucina and the Fates are summoned to mid-wife the magical child and Merlin is born full-grown in a circumstance of huge pagan import, as the child of an otherworldly union: *"Why Mother—I can be but half a man at best and that is your mortality—the rest in me is spirit!"* (III.iv) The reaction of Merlin's uncle to the sight of his uncanny nephew: *"A witch! A witch! A witch! Sister, rid him out of your company; he is either a witch or a conjuror; he could never have known this else!"* (III.iv) Later: *"Well, if thy mother were not my sister, I would say she was a witch that begot this..."* (IV.i)

The play sets about chronicling the various deeds and episodes credited to the Wizard of Camelot. The Welsh King Vortiger is building a castle. Every night, though, there is a strange earthquake and the construction keeps getting knocked down and there is no progress. So Vortiger issues a Proclamation summoning all workers in the arts mystic to come tell him what's up: all *"artists... that seek the secrets of futurity, the bards, the druids, wizards, conjurors, not an Aurasper with his whistling spells, no Capuomanster with his musty fumes, no witch or juggler, but is thither sent to calculate the strange and fear'd event..."* (IV.i)

So Merlin clairvoyantly figures out what no one else can and tells Vortiger that there are two dragons in a cave—a red one and a white one—and they fight every night—and the white one wins—and drives off the red—and the commotion makes the earth shake and the bricks and such to tumble.

So then Merlin explains the sad truth of the vision to Vortiger. The red dragon is Wales and the white dragon is England. The dream predicts Wales's defeat by the English.

Vortiger bucks up and takes it like a man.

Merlin presents himself to the English king Uter and divines the meaning of an awe-inspiring comet aflame overhead. A star appears (where does this sound familiar?), *"from out whose mouth two flaming snakes of fire stretch east and west."*

Merlin: *"So, so! Now observe, my lord... these bi-formed fires that from the dragon's mouth shoot east and west, emblem two royal babes which shall proceed from you, a son and daughter..."* The magical formulation—a girl and boy born at once—is seen in Artemis and Apollo; Viola and Sebastian in *Twelfth Night;* and Quicksilver and the Scarlet Witch in *The X-Men* and *The Avengers.* Here it is seen in the supernaturally presaged birth of—Arthur the Once and Future King and his sister!

Arthur's sister is variously named. At times—as in Geoffrey of Monmouth's *Historia Regum Britanniae,* as well as in *De Ortu Waluuanii* ("The Rise of Gawain"), and the *Chronicles* of Wace and Layamon—she is called *Anna,* which may be super-significant, as *Annu* was a major big-time territorial Celtic Goddess. The similarity in their names suggests that Arthur grew out of divine Celtic legends of heroism, rendered even more select (in the pro-female manner of the Celts) because of his relationship to his sister-counterpart, Annu the Land-Goddess.[351] Otherwise Arthur's sister is *Margawse;* other times she is super-significantly identified as *Morgaine,* the magical *Lady of Avalon*—again, an indication of two very select individuals.

Because of the astronomical omen, Uter takes the name *Pendragon.*

Merlin builds Stonehenge: *"I will erect a monument upon the verdant plains of Salisbury... with pendulous stones that I will hang by art... a dark enigma to thy memory, for none shall have the power to number them, a place... where no night-hag shall walk, nor ware-wolf tread."* (V.i) It is a superstition that—if you try to count the stones at Stonehenge—you will never ever come up with the same number twice; the same is said of the Rollright Stones. It is typical that the English connected their greatest wizard with their greatest prehistoric artifact, explaining the mystery of Stonehenge by means of Merlin's magic.

The play ends with hautboys (blasts on a trumpet); the crown-

---

351 John Matthews, *Gawain: Knight of the Goddess.* (Northamptonshire, England: The Aquarian Press, 1990), p. 41

ing of Uter; and a bit of a dumb show, in which appears a King in Armor (Arthur), to whom Princes kneel and offer their Crowns.

The climatic moment to *The Birth of Merlin* (sub-titled *The Child hath Found his Father*) is Merlin's rescue of his mother from her hellish paramour, the Devil (whom stage-notes tell us is now played with a Horrid Head or Mask):

Devil: *"Come forth, by thunder led, my Coajutors in the spoils of mortals!* [Thunder—a Spirit enters] *Claspe in your Ebon arms that prize of mine* [Merlin's mom], *mount her as high as palled* Hecate; *and on this rock Ile stand to cast up fumes and darkness o're the blew fac'd* [blue-faced] *firmament: from* Brittain *and from* Merlin *Ile remove her! They ne're shall meet agen."*

Merlin: *"Stay, you black slaves of night, let loose your hold, set her down safe, or by th'infernal Stix Ile binde you up with exorcisms so strong that all the black pentagoron of hell shall ne'er release you! Save yourselves and vanish!"*

Devil: *"Ha! What's he?"*

Merlin: "The Childe hath found his Father! *Do you know me?"*

Devil: *"Merlin!"*

Merlin: *"Thou didst beget thy scourge: storm not, nor stir; The power of* Merlins *art is all confirm'd in the Fates decretals. Ile ransack hell, and make thy masters bow unto my spells!"* [Imprisons the Devil within a rock.]

"Pentagoron" is a reference to the pentacle or pentagram—the sacred symbol for Wiccans and Witches. Being an instrument (like, say, Green Lantern's power-ring), the pentagoron can be used both for good (as Green Lantern uses his power-ring) and for evil (like the villainous Green Lantern Sinestro misuses his power-ring); likewise the light-saber of the Jedi is wielded both by Obi-Wan and Luke Skywalker, and by Darths Vader and Maul. The fact that Darth Vader utilizes a light-saber does not make the light-saber evil—it merely emphasizes its neutrality as an object.

The reference to the "black pentagoron of hell" means that Merlin will bind the Devil so tightly with magic-charms ("exorcisms"), the Devil will never be able to escape the Underworld again—even if he should utilize every bit of hell-fire energy ("the black pentagoron of hell") to assist him. It is altogether possible that Merlin makes use of his own pentagoron to subdue the Devil (sequel to *The Birth of Merlin*—*Merlin and the Pentagoron of Power*).

The confrontation between Merlin and the Devil is astonishingly like that between Luke Skywalker and Darth Vader; as well, arch-enemies Superman and Lex Luthor, or Harry Potter and Voldemort. Katharine Briggs further notes other elements of the *old and young god* myth—the miraculous *birth;* *threat* to the child's life; a *conflict* over a woman; the destruction of the *old god*.

Essentially, *The Birth of Merlin* is the most robust statement thus far of the firm English belief that—should a contest fall between the Devil and England's Highest Magician—fallen angel or no, *Satan is going down.*

The legends of Merlin were first systematically recorded by Geoffrey of Monmouth (c. 1135), in such works as *Historia Regum Britanniae* ("History of the Kings of Britain") and *Vita Merlini* ("The Life of Merlin"). Merlin is appended to the Arthur legends in the collection of the *Vulgate Cycle* (c. 1215–30), the first complete account of the Matter of Britain (the tale of Arthur and the Round Table), rendered in French prose. The Cycle (by an unknown author, but sometimes falsely attributed to Gautier [Walter] Map) consists of the *Prose Launcelot* series: *Launcelot; La Queste del Saint Graal;* and *La Mort le Roi Artu*, to which *L'Estoire del Saint Graal* has been added, in addition to Robert de Borron's (c. 1200) incorporated *Merlin*.[352] Merlin subsequently figures in such works as the *Post-Vulgate Romance* (c. 1230), which includes the *Suite du Merlin* ("Sequel of Merlin," a continuation of the Vulgate *Merlin*, by a writer pretending to be de Borron). Amusing fact—the early Welsh stories of Merlin call him *Myrddin*, which should translate into Latin as *Merdinus*. Geoffrey of Monmouth, however, records the Wizard's name as *Merlinus*—hence (in English) *Merlin*. Why Monmouth alters the name is a mystery, although it has been postulated that he was disturbed by the resemblance of *Merdin* to the French vulgarism *merde*. Maybe he was afraid people would think he was calling England's most pre-eminent magic-worker a "Shithead."[353]

Merlin, the cult of the deer, and divine madness

The first mentions of Merlyn (as Myrddin) are of a Welsh bard and seer of the sixth century; various poems and prophe-

---

[352] Cavendish, *King Arthur and the Grail*, p. 207
[353] *King Arthur and the Grail*, p. 106

cies ("studied and copiously annotated") are attributed to him.[354] Early traditions describe him as a tortured soul, driven raving mad by the horror of battle and by his own prophecy. Legend links Myrddin with the Battle of Arfderydd in 573 CE—Myrddin is so revolted and appalled by the slaughter that he flies to the solitude of the Caledonian forests, in the Scots Lowlands, living for years as a *wild man of the woods,* whilst developing a knack for foreseeing the future.[355] Various works—Welsh poems, Scots and Irish legends—take up the theme of Myrddin as an outcast *woods-dweller.*

In the early twelfth century, Geoffrey of Monmouth assimilated this figure to the legend of Arthur in his British *History.* Here Merlinus predicts to the British king Vortigern (pushed back to Wales) the coming difficulties with the invading Saxons. Merlin explains that the Saxons will press hard upon the Brits until the Boar of Cornwall (Arthur) comes along.

Monmouth apparently draws upon considerably earlier traditions regarding the wizard in his *Life of Merlin,* presenting in the *Vita Merlini* a prophetic madman wholly different from the mage in the *Historia.* In the *Life,* Merlin is a Welsh law-giver and prophet who loses his reason in battle and flees to Kelyddon (Caledonia, in Scotland), where he lives as a beast in the forest. Various people try to return him to civilization, but Merlin's sanity is too precarious for human contact and he escapes back to the peace of the woods. He is clairvoyant and other people have uncanny experiences with him. His sister Ganieda builds a house for him, where he spends the winters; the summers he roams in the forest with a wolf (motif: shamanic animal-association). Ganieda herself is eventually herself overcome by prophetic frenzy and Merlin renounces his own prophecy in order to care for her.[356]

Merlin will continue to be identified with a "return to nature" wildness that will be expressed as hermit-like existence *in the woods,* disdaining civilized contact, and as an intensely sympathetic *relationship to animals.* All of this will be compounded with a state of mind so shaky as to border on instability.

In the *Vita Merlini,* he retreats *into the woods,* living like a *beast,* losing his *wits* and behaving erratically when he emerges, such as

---

354 Markale, *Merlin,* p. 30
355 Cavendish, *King Arthur and the Grail,* p. 106
356 Markale, *Merlin,* p. 6

he does to attend his wife's remarriage in the singular circumstance of driving before him a *herd of deer* while mounted on a *stag*.

In the *Merlin* of the *Vulgate Cycle*, Merlin is found in the context of a *shape-shifter* and a *forest-dweller*, showing himself to messengers and to Uther Pendragon in the guise of a *woodcutter* and as a *deformed shepherd*, before assuming the form of a *young man*. Merlin helps Uther defeat the *"very wicked pagans"* (the Saxons), establishes the megalithic Stonehenge, and proclaims Arthur's rightness as king. He then disappears into the *forest;* in a later change-of-scene, he is a *Wild Man* summoned to prophesy before Caesar in Rome. The Wild Man identifies himself as a *great antlered stag* and as Merlin of Britain. He retires to *enchanted Broceliande Forest*, filled with *stags and sacred fountains*, where he dallies teaching magic to lovely Vivienne.[357]

Merlin became important to both the English and the Welsh (who interpreted his legend as symbolic of Welsh resistance to English aggression). As perhaps a political statement, and as an indication of how Welsh intellectuals of the early sixteenth century regarded their national hero, Elis Gruffud (a participant in the Camp of the Cloth of Gold at Calais in 1520) re-connects the Arthurian mage with his primal roots in a text called *Myrddin Wyllt* ("Myrddin the Wild Man"), reviving the old legends of the *mad man* and his *care-giver sister*.

Myrddin's mind is too unsteady to handle human society. Accordingly, he lives in the *woods*, in *caves* or in *shelters of foliage* (vegetation-motif). His sister Gwendydd brings him food and drink. Between his bouts with *insanity*, Myrddin prophesies to Gwendydd

---

357 *Merlin*, p. 14–16

and interprets dreams for her. *One concerns men chopping down a venerable grove of alders. Yews spring from the fallen alders.*[358] Myrddin explains this as representing the renewal of Britain after the assaults of the Anglo-Saxons; Gruffud apparently intends this to be understood as a statement of defiance to English domination. *The dream can also be interpreted as presaging the rebirth of the pagan spirit (represented by the grove of alders, groves being sacred spaces to the Celts) following the violent suppression of the Christians.*

All of these stories consider Merlin as a prophetic magic-worker because of his prolonged sojourns in the forests; his close affinity with animals; and his revelatory madness.

The *mad state* of uncommon knowledge and unnatural insight is actually a common reference of the times, which is interesting, in light of the number of people who report ecstatic visions. *Sir Orfeo* (in the eponymous romance-poem), having lost his wife, falls *mad with grief* and escapes to live like a *wild thing in the woods*. This is what *Lear* does as well, although he manages an impassioned scene about the vicissitudes of fortune before losing his reason altogether. *Launcelot,* having been scorned by Guinevere in *Morte d'Arthur* (XI–IX, XII–IV), runs similarly mad, *slaying a boar,* then *retiring* to a hermitage (XII–III), hence a Christian retreat, as opposed to the pagan retreat into the forest. He is found *sleeping* by a *well,* at *noon,* by *Elayne and her ladies,* who *heal* the knight of his *insanity* by means of the *Sangrael* (XII–IV). (Everything in this scenario is extremely Celtic, including the Grail/Graille/Graal/Grael, which appears in pagan Celtic myth before it becomes a Christian symbol.) *Yvain* spends an interlude of despairing madness, isolated in the country, in de Troyes's romance, as does *Orlando* (the peerless knight of the Charlemagne romances), most notably in a popular tale recorded by Ariosto as *Orlando Furioso,* printed in 1532 and dramatized by Robert Greene. In the Thornton *Perceval,* Percyvelle must find a woman who, *bereft of her senses,* has retreated *into the woods.* Percyvelle puts on a *goat-skin* and, after *nine days'* searching, finds her. A *magic draught* puts her into a *three days'* sleep, from which she *awakens restored to sanity.*[359]

Ecstatic madness is—of course—one sign of the *shamanic elevation,* the signal that one has been chosen by the fates and that

---

358 *Merlin,* p. 31
359 Nutt, *Studies on the Legend of the Holy Grail,* p. 38

one's consciousness has begun to open to the potentials of the shamanic infinite. Personal story: I am a Hare Krishna devotee, which I describe as being a Hare Krishna pagan, which means that I chant Hare Krishna while I practice paganism. This all started when I ran into this little mob of Hare Krishna guys out distributing transcendental literature one day. So shortly thereafter, I chance upon one of the devotees working a street-corner. "How goes the distributing of the transcendental literature?" I asked. "Not good," said he. "No one wants to be stopped to be enlightened. Their minds are all preoccupied with maya"—*maya* being the belief that the *physical world constitutes reality,* whereas *enlightened devotees* understand that it is actually the *spiritual realms that figure as truest reality.* "I know," I said. "It's weird—you can see it in their eyes…" Then I broke off in confusion, because I had never articulated a thought like that before. My Hare Krishna God-brother looked at me with deep understanding. "Your consciousness is changing," he explained gently. In some of that transcendental literature I found a story I love, of a Hindu some centuries ago, who became so enraptured by the Thought of Holy Lord Krishna, he sometimes "could not discern whether he was in a proper place or not." I find that to be a very apt way to describe religious delight.

In shamanic cultures, the shamanic initiation is sometimes said to overpower reason. Descriptions concerning knights like Launcelot, Yvain, and Orlando, suggest that the whirlwind-onset of shamanic consciousness figured heavily in Celtic myth. Tom Cowan has written about the shamanic elements of Celtic story, in *Fire in the Head*.[360] (Cowan takes his title from a Yeats poem: *"I went out to the hazel wood, because a fire was in my head…"*) The persistent depiction of Merlin as raving is strongly suggestive of a shamanic under-pinning to his magic and fore-telling.

As does his heavy identification with *beasts of the forest*. In the *Vita Merlini*, he rides a stag and commands a herd of deer, surely not the easiest creatures in the world to control and direct. As in Celtic hunting-mythology, deer are used symbolically in Arthurian story: white stags appear as pagan expressions of celestial beings in the Didot *Perceval;* the *Suite du Merlin*, of the Vulgate *Merlin;* and the *Morte d'Arthur.*

---

360 Tom Cowan, *Fire in the Head: Shamanism and the Celtic Spirit* (HarperSanFrancisco, 1993)

In the Vulgate *Merlin,* the wizard is identified with deer and emerges from the woods dressed in a wolf-skin.[361] This is like the "wolf-skins" and "bear-shirts" of the Teutonic sagas. A pre-Viking Swedish representation shows two figures—one naked, wearing horns on his head, the other human, wearing a wolf's pelt (including the head). The Oseberg Tapestry shows warriors in hooded garments, which may be bear-skins. Texts reveal a considerable aura of mystery and awe surrounding the bear—and wolf-shirts, who were believed to change themselves into animals, which power derived from their status as initiates into the cult of Odinn. Odinn's name comes from a word meaning "frenzied" or "mad," referring either to the frenzy of the warrior in battle, the ecstasy of the inspired poet, or the fortune-telling trance of the seer. Adam of Bremen writes of *"Wodan, id est Furor"*—"Wode, that is to say, Fury," and certain sagas describe customs of rhythmic howling and leaping among the "animal-skins."

Merlin's association with animals and the animal-identification of wearing skins reinforces his connection with the *divine madness* of the shaman and emphasizes his connectedness with the *animal-world*—another shamanic characteristic. In the Didot *Perceval* and in the Huth *Merlin,* the wizard has a mysterious companion who stays with Merlyn at his hermitage. This character is a man *Blaise;* in Welsh and Breton, *bleidd* or *bleiz* means "wolf," and a *St. Blaise* celebrates a holiday the second day after the fertility-holiday Imbolg.[362] According to legend, this St. Blaise, in "Master of the Animals" fashion, was found preaching to the creatures of the forest outside his hermitage. This implies that some legends gave Merlyn a wolf cohort, who is later humanized into a person. This not only connects Merlyn in a super-human manner to deer, but to wolves as well.

A substantial amount of human culture concludes that living in a harmonious sense of union and oneness with *nature* is the ideal way. Native humans of Southern and Northern America (through the direction of their Native shamans) sought to achieve as perfect a blend of the human with the natural as was possible. The Romantic Movement of poets such as Wordsworth was impassioned by the idea of Nature as a renewing and revivifying force.

---

361 Markale, *Merlin,* p. 164
362 *Merlin,* p. 164

This is the point of Shakespeare's *As You like It* as well, in which all the characters are reborn as a result of their dwelling within the peaceable acreage of Arden Forest. *Cymbeline, The Winter's Tale,* and Beaumont and Fletcher's *The Faithfull Shepherdess* also feature such bucolic fantasies.

The Celts and the Tuetons worshipped in the woods; it is significant that so many stories of the retreat to the woods seem to have religious overtones to them. In Celtic lore, *Finn mac Cumhaill* and his Fenian followers led the ideal life of dwelling as one with the surrounding forests; in later centuries, *Robin Hood* and *George a Green* would similarly achieve integrity and strength of character through the natural virtue of the woodlands. Merlin's retreats into the solitude of the forest must equally represent a being finding harmony and balance through a re-dedication to the *world of nature.*

All of this is such that Jean Markale takes to describing Merlin as a "Priest of Nature." Finding him a much more archaic figure than the one generally seen in the courtly Arthurian romances, Markale decides that it is "as if [he had] sprung from the night of time, his essential character that of the wild man restored to the primitive condition at the dawn of humanity."[363] The Trois Freres Sorcerer and the cults of Cernunnos and Herne are implicitly invoked, as Markale asks (since both the ecstatic madness of Merlin and his identification with deer are so shamanic) whether we can "conclude that the character of Merlin retrieves the memory of that ancient cult of the deer? It is not impossible."[364]

Wild-Ones of the Woods

Anderson notes that often the Green Man is called the *Wild Man* in instances where *hairiness* is the defining characteristic, and not *vegetation*. A period woodcarving of a Wild Man depicts him covered with a *coat of hair,* with a garland of vegetation about his forehead and modest middle, holding a tree branch in his hand. Every January the *Wilde Mann* of Basle (still, to this day) sails on a raft down the Rhine, before leading dancing in the streets (callin' out around the world); the Wilde Mann wears a suit of leaves and carries a small fir tree. These instances represent another aspect of the "spirit of nature" motif, this time

---

363 *Merlin*, p. 2
364 *Merlin*, p. 162

drawing upon identification with animals as expressions of the natural world. In the same way that the *Green Man* is the personified essence of *vegetative Nature,* the *Wild Man* is the personified essence of *animal Nature.*

The Wild Man became specifically identified with the *woodwose* or *wodehouse* (fans of Mr. P.G., take note). Like the Green Man, the Wodehouse is a popular subject of medieval legends, stories, and carvings, often depicted in churches.[365] The Wild Man/Woodwose is covered with shaggy hair, clothed in moss if at all, and lives in caves and communities (often with a Wild Woman companion) deep within the forest. Grimm identifies *woodwose* as a "satyrus," or "Faunus," as in the Roman manner. Otherwise, forest-folk are known as the *wood-wives,* or *holz-frau.* Other names for these creatures include: *moss-maiden, bush-grandmother, forest-father,* and *tree-host;* also: *wild-folk, forest-folk, wood-folk, moss-folk.*[366] As Anderson says, they are the "aboriginal creatures of medieval lore."[367] It is intriguing to suppose that they are like the famous *Sasquatch* of the American North.

Much folklore surrounded the wood-folk. Sometimes the wild-men rode stags. During hay-making or harvest, little heaps were left as the wood-maiden's due. Wood-wives were famous for wailing and howling, "You sound like a wood-wife!" being a good way to rebuke a noisy German person. Trees and temples were dedicated to the wood-sprites as late as the sixth and seventh centuries; in Lower Germany, the arms of many princes are supported by a *"salvage man,"* with an uprooted fir tree in his hand.[368] There was, according to Laroque, a "wild man dressed up in animal skins and foliage, who brandished torches in the Midsummer pageants. He was a both frightening and comical figure and he became a popular representation of madness."[369] *Note the reference to animal skins and seasonal holidays.*

For all that Wild-Folk lived in the forests, a species of them migrated indoors—according to Grimm, every German house contained *schrezlein*—or at least an individual *scrat, scato, schretz,*

---

365 Briggs, *Encyclopedia of Fairies,* p. 442
366 Grimm, *Teutonic Mythology,* vol. IV, p. 1426
367 Anderson, *Green Man,* p. 30
368 Grimm, *Teutonic Mythology,* vol. II, p. 481
369 Laroque, *Shakespeare's Festive World,* p. 57

or *schretzel*, who if fostered, brought goods and honor, drove the cattle and prepared the table.[370] The schrat is a "wild, rough, shaggy wood-sprite, very like the Lat. faun and the Gr. satyr, also the Roman silvanus"; in diminutive terms, called a *schratlein*. A monk of St. Gall tells of a schrat (a "frolicking, dancing, whimsical home-sprite, rough and hairy to look at"), that lived in the home of a smith, amusing himself by playing with the man's hammer and anvil, and filching bottles out of the cellar.

In the eighth-century Irish story *Briciu's Feast* (the precursor to *Sir Gawain and the Green Knight*), the Celtic hero *Cu-chulaidh* is challenged by a *bachlach*, a wild man hideous to look upon. A twelfth-century story tells of fishermen who caught an aquatic Wild Man (a medieval Aquaman, if you will) in nets on the North Sea. He was kept in Orford Castle, maintained on a diet of fish, and could never be induced to say a word.[371] Professor Russell notes that the Wild Man of forest legend may be associated with the "wild men" who rode in the Wild Hunt; the male leaders of the Hunt, Russell indicates, were "originally fertility spirits" and the Wild Woman serves as a "prototype of the witch."[372]

The Wild-folk clearly represent our primitive past—our "Quest for Fire" past, our way primitive past. The Wild-folk are the atavistic impulses which live in each of us, the same part of us that responds to drums and dancing around a fire at night with no clothes on and your body painted. It is interesting that our medieval ancestors had the Wild-One archetype ingrained into their customs; our own super-civilized culture banishes the Bigfoot to the mythological outskirts of lumber camps. In pop-psychology terms, they clearly integrated their wild-people—they saw something beneficial in an occasional return to primitivism.

Other folkloric creatures are identified by hairiness (notably the members of Magnus's Faery-Ring). Among several instances of the Horned-God-as-Wild-Man European Deity recorded by Chadwick Hansen is the Austrian *Krampus*, whom Hansen calls an "Alpine version of the fertility god."[373] Krampus is said to be black and furry, with horns. He has become associated primarily

---

[370] Grimm, *Teutonic Mythology*, vol. II, p. 481
[371] Anderson, *Green Man*, p. 30
[372] Russell, *Witchcraft in the Middle Ages*, p. 50
[373] Chadwick Hansen, *Witchcraft at Salem* (New York: George Braziller, 1969), p. 3

with children at the Solstice Season, otherwise called Christmas—Krampus sees to the bad children while St. Nicholas attends to the good. But, as Hansen points out, the Krampus's "chief attribute is evidence that he is not really a children's deity." Should the Krampus strike one with the bundle of dried twigs carried by him, one will become sterile for a year—as Hansen says, not really a Deity for kids. In Styria, Krampus is baked as bread and eaten—further proof of a fertility past.

A further example of the Beast-God of the Forest would be *Puck-Hairy*, of Ben Jonson's *The Sad Shepherd* and my own book *A Briefe Historie of Wytches*.

Another

There is another who is without doubt hugely invested in forest-mythology, having been postulated as a version of the European Woods-God. Others argue that he was a real person, whom (like the British chieftain Arthur) time transformed into a legend. He is of course the Green Man of Sherwood Forest, the outlaw devoted to good—*Robin Hood*, whose first name connects with the Goodfellow and whose last recalls Odinn Grimr, Odinn the Hooded One. Robin Hood is so identified with the Green Man that many pubs and taverns in England (so William Anderson tells us) named for the Green Man show Mr. Hood on their sign. The mythology of Robin has grown archetypal; in the twentieth century, Robin Hood was portrayed in movies by Douglas Fairbanks, Errol Flynn, Sean Connery, Kevin Costner, and (in Mel Brooks's *Men in Tights*) by Cary Elwes. Only Hamlet receives so much play otherwise.

Whoever he was or whatever he may have been, he is a very long story and I am weary. So I wish to include him by mentioning him, and save him for another day.

Thank you.

Bibliography

The Plays

Adams, Joseph Quincy, ed. *Chief Pre-Shakespearean Dramas.* Houghton-Mifflin, 1924.

Adams, Robert M., ed. *Ben Jonson's Plays and Masques: Texts of the Plays and Masques; Jonson on his work; Contemporary Readers on Jonson; Criticism.* New York: W.W. Norton & Co, 1979.

Bowers, Fredson, general ed. *The Dramatic Works in the Beaumont and Fletcher Canon.* Cambridge University Press, 1976.

Craik, T.W., ed. *The Merry Wives of Windsor.* Oxford: Oxford University Press, 1994.

Farmer, John S., ed. *Early English Dramatists: Five Anonymous Plays.* New York: Barnes and Noble, Inc., 1966 edition.

Gassner, John ed. *Medieval and Tudor Drama.* New York: Applause Books, 1987.

Glover, Arnold, A.R. Waller, ed. *The Works of Francis Beaumont and John Fletcher, in ten volumes.* New York: Octagon Books, 1969.

Kozlenko, William, ed. *Disputed Plays of William Shakespeare.* New York: Hawthorn Books Inc., 1974.

Laroque, Francois. *Shakespeare's Festive World: Elizabethan Seasonal Entertainment and the Professional Stage.* New York: Cambridge University Press, 1991.

Hazlitt, W. Carew, ed. *A Select Collection of Old English Plays,* 4th edition. New York: Benjamin Blom, Inc., 1964 (first published by Robert Dodsley in 1744).
Manly, John Matthews. *Specimens of the Pre-Shakespearean Drama.* New York: Dover Publishers, Inc., 1967.
McIlwraith, A.K., ed. *Five Elizabethan Comedies.* London: Oxford University Press, 1965 edition.
Melchiori, Giorgio, ed. *The Merry Wives of Windsor, the Arden Shakespeare, third series.* Thomas Nelson and Sons, Ltd., 2000.
Neilson, William Allan, ed. *The Chief Elizabethan Dramatists: Excluding Shakespeare.* Boston: Houghton-Mifflin Co., 1939 edition.

Other Works

Alford, Violet. *The Hobby Horse and Other Animal Masks.* London: The Merlin Press, 1978.
Anderson, William. *Green Man: The Archetype of our Oneness with the Earth.* New York: HarperCollins, 1990.
Barstow, Anne Llewellyn. *Witchcraze: A New History of the European Witch Hunts.* San Francisco: Pandora, 1994.
Branston, Brian. *Lost Gods of England.* London: Thames and Hudson, 1957.
Briggs, Katharine. *The Anatomy of Puck: An Examination of Fairy Beliefs among Shakespeare's Contemporaries and Successors.* New York: Arno Press, 1977 edition.
———*British Folk-Tales and Legends: A Sampler.* London: Routledge Classics, 2002.
———*An Encyclopedia of Fairies.* New York: Pantheon Books, 1976.
———*Pale Hecate's Team: An Examination of the Beliefs on Witchcraft and Magic among Shakespeare's Contemporaries and His Immediate Successors.* New York: The Humanities Press, 1962.
Bulfinch, Thomas. *Bulfinch's Mythology: The Age of Chivalry and Legends of Charlemagne or Romance in the Middle Ages.* Meridian Books, 1995.
Cavendish, Richard. *King Arthur and the Grail: the Arthurian Legends and their Meaning.* New York: Taplinger Publishers, 1978.
Comfort, W.W., trans. *Chretien de Troyes: Arthurian Romances.* Dutton, New York: Everyman's Library, 1978 edition.
Conner, Randy P. *Blossom of Bone: Reclaiming the Connections between Homoeroticism and the Sacred.* HarperSanFrancisco, 1993.

Cowan, Tom. *Fire in the Head: Shamanism and the Celtic Spirit*. HarperSanFrancisco, 1993.
Davidson, H.R. Ellis. *Myths and Symbols in Pagan Europe: Early Scandinavian and Celtic Religions*. Syracuse University Press, 1988.
Evans, Arthur. *Witchcraft and the Gay Counterculture*. Boston: Fag Rag Books, 1978.
Farrar, Janet and Stewart. *The Witches' God*. Custer, Washington: Phoenix Publishing, 1989.
Ginzburg, Carlo. *Ecstasies: Deciphering the Witches' Sabbath*. New York: Pantheon Books, 1991.
———*The Night Battles: Witchcraft and Agrarian Cults in the Sixteenth and Seventeenth Centuries*. New York: Penguin Books, 1985.
Grahn, Judy. *Another Mother Tongue: Gay Words, Gay Worlds*. Boston: Beacon Press, 1984.
Green, Miranda J. *Dictionary of Celtic Myth and Legend*. Thames and Hudson, 1992.
Grillot de Givry, Emile. *Illustrated Anthology of Sorcery, Magic and Alchemy*. Zachary Kwinter Books, Ltd., 1973.
Grimm, Jacob. *Teutonic Mythology, vols. I–IV*. Gloucester, Massachusetts: Peter Smith, 1966 edition.
Guiley, Rosemary Ellen. *The Encyclopedia of Witches and Witchcraft*. New York: Facts on File, 1989.
Hansen, Chadwick. *Witchcraft at Salem*. New York: George Braziller, 1969.
Jones, Prudence, Nigel Pennick. *A History of Pagan Europe*. New York: Routledge, 1995.
Kittredge, George Lyman. *Witchcraft in Old and New England*. New York: Russell and Russell, 1956 edition.
Kors, Alan C., Edward Peters. *Witchcraft in Europe: 1100–1700: A Documentary History*. Philadelphia: University of Pennsylvania Press, 1984
Larrington, Carolyne, trans. *The Poetic Edda*. Oxford: Oxford University Press, 1996.
Lethbridge, T.C. *Witches: Investigating an Ancient Religion*. London: Routledge and Kegan Paul, 1962.
Manley, John. *Atlas of Prehistoric Britain*. New York: Oxford University Press, 1989.
Markale, Jean. *Merlin: Priest of Nature*. Rochester, Vermont: Inner Traditions, 1995.

Marshall, Sybil. *Everyman's Book of English Folktales.* London: J.M. Dent & Sons Ltd., 1981.

Matthews, John. *Gawain: Knight of the Goddess.* Northamptonshire: The Aquarian Press, 1990.

Medway, Gareth J. *Lure of the Sinister: The Unnatural History of Satanism.* New York University Press, 2001.

Metzner, Ralph. *The Well of Remembrance: Rediscovering the Earth Wisdom Myths of Northern Europe.* Boston: Shambhala, 1994.

Michell, John. *Megalithomania: Artists, Antiquarians, and Archaeologists at the Old Stone Monuments.* Ithaca, New York: Cornell University Press, 1982.

Monter, E. William. *Witchcraft in France and Switzerland: The Borderlands During the Reformation.* Ithaca: Cornell University Press, 1976.

Murray, Margaret. *The Witch-Cult in Western Europe.* Oxford: The Clarendon Press, 1962 edition.

———*The God of the Witches.* London: Faber and Faber, Ltd., 1952 edition.

Nutt, Alfred. *Studies on the Legends of the Holy Grail, With Especial Reference to the Hypothesis of its Celtic Origin.* New York: Cooper Square Publishers, 1965.

Pegg, Bob. *Rites and Riots: Folk Customs of Britain and Europe.* Poole, Dorset: Blandford Press, 1981.

Purkiss, Diane. *At the Bottom of the Garden: A Dark History of Fairies, Hobgoblins, and Other Troublesome Things.* New York: NYU Press, 2001.

Rosen, Barbara, ed. *Witchcraft.* New York: Taplinger Publishing, 1972.

Russell, Jeffrey Burton. *A History of Witchcraft: Sorcerers, Heretics, and Pagans.* New York: Thames and Hudson, 1980.

———*Witchcraft in the Middle Ages.* Ithaca, New York: Cornell University Press, 1972.

Scott, Walter. *Letters on Demonology and Witchcraft.* New York: Bell Publishing, 1970 reprint of 2nd edition.

Starhawk. *The Spiral Dance: A Rebirth of the Ancient Religion of the Great Goddess.* HarperSanFrancisco, 1989 edition.

Tatar, Maria. *The Annotated Classic Fairy Tales.* New York: W.W. Norton and Co., 2002.

Underdown, David. *Revel, Riot, and Rebellion: Popular Politics and Culture in England: 1603–1660*. Oxford: Clarendon Press, 1985.
Valiente, Doreen. *An ABC of Witchcraft: Past and Present*. Custer, Washington: Phoenix Publishing, 1973.
———*Natural Magic*. Custer, Washington: Phoenix Publishing, 1975.
———*Witchcraft for Tomorrow*. Custer, Washington: Phoenix Publishing, 1978.
Wolkstein, Diane, Samuel Noah Kramer. *Inanna, Queen of Heaven and Earth: Her Stories and Hymns From Sumer*. Harper and Row, 1983.
Young, Jean I. *The Prose Edda of Snorri Sturluson: Tales from Norse Mythology*. Berkeley: University of California Press, 1954.

Acknowledgement

I would like to acknowledge the formidable erudition, indefatigable spirit, and boundless patience of Marilyn Dillon at Three Moons Media, without whom this volume would not have been possible.

Made in the USA
Columbia, SC
30 April 2021